THE MAKING OF A WORLD TRADING POWER

T0300471

Modern Economic and Social History Series

General Editor: Derek H. Aldcroft

Titles in this series include:

The Making of a World Trading Power

The European Economic Community (EEC)
in the GATT Kennedy Round Negotiations
(1963–67)

LUCIA COPPOLARO
Institute of Social Sciences – University of Lisbon

Routledge
Taylor & Francis Group

LONDON AND NEW YORK

First published 2013 by Ashgate Publishing

2 Park Square, Milton Park, Abingdon, Oxon OX14 4RN
711 Third Avenue, New York, NY 10017, USA

Routledge is an imprint of the Taylor & Francis Group, an informa business

First issued in paperback 2016

British Library Cataloguing in Publication Data
Coppolaro, Lucia.
 The making of a world trading power : the European Economic Community (EEC) in the GATT Kennedy Round Negotiations (1963-67). -- (Modern economic and social history)
 1. European Economic Community--History. 2. Kennedy Round (1964-1967 :
 Geneva, Switzerland) 3. Foreign trade regulation--History--20th century.
 4. European Union countries--Commercial policy.
 I. Title II. Series
 382.9'4-dc23

Library of Congress Cataloging-in-Publication Data
Coppolaro, Lucia.
 The making of a world trading power : the European Economic Community (EEC) in the GATT Kennedy Round negotiations (1963-67) / by Lucia Coppolaro.
     p. cm. -- (Modern economic and social history)
 Includes bibliographical references and index.
 ISBN 978-1-4094-3375-0 (hbk.) 1. European Economic Community countries--Foreign economic relations. 2. European Economic Community countries--Commercial policy--History.
 3. Europe--Commercial policy--History. 4. Europe--Foreign economic relations--United States.
 5. United States--Foreign economic relations--Europe. 6. European Economic Community--History. 7. General Agreement on Tariffs and Trade (Organization) 8. Kennedy Round (1964-1967 : Geneva, Switzerland) I. Title.

 HF1532.5.C67 2013
 382'.9209409046--dc23

                                                                    2012034225

ISBN 978-1-4094-3375-0 (hbk)
ISBN 978-1-138-24944-8 (pbk)

For Little T.

Contents

Contents

List of Figures and Tables

Acknowledgments

This book originated in a Ph.D. dissertation submitted to the European University Institute (EUI) in Florence in December 2006. Throughout the writing of the thesis and then of the book, I was fortunate to receive precious help, support, and encouragement from many people, without which the process would have been much more difficult. All have contributed in different but crucial ways.

At EUI I was fortunate to have Professor Alan S. Milward as supervisor. His confidence in me was a great support during the entire period of writing. I consider it a privilege to have had such an outstanding scholar as a guide and interlocutor in discussing the topics of this book.

The preparation of the manuscript has entailed a fascinating journey in the Iberian peninsula during which my debts have accumulated. I am, first of all, indebted to Fernando Guirao. For nine months beginning in September 2006 he gave me the opportunity to visit the Universitat Pompeu Fabra in Barcelona as a postdoctoral researcher. During this period he carefully and patiently read my dissertation, and his incisive comments and criticisms helped to improve the argumentation of this book. Moreover, he gave me the opportunity to make my debut as a teacher at this very stimulating university. I am most grateful to Fernando for all this and also—let's be frank—for allowing me to enjoy the terrific city of Barcelona.

In 2008, I started a postdoctoral program at the Institute of Social Sciences of the University of Lisbon. This position provided the opportunity to continue my research on international trade and European integration and to complete the writing of this book in an intellectually inspiring environment. I benefited from the scholarly advice of Pedro Lains—and enjoyed his mild but very acute sense of humor and irony—and that of José Luís Cardoso on countless matters, and from their constant support. I am most grateful to both. I would also like to express my gratitude to my friend and colleague Nina Wiesehomeier, with whom I enjoyed many lunch breaks. My thanks go also to Maria Eugénia Rodrigues for general administrative support.

Several people have read parts of the thesis and of the book and proffered useful criticism. I wish to record my thanks to David M. Andrews, Michael J. Geary, Ann-Christina Lauring Knudsen, N. Piers Ludlow, Francine McKenzie, Sigfrido Manuel Perez Ramirez, Pascaline Winand, Thomas W. Zeiler, and Hubert Zimmermann. I am indebted especially to Piers Ludlow for being available whenever I needed good advice.

I wish to thank Ashgate for assistance through the publishing process and for having recruited two anonymous reviewers who gave thoughtful advice. I acknowledge with gratitude the assistance provided by Richard Isomaki in the proofreading of the book manuscript.

The revision and proofreading of this manuscript were financed by the Portuguese Foundation for Science and Technology and the Institute of Social Sciences of the University of Lisbon. I am grateful to both institutions for their financial support.

Finally, I am thankful to my family—my parents and my sisters—for their support and to Davide for his outstanding help with computer problems. I must also mention Fabrizio, who during the writing process patiently suffered my stress and tension. During the latter preparations of the book, he bore my commuting and was always eager to visit me first in Barcelona and then in Lisbon. I suspect that the beauty of the cities and the local football teams were a great incentive. His indifference to the finer points of international trade, GATT, and European integration was a stabilizing influence throughout this endeavor.

Lisbon, June 2012

Key to Archives

AAPD	Akten zur Auswärtigen Politik des Bundesrepublik Deutschland
AECB	Archives European Commission, Brussels
AN	Archives Nationales Contemporaines, Fontainebleau (France)
CM EC	Council of Ministers, Brussels
DDF	Documents Diplomatiques Français
EM	Personal Paper Edoardo Martino
FRUS	Foreign Relations of the United States
HAEC	Historical Archives European Community, Florence
JFKL	John Fitzgerald Kennedy Library
JM	Personal Paper Jean Monnet
LBJL	Lyndon Bains Johnson Library
MAE	Ministero Affari Esteri (Italy)
MAEF	Ministère des Affaires Etrangères (France)
NARA	US National Archives and Records Administration College Park, MA
OW	Personal Paper Olivier Wormser
PPJR	Personal Paper Jean Rey
PRO BT	Public Record Office, Board of Trade
PRO CAB	Public Record Office, Cabinet
PRO FO	Public Record Office, Foreign Office
PRO PREM	Public Record Office, Premier
PRO T	Public Record Office, Treasury
WHCF	White House Central Archives

Key to Archives

Abbreviations and Acronyms

ASP	American Selling Price
BLEU	Belgium and Luxembourg
BTN	Brussels Tariff Nomenclature
CAP	Common Agricultural Policy
CCP	Common Commercial Policy
CET	Common External Tariffs
COREPER	Comité des représentants permanents (Committee of Permanent Representatives)
EC	European Community
EEC	European Economic Community
EFTA	European Free Trade Association
EPU	European Payments Union
EU	European Union
GATT	General Agreement on Tariff and Trade
IMF	International Monetary Fund
IWA	International Wheat Agreement
ITO	International Trade Organization
LDC	Less-developed countries
LTA	Long-term Agreement on Cotton Textiles
MDS	Montant de soutien
MFN	Most-favored nation
NATO	North Atlantic Treaty Organization
NTB	Nontariff barrier
OECD	Organisation for Economic Co-operation and Development
OEEC	Organization for European Economic Cooperation
QMV	Qualified Majority Vote
QR	Quantitative restriction
RTA	Regional Trade Agreement
SITC	Standard International Trade Classification
SSR	Self-sufficiency rate
TEA	Trade Expansion Act
TNC	Trade Negotiation Committee
UGPs	Unified Grains Prices
UNCTAD	United Nations Conference on Trade and Development
USDA	U.S. Department of Agriculture
US SRTN	U.S. Special Representative for Trade Negotiations
WTO	World Trade Organization

Modern Economic and Social History Series
General Editor's Preface

Economic and social history has been a flourishing subject of scholarly study during recent decades. Not only has the volume of literature increased enormously but the range of interest in time, space and subject matter has broadened considerably so that today there are many sub-branches of the subject which have developed considerable status in their own right.

One of the aims of this series is to encourage the publication of scholarly monographs on any aspect of modern economic and social history. The geographical coverage is world-wide and contributions on the non-British themes will be especially welcome. While emphasis will be placed on works embodying original research, it is also intended that the series should provide the opportunity to publish studies of a more general thematic nature which offer a reappraisal or critical analysis of major issues of debate.

Derek H. Aldcroft
University of Leicester

Introduction

The Role of the EEC in Trade and Beyond

On 9 May 1967, Jean Rey, the Belgian member of the European Commission and chief negotiator for the EEC during the Kennedy Round of trade negotiations, and William W. Roth, the U.S. special trade representative, met in an attempt to bring the round to a conclusion. Bargaining had dragged on since 1963 under the aegis of the General Agreement on Tariffs and Trade (GATT). In the last days of the talks, the discussions between the two sides were stalled on, among other issues, duties on canned ham, canned peaches, and organic chemicals. The meeting between Rey and Roth went on into the night, and mediation by the GATT executive secretary, Eric Wyndham White, failed to narrow the differences between the parties. By four o'clock in the morning, the discussions had deadlocked on all fronts, and a final agreement was nowhere in sight.

The following day, Nils Montan, the Swedish diplomat representing the Scandinavian countries, organized a lunch at a Geneva restaurant for Rey, Roth, and W. Michael Blumenthal, his deputy, hoping that the EEC and the United States could find common ground on which to salvage the negotiations. "There, over a lunch of smoked salmon, filet mignon, and numerous glasses of wine," the three men were able to establish a schedule they would follow to conclude the round, a schedule the negotiators in fact adhered to in reaching the final agreements.[1]

This luncheon is telling, not just because of the crisis atmosphere, which commonly surrounds the final phase of such negotiations, or the mundane subject—canned peaches and ham—of an international bargain on tariffs, or the role a congenial meal can play in smoothing out differences that have blocked major trade talks. The meeting over food and wine is, above all, revealing about the status of the EEC. It shows that, for the first time in its history, the Community was bargaining with a single voice in the final phase of far-reaching negotiations. Moreover, the European Commission, the EEC's supranational institution, through its representative, Jean Rey, was able to speak on behalf of the member states. Equally important, the EEC was able to bargain as an equal partner with the United States.

The Kennedy Round was of major importance in the history of world trade, as the climax of post-World War II international cooperation and reduction of trade barriers. The round slashed duties by 35 percent on average, with about two-thirds of the cuts reaching 50 percent, substantially more than had been achieved

---

[1] Steven Dryden, *Trade Warriors: USTR and the American Crusade for Free Trade* (New York, 1995), 107.

in any previous GATT round.[2] The participation of the EEC in these momentous negotiations is the topic of this book, which provides the first historical account of the Community's behavior in major trade talks. I argue that the negotiations were a critical process in the history of the Community, marking its emergence as a world trading power, and shaping its stance in world trade. This, in barebones outline, is the story told in this book. My approach is a means to understand how the EEC became a powerful actor in international trade and its impact as a regional trading area on the multilateral system. I believe that such an analysis is essential if we are to understand the actual stance of the European Union in world trade and in the World Trade Organization (WTO) and to grasp its economic diplomacy.

Trade has played a fundamental role in European integration and in the evolution of the EU. In the first place, the EEC was established with a customs union as its basis. Second, trade policy was the initial field where the original members chose to pool their sovereignty, delegating to the EEC the authority to wield it. This decision was a major accomplishment in itself, transferring to the Community a crucial aspect of national independence, that is, the capacity to use trade policy to regulate the economy. Third, it was in the field of world trade that the EEC established itself as a single actor and acquired international status. Even now, more than four decades after the conclusion of the Kennedy Round, international trade is one of the few fields where the EU is able to speak with a united and powerful voice. All these considerations make the trade policy and policymaking of the EU and its stance in the world regime fundamental to understanding the EU, international trade, international trade negotiations, and the GATT/WTO system.

Despite the relevance of these topics, the literature in this field is relatively small, and only recently has theoretical and empirical research been developed. Moreover, the scholarship that exists is dominated by political scientists and economists, while historians have been relatively inactive.[3] While two excellent historical studies have been dedicated to the commercial background to the establishment of the EEC and the tariff policy of the Western European countries

---

[2] For the relevance of the Kennedy Round for world trade see Ronald Findlay and Kevin O'Rourke, *Power and Plenty: Trade, War and the World Economy in the Second Millennium* (Princeton, NJ, 2007), 491. For an assessment of the Kennedy Round tariff cuts see Bela Balassa and Mordechai E. Kreinin, "Trade Liberalization Under the Kennedy Round: The Static Effects," *Review of Economics and Statistics* 49, 2 (1967), 125–37 and J. Michael Finger, "Effects of the Kennedy Round Tariff Concessions on the Exports of Developing Countries," *Economic Journal* 86, 341(1976), 87–95.

[3] See among, the others, Sophie Meunier, *Trading Voices: The European Union in International Commercial Negotiations* (Princeton, 2006). Mark A. Pollack, *The Engines of European Integration: Delegation, Agency, and Agenda Setting in the EU* (Oxford, 2003), has analyzed the functioning of the EEC/EU in international negotiations. Vinod K. Aggarwal and Edward Fogarty, in *EU Trade Strategies: Between Regionalism and Globalization* (Basingstoke, 2004), illustrate the EU's role in world trade, focusing on the logic of the interregionalism pursued by the EU.

in the 1950s,[4] historians have given scarce attention to the development of the EEC's trade relations and policies.[5] Several books on the Kennedy Round have been written, but none of them analyze the stance of the EEC, considering instead the U.S. or British point of view.[6] Providing an account of the EEC's participation in these talks, this book examines a hitherto unsketched component of the history of both EU and international trade.

This is not a study, however, of trade and tariffs alone. My narrative of the EEC's participation in the Kennedy Round reveals new aspects of the development of the Community in the 1960s. The GATT talks were intertwined with other events critical to the EEC, among them the British applications in 1963 and 1967 to join the Community and the French vetoes in response, the definition and settlement of the Common Agricultural Policy (CAP), the crisis of the Empty Chair and the Luxembourg Compromise of 1965–66, the role of the European Commission in European integration and, broadly, tensions among the six member states over the agenda and development of the Community. These occurrences influenced and, at the same time, were influenced by the GATT talks, an international context that historians have often overlooked but is essential to the EEC's evolution. The internal development of the EEC dictated the rate and timing of progress at the Kennedy Round, but the need to make progress at the GATT talks led EEC members to move forward with the elaboration of the CAP and the common commercial policy (CCP) in Brussels. GATT was used as a lever to enhance the

---

[4] Alan S. Milward, *The European Rescue of the Nation-state* (London, 2000) and Wendy Asbeek Brusse, *Tariffs, Trade, and European Integration, 1947–1957: From Study Group to Common Market* (New York, 1997).

[5] The exceptions are N. Piers Ludlow, "The Emergence of a Commercial Heavy-weight: The Kennedy Round and the European Community of the 1960s," *Diplomacy and Statecraft* 18, 2 (2007), 351–68; and Ynze Álkema, "Regionalism in a Multilateral Framework: The EEC, the United States and the GATT Confronting Trade Policies, 1957–1962," thesis, European University Institute, Florence, 1996, dedicated to the EEC and GATT from 1957 to 1962.

[6] The following books investigate the Kennedy Round from an American perspective: Ernest H. Preeg, *Traders and Diplomats: An Analysis of the Kennedy Round of Negotiations under the GATT* (Washington, DC, 1970); John W. Evans, *The Kennedy Round in American Trade Policy: Twilight of the GATT* (Cambridge, MA, 1971); Thomas B. Curtice and John R. Vastine Jr, *The Kennedy Round and the Future of American Trade* (New York, 1971); Thomas W. Zeiler, *American Trade and Power in the 1960s* (New York, 1995); Steven Dryden, *Trade Warriors: USTR and the American Crusade for Free Trade* (Oxford, 1995); Alfred E. Eckes Jr, *Revisiting U.S. Trade Policy: Decisions in Perspective* (Athens, OH, 2000); and Francine McKenzie, "GATT–EEC Collision: The Challenge of Regional Trade Blocs to the General Agreement of Tariffs and Trade, 1950–1967," *International History Review* 33, 3 (2010), 229–52. Donna Lee, *Middle Powers and Commercial Policy: British Influence at the Kennedy Round* (New York, 1999) is dedicated to the British stance. Gian Paolo Casadio, Transatlantic Trade: USA–EEC Confrontation in the GATT Negotiations (Farnborough, 1973) analyzes the EEC's position; however it is not based on historical archives.

internal developments. An analysis of the adoption of the CAP from the point of view of the Kennedy Round shows that this policy was not elaborated and adopted in isolation in Brussels. First, Germany, the Netherlands and Italy considered the effect of this policy on third countries, not because they were concerned about the trade balance of these countries, but because they hoped to maintain their flow of cheap imports from outside the EEC thanks to the Geneva talks. Second, the CAP was negotiated under the pressure of the Kennedy Round. The Germans had to resign themselves to the fact that, to attend Kennedy Round as they wished to, they also had to permit a faster elaboration of this policy than they had hoped.

The importance of the Kennedy Round, in sum, extends well beyond trade. The EEC's participation in the round sheds new light on the development of the Community in the 1960s and on the political and economic history of European integration.

Argument and Plan of the Book

This study has three domains of analysis and overriding argument. The first is the bargaining among the EEC's members ("the Six") in Brussels for the purpose of establishing a common position in the Geneva negotiations. Here I describe the preferences of the member states and how their divergent interests were reconciled in a common position on trade. My argument is that the member states had a critical stake in attending the round as a regional unit, an interest driven by the same factors that had led to the creation of the Community, with a customs union as its foundation. Unity had been considered essential to export-led economic growth through the liberalization of trade in a regional area protected from international competition. Thus the Six responded to the internationalization of trade by means of a regional agreement, fostering a new form of international cooperation, that is, integration. National governments pooled their sovereignty over trade and blended six national commercial policies in one common commercial policy. This approach required the maintenance of EEC regionalism within GATT and, consequently, negotiating as a unit in the new round. Crucially, member states were spurred to compromise over their conflicting trade interests so as to converge on a CCP that could be deployed in the GATT round. Equally important, their ability to maintain regionalism in the Kennedy Round permitted the EEC's member states to speak with one voice and so become an international actor and a world trading power. Significantly, they were able to sustain their unity during negotiations despite quarrels over other crucial matters, such as the enlargement of the Community and the establishment of the CAP. This solidarity shows the fundamental role trade integration played in the politics and economics of the member states, an impetus historians have often underestimated.

The second domain of analysis is the EEC's trade policymaking. Here my focus is the role of the member states and the EEC's institutions in formulating the common position in Brussels and in conducting negotiations with other countries in Geneva. This topic has previously been investigated primarily by political scientists, and it can be useful to begin with their conclusions in framing this topic. Among many other aspects of trade policymaking, scholars have analyzed the role of the Council of Ministers and the Commission, the two institutions most closely involved in settling on policy. Researchers have asked whether one institution outweighed the other, or the two shared equal influence over the outcome of negotiations. Aggarwal and Fogarty, De Bièvre and Dür, Meunier, and Moravcsik, highlighting the instruments member states have at hand to control the Commission, underline its relative weakness. These scholars note that member states nominate the commissioner responsible for trade, set the mandate under which the Commission negotiates with other countries, and monitor it through the national experts' committee during such talks. In addition, member states must ratify agreements negotiated with other countries. They thus wield a number of tools through which they can rein in the Commission. These scholars conclude, therefore, that the sovereign states determined the policy outcome.[7] By contrast, Coleman and Tangermann, Woll, and Zimmermann stress the relative autonomy of the Commission, pointing out that negotiating with other countries gives it access to information unavailable to member states. Moreover, the Commission is able to determine strategy and use its right of initiative to present member states with proposals and package deals that correspond to its own preferences. Given these powers, these latter researchers conclude that the Commission is fully able to influence policy.[8] While historians have studied the actions of the Commission and the Council of Ministers in other fields, such as the enlargement of the Community or the elaboration of the CAP, they have neglected trade policymaking.[9] Only Ludlow has dealt with it, siding with those who regard the ministers as the

---

[7] Aggarwal and Fogarty, *EU Trade Strategies*; Dirk De Bièvre and Andreas Dür, "Constituency Interests and Delegation in European and American Trade Policy," *Comparative Political Studies* 38, 10 (2005), 1271–96; Meunier, *Trading Voices; Andrew Moravcsik, The Choice for Europe: Social Purpose and State Power from Messina to Maastricht* (Ithaca, NY, 1998).

[8] William D. Coleman and Stefan Tangermann, "The 1992 CAP Reform, the Uruguay Round and the Commission: Conceptualizing Linked Policy Games," *Journal of Common Market Studies* 37, 3 (1999), 385–405; Cornelia Woll, "The Road to External Representation: The European Commission's Activism in International Air Transport," *Journal of European Public Policy* 13, 1 (2006), 52–69; Hubert Zimmermann, *Wege zur Verhandlungen um die Aufnahme Chinas in die WTO, 1985–2001* (Baden-Baden, 2007). For a complete review of the literature see Andreas Dür and Hubert Zimmermann, "Introduction: The EU in International Trade Negotiations," *Journal of Common Market Studies* 45, 4 (2007), 771–87.

[9] On the enlargement see Michael J. Geary, *The European Commission and the First Enlargement of the European Union: Challenging for Power?* (London, forthcoming); on the CAP see Ann-Christina L. Knudsen, *Farmers on Welfare: The Making of Europe's Common Agricultural Policy* (Ithaca, NY, 2009).

predominant power within the dyad, and concluding that "Commission autonomy was … strictly framed by a variety of Council controls."[10]

The focus of this book is on the role of the Commission relative to that of the member states, and my analysis will support a robust view of the institution's capacities. I consider two distinct moments: the negotiations in Brussels over a common stance in the Kennedy Round and the bargaining in Geneva between the Commission and the other participants. My aim is to assess the Commission's role in order to understand in what respects and under which conditions it can influence policy outcomes. The analysis, first, considers whether the Commission was decisive in reaching an agreement in Brussels and later in Geneva, and, second, ascertains whether the final outcome incorporated the Commission's proposals and preferences.

I will argue that the Commission had its own preferences, which in some cases differed from those of its constituents, and advanced them through its right of presenting proposals and its role as negotiating agent in Geneva on behalf of member states. Yet there were clear limits to its freedom to act and capacity to determine the final outcome. Member states made the final decisions. The Commission could realize its preferences only when they appealed to the Council of Ministers, and it could act only within the constraints posed by the member states' preferences. Moreover, the Council of Ministers defined the limits of the Commission's room for maneuver in Geneva. Within this general arrangement, however, there were evolutionary changes, and during the progress of the Kennedy Round the Commission gained new capacities. Whereas from 1963 to early 1967 member states strictly controlled the Commission, in the last phase they enlarged the discretion of their negotiating agent in order to improve the efficiency of the decision-making process and conclude the round. Thus, the autonomy of the Commission varied considerably over time as a function of the phase of the negotiations in Brussels and in Geneva. The member states pragmatically set limits to the actions of their agent, guided by the goal of enhancing their own trade interests. Ultimately, member states allowed the Commission to strengthen its role and become the sole negotiating agent even in sectors for which it lacked legal authority under the Treaty of Rome. They did so because this greater power aligned with their self-interest—evidence that the Commission was instrumental to the aims of the member states.

The third focus of analysis here is the history of the GATT and international trade, and the role of the EEC in their development. This book explains the conditions under which the EEC reduced its trade barriers and its contribution, by means of this streamlining, to the liberalization of international trade. In so doing, this study also ascertains the circumstances in which trade is more generally liberalized in the GATT and the impact a regional trade agreement can have on the multilateral trading system.

---

[10]   Ludlow, "Emergence of a Commercial Heavy-weight."

As Findlay and O'Rourke note, after World War II, the only countries that did not follow protectionist policies were the northern Atlantic economies of Western Europe and North America. Here, under U.S. leadership, governments slowly started to lower barriers within the framework of the GATT and of European regional institutions.[11] The U.S. decision to propose a new round of GATT negotiation and the EEC's agreement to join it confirmed this policy of liberalization in the Atlantic economies. I argue that the formation of the EEC encouraged the Kennedy administration to propose a far-reaching reduction of tariffs and provided the decisive push towards genuinely multilateral, across-the-board negotiations. For the first time since 1947, on the other side of the Atlantic there existed a credible negotiating partner for the Americans, capable of making valuable counter concessions thanks to the size of its market. Thus, the very existence of a regional bloc made possible the decisive step towards a sweeping reduction of tariffs with genuinely multilateral negotiations, giving impetus to the GATT itself.

In taking a position on Kennedy's initiative, the EEC had to delineate its international trade policy and define its role in the world trade regime. With regard to the industrial sector, members agreed to attend the round in order to reduce protectionism and increase their exports. To this end, they were ready to reduce the Common External Tariff (CET) so as to obtain reciprocal reduction of duties imposed by the United States and the European Free Trade Association (EFTA). Improvements in European competitiveness made liberalization on a multilateral scale bearable. The growth of the EEC's exports to the United States and the rest of Western Europe guided the Six to complementary tariff reductions at regional and multilateral levels, in order to sustain the flow of exports. While concerned to protect certain sectors, member states were disposed to reduce tariffs to enhance the outward flow of goods to the EFTA countries and the United States. The EEC aimed to maintain the CET at a level that would defend the region, but it was in members' best interests to reduce barriers so as to increase exports. From behind the wall of the CET, even such traditionally protectionist countries as France and Italy were ready to compete worldwide and reduce tariffs multilaterally. Moreover, negotiating with a single voice gave the EEC the power to bargain as an equal partner with the United States and to question U.S. trade policy, a capacity the Europeans had lacked in the 1950s.

The Six's behavior in the agricultural sector was totally different from their approach to industrial products. An analysis of the way agriculture was treated in the round is of crucial importance, for the issue still has contemporary resonance: agriculture remains a stumbling block in the Doha Millennium Round, initiated in 2001 and still in process. The Six had decided to set up a strictly protected and regulated regional agricultural market, supporting the sector as a kind of welfare policy. Thus they refused to reduce protections in this area. As a result, the EEC ended the round as a liberal actor in the industrial sector, contributing to freer trade, but as an obstacle in agriculture, a role the EU plays to this day, troubling the Doha Round.

---

[11]   Findlay and O'Rourke, *Power and Plenty*, 392.

The EEC's stance sheds light on the conditions under which trade is liberalized in talks in Geneva. The first aspect of this history worth highlighting is that the GATT works like a bazaar. Governments reduce barriers only when they can obtain in return a valuable concession from another participant in the round. It is, therefore, the bargaining power each government brings to the table that induces others to reduce trade protection by offering something valuable in exchange. During the Kennedy Round, the United States could not offer the EEC any prize that would soften its stance on agriculture because the Six had a critical concern in maintaining their regionalism and no significant interest in enhancing agricultural exports to the United States.

The second point to underline is that the GATT responded perfectly to the political economy of trade liberalization of the Western countries, which consisted in reducing trade barriers in the most dynamic sectors, while giving shelter to less competitive ones, those considered strategic for industrial development or more sensitive from a political point of view. The GATT, which permits many exceptions to its fundamental most-favored-nation (MFN) rule, fostered a mixture of Keynesian economic nationalism and liberal economic internationalism, of neomercantilist policy and free trade ideology, a blend that characterized the political economy of the Western countries in the 1950s and 1960s. The regime developed within the GATT combined a shrewd mixture of freer trade and protectionism, accurately embodying Western countries' interests and proving a flexible instrument able to adapt to the requirements of its developed economies. This phenomenon is central for interpreting the history of liberalization of international trade in the GATT/WTO regime.

Liberalization achieved during the Kennedy Round affected trade among rich and developed countries, while the less-developed countries (LDCs) did not benefit from it. Despite the fact that the round had been launched with a development-focused agenda, it soon became evident that developed members would not rush to act for the benefit of LDCs. As a result, trade in commodities of major interest to LDCs was not made freer. Two historical elements contributed to this result. First, the preferential agreements the EEC had negotiated under the Yaoundé convention of 1964 with its former colonies did not favor liberalization at the multilateral level. The EEC as a whole—even if different positions existed among the nations in Brussels—opposed any reduction in preferences, and some states even asked for an increase in the preferential duties against nonassociated countries. Second, and perhaps most crucially, the LDCs were not playing the GATT "bazaar game." They predominantly pursued industrialization based on import substitution, and their policy was endorsed by the GATT, which accepted the idea that LDCs were not obligated to liberalize.[12] They asked for concessions from the developed economies, but were not disposed to reciprocate with reductions of their own trade barriers. In the Kennedy Round they were formally

---

[12]   On this aspect see Ann O. Krueger, "Trade Policy and Economic Development: How We Learn," *American Economic Review* 87 (1997), 1–22.

granted the right not to exchange concessions with the developed countries. Yet this exemption had the perverse effect of keeping them outside the productive actions of the GATT, where, as I have previously illustrated, trade is made freer when concessions are reciprocal. The results of the Kennedy Round confirmed that the GATT's commitment to development was lackluster and that the GATT was a "rich-man's club."

It may be helpful to the reader to have an advance view of the way in which the framework of the book has been fitted to its purposes and three domains of analysis. Chapter 1 illustrates the background of the Kennedy Round. It describes how U.S. commitment to promoting an open, nondiscriminatory international economic system at the end of World War II was reconciled with strong support for European regional integration. I explain the reasons that led the Kennedy administration in 1962 to launch a new GATT conference. The existence of the EEC led Kennedy to propose a sweeping liberalization of international trade, in both the industrial and the agricultural sectors, in order to increase U.S. trade, boost U.S. economic growth, and integrate the EEC region into the multilateral trading system and the Atlantic Alliance.

Chapter 2 describes the reaction of the EEC to the proposal of a new round. The U.S. initiative placed the Community in the position of having to delineate its stance in world trade as well as the pattern of its regional and multilateral integration. My account emphasizes the priority member states attached to trade at the EEC regional level so as to favor their economic growth, and demonstrates their primary interest in attending the round as a trading unit in order to defend the EEC's regionalism within the GATT. The chapter illustrates the clear reaction of the Six: in the industrial sector, they accepted the reduction of duties in order to obtain, on a reciprocal basis, the reduction of U.S. and other European countries' duties and, therefore, enhance EEC exports. Totally different was their response in the agricultural sector. In implementing the CAP, the Europeans had decided to set up a strictly protected and regulated regional agricultural market. None of the EEC members had a major interest in increasing their agricultural exports outside the region, and, consequently, none were eager to reduce barriers to obtain reciprocal concessions from other GATT members.

In Chapter 3, the attention shifts to the beginning of the negotiations in Brussels to establish a common position on the GATT talks; in parallel, I consider the negotiations in Geneva from January 1963 to May 1964 between the EEC and other participants over the agenda and the rules of the round. The narrative demonstrates that the EEC members were able to reach a common position from which to negotiate as a single unit in Geneva, despite internal tensions caused by the elaboration of the CAP and the French veto of British membership in the EEC in January 1963. The customs union kept its members together. The chapter illustrates the EEC decision-making process, highlighting the difficulties the Commission experienced in assuming its role as negotiating agent on behalf of the member states.

Chapter 4 discusses the complicated period running from June 1964 to July 1966, during which the EEC's internal quarrel over the elaboration of the CAP became an intricate transatlantic dispute and the crisis of the Empty Chair unfolded. Investigating this internal dispute in the context of the GATT, I am able to shed new light on the Community in the 1960s and on the elaboration of the CAP. I argue that the Kennedy Round and the EEC's internal negotiations over the CAP had mutual effects: the internal development of the EEC dictated the rate and timing of progress in Geneva; at the same time, the need to move ahead with the GATT talks in the agricultural sector pushed the EEC's members to move forward with the CAP in Brussels. The GATT was used as a lever to enhance the CAP, whose elaboration also has an international dimension. Examining the crisis of the Empty Chair within the context of the GATT reveals new facets of the story. First, member states maintained their unity in Geneva, despite the French boycott of meetings in Brussels. This shows, once again, the significance of the regional trade dimension of the EEC and the importance member states attached to attending the GATT talks as a trading unit. Second, the crisis did not affect the role of the Commission in the EEC's trade policymaking, contrary to what is commonly maintained.

Chapters 5 and 6 address the concrete history of the trade talks and the role of the EEC in international trade liberalization. Chapter 5 examines the negotiations in the industrial sector, focusing on the bargaining among the Six in Brussels and then the talks with other countries in Geneva from November 1964 to December 1966. I argue that member states' interest in enhancing their exports worldwide led them to adopt a liberal stance in the industrial sector so as to obtain, on a reciprocal basis, the reduction of other countries' trade barriers. They delineated the CCP along liberal lines. In the Geneva negotiations with the other participants, the EEC agreed to reduce its protectionism, thus contributing to the liberalization of international trade. I also discuss the EEC's trade policymaking, demonstrating that the Commission could inscribe its preferences in the EEC's final position only so long as they were supported by member states. In Geneva, in this phase, member states gave the Commission no flexibility in bargaining with other countries.

The differing status of agriculture, the subject of Chapter 6, is fundamental to understanding how the EEC became a protectionist actor in this sector. Despite the conflicting interests of the its members, none of them aimed to increase exports outside the EEC and none, therefore, needed to reduce barriers so as to obtain reductions from other countries. As a result, when the negotiations over agriculture started in Geneva, after a protectionist and non-negotiable CAP had been approved in Brussels, there was nothing to talk about. The EEC's lack of interest in enhancing its exports, combined with its desire to establish a welfare policy in agriculture, explains the lack of bargaining power on the part of the United States and other participants that might spur the EEC to modify its stance. It is important also to consider here how the EEC made trade policy. The Commission played a key role in setting the agricultural mandate. Thanks to its technical expertise and ability to engineer compromises, the Commission played to perfection its part as broker and was able to structure the entire debate and, consequently, influence the final outcome in Brussels. The EEC's stance in the agricultural sector well reflected the Commission's vision of the organization of world markets. Yet the Commission's preferences were exploited and manipulated by member states, primarily France, to achieve their own goals. This became evident in the final phase of the talks, when the proposals of the Commission were utterly written off. As in the industrial negotiations, in this phase member states did not concede flexibility to their negotiating agent in its bargaining with other countries.

Chapter 7 portrays the last phase of the GATT talks, from January to May 1967, analyzing the negotiations among the EEC members in Brussels and with other Kennedy Round participants in Geneva. I describe the main results of the trade talks, their impact on world trade, and their implications for the EEC, showing how the Community defined its position in world trade. It concluded the GATT talks with a liberal common commercial policy, contributing to the opening up of international trade in the industrial sector, and, while maintaining regionalism, was not an impediment to freer trade. In the agricultural sector, on the other hand, the EEC's refusal to reduce its protectionism led to a complete failure of the negotiations in Geneva, and the EEC did effectively become a stumbling block to free trade in agriculture.

During these years, by demonstrating its ability to participate in a major negotiation with a single voice, the EEC became one of the leading commercial agents in the international trading system. The Kennedy Round marked the EEC's emergence as a single powerful actor in world trade, gave it an international political identity, and showcased the first manifestation of a common EEC foreign policy.

Chapter 7 also considers the EEC's trade policymaking, demonstrating that member states were aware that more flexibility was required in Geneva to achieve final concessions and conclude the round. This recognition led them to give the Commission more room to maneuver. A trade-off took place between member states' control over the Commission, on the one hand, and the speed and efficiency of the decision-making process on the other. In this last phase, when an agreement had to be reached in Geneva—and when no linked issue was pending in Brussels, once the question of the CAP had been settled—member states allowed the Commission a greater degree of freedom, increasing its power because it was in their interest to do so. Once more, the Commission was instrumental to addressing national interests, and the source of its power lay firmly in the hands of the member states.

This study ends with a synthesis of the main empirical findings in order to underline the key insight for each of the three domains of investigation. Moreover, the conclusion shows how that policy choices of the 1960s and the results of the Kennedy Round impacted the EEC and the entire multilateral trading system in the following decades.

A multilevel study on the EEC common commercial policy necessarily requires certain self-selected restrictions in the issues examined. These self-imposed limitations are adopted only to serve the brevity and clarity of argumentation.

However, they should not be interpreted as a concession to one-dimensional explanation. As for the first such limitation, the book deals predominantly with the trade policy of national governments. I consider nation-states as unitary actors in the international framework of trade relations and do not offer a deeper analysis of events at lower domestic levels that shaped national policy. This choice had to be made because the systematic treatment of decision-making processes at domestic level, involving the role of business sectors and political parties, would require another book's worth of empirical research and exposition. Even so, where possible, I highlight the interaction between domestic decision-making and trade bargaining in Brussels and Geneva. A further circumscription concerns the analysis of the relations between the United States and the EEC, the two major actors during the round. A description of the U.S. position in the round, while not my primary purpose, is essential to understanding the stance of the EEC. Washington led the negotiations, and the EEC's diplomacy was considerably shaped by the way it responded to the U.S. initiatives. By taking into consideration the U.S. position in the round—even if just as a background—I am able to analyze U.S. economic diplomacy directed towards European regionalism and integration, an issue that is underestimated in existing accounts of the GATT talks. However, since I concentrate on the trade relations between the EEC and the United States, the book leaves in the background crucial monetary and security problems that considerably strained transatlantic relations in the 1960s.

Sources

This monograph is the outcome of multiarchival research. As Ludlow notes, with the establishment of the EEC and the pooling of their sovereignty, member states exercised their influence collectively, while EEC institutions began to play a part in the organization's decision-making process. To understand the development of the EEC, it is necessary to analyze not only the relations between the member states, but also their interplay with the EEC's institutions. Consequently, investigation of the archives of these institutions is essential to grasp the evolution of the Community.[13] In writing this book, I have focused on the historical archives of the EU and its institutions—the Council of Ministers, Comité des Représentants Permanents (COREPER), the 111 Committee, and the Commission—both in Brussels and in Florence, so as to compile data from essential sources. The historical archives of the European Union in Florence include the useful personal papers of Jean Monnet, Max Kohnstamm, Edoardo Martino, Emile Nöel, and others who were not involved in the Kennedy Round but were in constant contact with participating officials. In Brussels, I also conducted research in the personal

---

[13]   N. Piers Ludlow, *The European Community and the Crises of the 1960s* (London, 2006), 11.

archives of the commissioner responsible for the Kennedy Round, Jean Rey of Belgium, whose papers are deposited at the Université Libre de Bruxelles.

The major attention given to EEC sources does not imply that I gave no consideration to the national archives. In an ideal world, the national archives of all the member states would have been used. Unfortunately, the ideal must be tempered by the accessibility of archives and the languages the author wields. As a result, this book is grounded on the French archives of the Ministère des Affaires Etrangères, the Archives Nationales Contemporaines (Fontainebleau), the Couve de Murville cabinet papers, and the Documents Diplomatiques Français. It is also grounded in the Akten zur Auswärtigen Politik des Bundesrepublik, Deutschland. However, it is not based on the archives of Italy and the Benelux countries (Belgium, the Netherlands and Luxembourg). To overcome this limitation, I undertook careful research in the British and American archives, which provide substantial alternative sources of information: German, Italian, and Benelux officials involved in the Kennedy Round had the good habit—good, that is, for the sake of this study—of keeping London and Washington well informed about the debates taking place in the Council of Ministers, and about the stances of the member states and the Commission. These accounts, while obviously partisan, were frank and open in tone and allowed me to supplement the information acquired from the EEC and national archives of the member states. The British archives, moreover, provided a most useful description of relations between the Americans and the EEC. Among British sources, the National Archives in Kew Gardens were central. American sources included the Kennedy and Johnson Libraries and the U.S. National Archives and Records Administration in College Park, Maryland. A careful reading has also been conducted of the volumes of the *Foreign Relations of the United States* (FRUS) dedicated to the Kennedy and Johnson administrations.

The archival sources have been integrated with interviews with officials or politicians involved in the Kennedy Round. Paul Luyten and Jean-Michel Jacquet of the European Commission), Valéry Giscard d'Estaing, the French Minister of Finance, and Richard N. Gardner of the Kennedy administration provided valuable perspectives in interview. The GATT Basic Instruments and Selected Documents and the GATT online archives were also fruitful. Finally, a vast collection of statistical data on trade was critical to this project, especially the *Direction of Trade Statistics Historical, 1948–1980* (Washington, DC: International Monetary Fund, 2002), and *OECD SITC Rev. 2—Historical Series 1961–1990* (Paris: OECD, 2000).

Chapter 1

Kennedy's Initiative for a New GATT Round: Liberalizing International Trade and Strengthening the Atlantic Alliance

From Bretton Woods to the Treaty of Rome: The United States between Multilateralism and European Integration (1944–58)

Well before the end of World War II, President Roosevelt and Secretary of State Cordell Hull were convinced that the lack of an open world economy during the 1930s had been one of the causes of the war. As they planned a new postwar economic order, it became imperative that the protectionism and unilateralism that had characterized the prewar years be prevented from reappearing. As Irwin notes, "After the interwar catastrophe, the notion that a beneficent, decentralized, noncooperative equilibrium (like that prior to World War I) could possibly emerge after World War II seemed fanciful."[1] As the "nonsystem" of the late nineteenth century would not be automatically re-established, by the end of 1941 the United States and the United Kingdom were already planning a postwar system grounded on new and multilateral institutions that would ensure the stability of monetary relations, reduce trade barriers, and limit discriminatory tariff preferences. Multilateralism and liberalization would favor the expansion of international trade, considered necessary to the achievement of fundamental U.S. goals as set by the New Dealers, notably economic growth, rising per capita real income, and full employment. The correlation between multilateralism and security, between the domestic and the international dimensions of the New Deal, was firm in the minds of Democratic leaders and represented a fundamental issue in U.S. foreign policy. To enforce the envisaged multilateral system and perform the key functions of regulating international trade and payments, the International Monetary Fund (IMF) and the International Bank for Reconstruction and Development (World Bank) were established at the international conference at Bretton Woods in 1944.[2] In 1947 the General Agreement on Tariffs and Trade (GATT) was established, as a forerunner of the International Trade Organization (ITO), to provide a set

---

[1]   Douglas A. Irwin, "The GATT in Historical Perspective," *American Economic Review* 85, 2 (1995), 323–8.

[2]   For a description of the Bretton Woods negotiations see Richard N. Gardner, *Sterling–Dollar Diplomacy: The Origins and the Prospects of Our International Economic Order*, rev. edn (New York, 1980).

of rules directed to the substantial reduction of tariffs and other barriers to trade and to the elimination of discriminatory treatments. The General Agreement was grounded on the *most-favored-nation* (MFN) rule, which provided the foundation for the multilateral trading system.[3] After the failure of the ITO in 1950, only the GATT was left to reduce discrimination, and it soon established itself as the key international agreement dealing with international trade. As Zeiler notes, it survived because it shrewdly combined freer trade principles with protectionism and it accurately embodied the political economy of its members.[4]

Despite its strong proclamation of free trade, the GATT allowed for discrimination. This flexibility was evident in the exceptions to the MFN rule. The most noteworthy one, provided by Article XXIV, would turn out to be of great importance for the establishment of the EEC in 1957. This article permitted contracting parties to form a customs union and a free trade area, giving preferential treatment to imports coming from other member countries of the regional agreement.[5] Article XXIV reflected the position of the U.S. government that regional trade agreements (RTAs) were stepping-stones to freer global trade. For the U.S. drafters of the GATT, multilateralism and regionalism were part of the same process of liberalizing international trade, regionalism being one fundamental component in the establishment of an open and multilateral trading system.[6]

The beginning of the Cold War obstructed the United States' intention to shape the GATT as a global actor with universal membership, with the consequence that

---

[3]   On the origins of GATT see Douglas A. Irwin, Petros C. Mavroidis and Alan O. Sykes, *The Genesis of the GATT* (Cambridge, 2008). On the GATT system see, among the others, Jackson, John *The World Trading System: Law and Policy of International Economic Relations* (Cambridge, MA, 1992); John H. Barton, Judith L. Goldstein, Timothy E. Josling, Richard H. Steinberg, *The Evolution of the Trade Regime. Politics, Law, and Economics of the GATT and WTO* (Princeton, NJ, 2006). Bernard Hoekman and Michael M. Kostecki, *The Political Economy of the World Trading System: The WTO and Beyond* (Oxford, 2009).

[4]   On the failure of ITO see Thomas W. Zeiler, *Free Trade, Free World* (Chapel Hill, NC, 1999) and William Diebold Jr, *The End of ITO* (Ann Arbor, MI, 1981). On the first years of activities of GATT see Gerard Curzon, *Multilateral Commercial Diplomacy: The General Agreement on Trade and Tariffs and its Impact on National Commercial Policies and Techniques* (New York, 1965); Karin Kock, *International Trade Policy and the GATT 1947–1967* (Stockholm, 1969).

[5]   For a legal history of Article XXIV see Jorg Mathias, *Regional Trade Agreements in the GATT/WTO: Article XXIV and the Internal Trade Requirements* (The Hague, 2002), 2–4.

[6]   Jacob Viner, *The Customs Union Issue* (New York, 1950) and Kenneth W. Dam, *The GATT: Law and International Economic Organisation* (Chicago, IL, 1970), 274–83. For an assessment on the issue multilateralism vs regionalism see also Jaime De Melo, and Arvin Panagariya (eds), *New Dimensions in Regional Integration* (Cambridge, 1993); Richard H. Snape, "History and Economics in GATT's Article XXIV," in Kym Anderson and Richard Blackhurst (eds), *Regional Integration and the Global Trading System* (New York, 1993), 273–91.

multilateralism had to be adapted to the new bipolar strategic perspective.[7] Equally important, it led Washington to foster Western European regional integration as a way of reinforcing the area politically and economically, and integrating a new West German state into the Western camp. As early as World War II, the U.S. government had considered whether to encourage European integration and, in particular, a customs union. An economically unified Europe would yield a more economically efficient European market than the single markets of the individual countries. It could enhance European economic growth that could, in turn, advance political stability, and it could provide a bigger market for outsiders' exports. European unity would also house a new German state's economic resources and integrate it economically and politically with its European partners.[8] By 1946 the Western European governments already appeared to be unconvinced that worldwide competition, multilateral liberalization, and the full convertibility of their currencies supported by the Bretton Woods system represented the path to follow in postwar reconstruction. The reconstruction of Western Europe required the return of Germany to full production through a return to statehood and the reduction of trade barriers among the Western European nations. It was with these two goals that in 1947 Washington launched the Marshall Plan. Western Europeans were stimulated to take steps that would enable them not just to grow economically, but to move towards open trading policies with each other and, then, with the rest of the world. The U.S. initiative was a key moment in Western Europe's path towards internal freer trade, and more generally towards a broadly liberal trade policy. In 1947, to pursue its policy of reconstruction, Western Europe opted for a regional and, therefore, smaller and discriminatory framework within which to gradually and slowly liberalize trade. The Organization for European Economic Cooperation (OEEC), established in 1948, and the European Payments Union (EPU), set up in 1950, among many other efforts, promoted a common reconstruction program, the removal of quantitative restrictions, and the convertibility of currencies between the participating countries.[9]

The liberalization of Western European trade started on a regional basis and through regional institutions, bypassing Bretton Woods multilateralism. Any general principles contrary to West European governments' own reconstruction principles were pushed into the background. In 1947, in the same year that

[7]   On the consequences of the Cold War on GATT see Michael M. Kostecki, *East–West Trade and the GATT System* (London, 1979).

[8]   On the U.S. stance towards European Integration see Pascaline Winand, *Eisenhower, Kennedy and the United States of Europe* (New York, 1993), 10–15; and Geir Lundestad, *"Empire" by Integration: The United States and European Integration, 1945–1997* (Oxford, 1998), 7–19.

[9]   The best account on the reconstruction of Western Europe remains Alan S. Milward. *The Reconstruction of Western Europe, 1945–51* (London, 1984). See also Barry J. Eichengreen, *The European Economy since 1945: Coordinated Capitalism and Beyond* (Princeton, NJ, 2007), 52–130.

the Truman administration signed the General Agreement, it also launched the Marshall Plan. While the GATT represented U.S. support for a multilateral, nondiscriminatory, and global trade system, the OEEC and EPU endorsed the principle of discrimination by the participants in the Marshall Plan. U.S. support for European regional integration came to coexist with the GATT's multilateralism, and doubts about the consequences of discriminatory European integration were put aside. According to the U.S. plan, in the long run European integration would reinforce Western Europe economically and would finally make possible the implementation of a multilateral trade and payments system. For the time being, however, Western Europe would discriminate in its trade relations and would do so with the full encouragement of the ally discriminated against.[10] Following this policy, in 1951 the Truman administration endorsed the Treaty of Paris establishing the European Coal and Steel Community (ECSC). Despite the inconsistency of the treaty with the rules of the GATT, under U.S. leadership a waiver was granted.[11]

President Eisenhower did not alter the U.S. stance on European integration, as he held that the original reasons for U.S. support were still valid. When, in 1955, the Benelux countries, France, the Federal Republic of Germany, and Italy started negotiations leading to the EEC, the Eisenhower administration adopted the same stance of full support as had Truman. The State Department was aware of the potentially discriminatory effects of the EEC. Nonetheless, it held that the political and economic advantages that European integration could provide were worth some trade discrimination.[12]

U.S. support became evident when the Treaty of Rome establishing the EEC with a customs union as its basis was presented to the GATT in 1958. Article XXIV required the members of a regional trading area to present the instituting treaty in Geneva in order to ensure its consistency with the GATT. Recommendations by the other contracting parties could lead to reconsiderations and revisions in the customs union treaty. The discussion over the Treaty of Rome resulted in the first significant test for the relationship between multilateral and regional trade in the GATT and for the U.S. policy of support for European integration and the multilateral trading system.

Notwithstanding the assurances of the EEC members, the Treaty of Rome in its most salient features did not comply with the GATT. On almost 80 percent of tariffs, the Treaty of Rome had set the level of the CET at the level of the arithmetical average of the duties applied in the four customs territories covered

---

[10] On this aspect of U.S. policy see Milward, *The Reconstruction of Western Europe*, and Wendy Asbeek Brusse, "The Americans, the GATT, and European Integration, 1947–1957: A Decade of Dilemma," in Francis Heller and John R. Gillingham (eds), *The United States and the Integration of Europe. Legacies of the Postwar Era* (New York, 1992), 221–52.

[11] Kock, *International Trade Policy and the GATT*, 54–6.

[12] On the attitude of the Eisenhower administration towards the EEC see Winand, *Eisenhower, Kennedy and the United States of Europe*, 63–85; and Lundestad, *"Empire" by Integration*, 40–57.

by the Community on January 1 1957. As a result, higher French and Italian duties were averaged with lower German and Benelux ones. Article XXIV provided that the CET on the whole could not be more restrictive than the general incidence before the creation of the customs union; where the common external tariff involved an increase in any rate previously bound in the GATT, a release had to be negotiated with the other contracting parties that were beneficiaries of that binding. These paragraphs became sources of everlasting debate. The EEC member states asserted that they had incorporated GATT provisions into the Treaty of Rome, as outside countries would be compensated for any increase in the low tariffs by the simultaneous reductions of high tariffs. By contrast, other GATT members rightly pointed out that the volume of trade affected by the changes in the duties had also to be considered. No less problematic was the issue of quantitative restrictions. According to the interpretation of EEC members, they could remove quantitative restrictions among themselves without extending the same liberalization to third countries. The other GATT members held that quantitative restrictions had to be eliminated against third countries in any case, as they were contrary to the GATT. The agricultural sector was included in the Treaty of Rome, but no details were given on how it would be regulated. This vagueness was considered as contravening the GATT. Conflict arose as well over the treaty's association agreement with overseas territories, by which each member's colonies would enjoy a preferential trading arrangement with the entire Community. Critics correctly argued that it did not establish a free trade area, but an old system of preferences, contravening the GATT on a point of maximum importance.[13]

A special GATT committee was set up with the task of assessing the conformity of the Treaty of Rome with the GATT. However, the core obstacle was that the commercial and political weight of the EEC made it impractical to condition its existence on consistency with the General Agreement. Against this backdrop, the risk Washington wanted to avoid was that the EEC be declared in formal violation of the General Agreement. Washington aimed at finding an ad hoc political solution, which could resolve the problem in a pragmatic way, so as to reconcile the unwillingness of the EEC to compromise with the mistrust of the other contracting parties and with the credibility of the GATT itself. The EEC was the cornerstone of U.S. policy in Western Europe, while the GATT represented the multilateral system. A settlement was indispensable. Thus, after a year of tough negotiations, under the leadership of Washington the legalistic confrontation was put aside for a pragmatic approach. The GATT would monitor the commercial policy of the EEC to ensure that an outward-looking Community developed and would look to the possibility of obtaining compensation from the EEC in future negotiation rounds. As a result, no formal decision on the compatibility of the Treaty of Rome

---

[13]   This reconstruction of the negotiations over the conformity of the Treaty of Rome to the GATT rules is grounded on Kock, *International Trade Policy and the GATT*, 122–31 and Ynze Alkema, *Regionalism in a Multilateral Framework: The EEC, the United States and the GATT. Confronting Trade Policies, 1957–62*, EUI Ph.D. dissertation, 1996, 65–117.

was made, and any problems that arose would be pragmatically resolved in future GATT rounds. As Romero puts it, "This new, crucial advancement of European integration was allowed to entrench itself behind the shelter of the USA's friendly diplomacy."[14] The priority of having the EEC fully settled pushed the Eisenhower administration to put aside any doubts on the potential discriminatory effects of the Treaty of Rome and any negotiations on its most controversial aspect, until after the EEC was firmly established.

In truth, not all members of the Eisenhower administration shared a belief in the wisdom of this approach, and latent concerns remained. The Treasury, Commerce, and Agricultural departments together with the Federal Reserve took a more critical position and held that any negotiations after the Treaty of Rome had gone unchallenged in Geneva might come too late to change it. However, the State Department and the U.S. president were in full support, and with the U.S. economy in good condition, it was unproblematic for them to affirm that European integration was worth some economic sacrifices.[15]

GATT Activities in the 1950s and the Dillon Round (1960–62)

In order to understand the reasons behind the launching of the Kennedy Round, it is necessary to briefly describe GATT activities in the 1950s and then the Dillon Round. The first GATT round took place in 1947. Under the authority of the Reciprocal Trade Agreement Act (RTAA), with which Congress authorized the U.S. government to enter into trade negotiations, the Truman administration was eager to start a new round. Its aim was to achieve a substantial reduction of tariffs and elimination of preferences, and notably the Commonwealth preference, although this latter goal turned out to be unattainable. Under the RTAA, the U.S. government lacked the authority to achieve the sweeping reductions of tariffs and nontariff barriers that would have pushed the British and the Commonwealth countries to eliminate their preferences. The RTAA—firmly grounded on the traditional American practice of accumulating bilateral, product-by-product tariff agreements, which could be altered by various congressional safeguard clauses and conditions—did not offer a convincing opportunity for long-term bargains. Consequently, the United Kingdom aimed at maintaining its preferences as a bargaining chip for future negotiations, hoping to get guaranteed easier access to the American market. At the same time, Commonwealth countries had no

---

[14]   Federico Romero, "Interdependence and Integration in American Eyes: From the Marshall Plan to Currency Convertibility," in Alan S. Milward (ed.), *The Frontier of National Sovereignty: History and Theory 1945–1992* (London, 1994), 155–82. Quote from 171.

[15]   On the doubts that existed within the Eisenhower administration see Winand, *Eisenhower, Kennedy and the United States of Europe*, 63–85; and Lundestad, *"Empire" by Integration*, 40–57.

intention of giving up their preferences on the British market while Congress kept Commonwealth agricultural exports out of the American market.[16] The round was rescued by the decision of the American delegation to accept small British concessions. The first round established the method for GATT negotiations, consisting of more than 100 separate, carefully bilateral negotiated accords that could be multilateralized. Despite the cumbersome method, the first round proved to be a successful test for the MFN rule technique of negotiating, as it achieved satisfying results, an average reduction of tariffs of 19 percent.[17]

The Annecy and Torquay conferences were held respectively in 1949 and 1951 and consisted of accession negotiations of new members. Combined, the two rounds yielded a 5 percent reduction of duties. Facing the prospect of the loss of protection through the elimination of quota restrictions in the OEEC framework, some major European countries such as the United Kingdom, France, Italy, and Germany reacted either by reintroducing previously suspended, prewar tariff schedules or by establishing new rates, often with generous "bargaining" margins aimed at negotiations in GATT rounds. The OEEC's practice of focusing on quotas and leaving tariff cuts to the GATT's cumbersome item-by-item procedure favored protectionism in Europe as, indirectly, it encouraged high-tariff countries to reactivate their customs schedules. The tariffs registered at the Annecy Round were generally high, and, although for the most part intended as bargaining positions, they started to be applied in 1950 as quotas began to be removed. As a result, by the early 1950s tariffs had made a reappearance as instruments of protection.[18] Moreover, the unwillingness of the Commonwealth countries to reduce their preferences meant that no tariff cuts were obtained between the United States, on the one hand, and the United Kingdom, Australia, and New Zealand on the other. The Geneva Tariff Conference of 1956, the fourth round, was unique. Only 25 out of 39 contracting parties agreed to participate, and, among them, concessions were agreed upon only by 22. The average tariff cut of the round was 2 percent.[19]

One of the causes of these small cuts should be looked for in the politics of the Europeans. Italy and France, holding that U.S. products were more competitive, resisted any meaningful multilateral reduction. The United Kingdom refused to dismantle or even reduce its colonial preferences. Only Germany took a more liberal stance. Despite these differences, one fact appeared evident to all: one of the conditions for joining in sweeping and across-the-board tariff reductions was that the United States would have to be able to make large tariff cuts. Washington

---

[16]   On British economic policy at the end of World War II see Alan S. Milward and George Brennan, *Britain's Place in the World Import Controls 1945–60* (London, 1996).

[17]   On the first GATT round see Zeiler, *Free Trade, Free World*, 55 and Kock, *International Trade Policy and the GATT 1947–1967*, 89–95.

[18]   Wendy Asbeek Brusse, *Tariffs, Trade, and European Integration, 1947–1957: From Study Group to Common Market* (New York, 1997), 84–6.

[19]   Hoekman and Kostecki, *The Political Economy of the World Trading System*, 103; and Kock, *International Trade Policy and the GATT*, 89–95.

would have to offer substantial and, above all, long-term and stable export benefits that would permit the Europeans to increase their exports. However, during the entire decade of the 1950s, the U.S. government never obtained from Congress the authority to reduce tariffs because of the domestic opposition to widespread, across-the-board tariff reductions, while nontariff barriers (NTBs) reinforced the protection and made any tariff cut unstable. The American legislative body attached protective clauses to the RTAA. It adopted the escape clause—which permitted the withdrawal of a tariff concession that might injure an industry—as a legitimate device in trade negotiations, while the peril point provision—which set a point at which a tariff concession could hurt a domestic producer—became a staple part of the RTAA. The U.S. policy made tariff rates inherently unstable and tariff negotiations precarious, offering few prospects for long-term benefits to its trading partners.[20]

Nor did the cumbersome reduction procedure used in Geneva favor a major scaling down of tariffs. Governments bargained bilaterally on an item-by-item basis and then, if agreement was reached, the reduction was multilateralized. This bilateral–multilateral method had been designed by U.S. drafters of the GATT, who presumed that the United States, being the major supplier of most goods, would take the lead in offering major tariff cuts. However, the plan underestimated the impact of the protectionist mood of Congress.[21]

Unwillingness to reduce tariffs and disagreement on how to do so account for the stalemate of the GATT in the 1950s. The U.S. government was not able to offer substantial cuts, and not all the Europeans were ready to reduce tariffs on a multilateral basis. As a result, tariffs remained fairly stable between the Annecy Round and the preliminary phase of the Dillon Round, as Table 1.1 illustrates.

Still, the GATT was not irrelevant. As noted by Irwin and Asbeek Brusse, the GATT's major contribution in the 1950s was not reducing tariffs, but rather securing binding agreements on early tariff reductions and, consequently, preventing the Europeans from setting higher tariffs as quotas and foreign exchange controls were progressively removed.[22]

The signing of the Treaty of Rome led the Eisenhower administration to promote a new round, with the aim of reducing both the discrimination of the EEC and, more broadly, barriers to international trade. In the State Department's strategy, a new round was another piece of a pragmatic solution to the problem of fitting the EEC into the GATT and monitoring its development. In 1958 Congress renewed the RTAA for three years to reduce tariffs by up to 20 percent over a four-year period. In truth, the available bargaining power granted to the U.S.

---

[20]   Asbeek Brusse, *Tariffs, Trade, and European Integration*, 84–6. On the U.S. trade policy see, among the others, Alfred E. Eckes, Jr, *Revisiting U.S. Trade Policy: Decisions in Perspective* (Athens, OH, 2000), 49–51.

[21]   Asbeek Brusse, *Tariffs, Trade, and European Integration*, 119 and 131–9.

[22]   Irwin, "The GATT in Historical Perspective"; Asbeek Brusse, *Tariffs, Trade, and European Integration*, 119.

Table 1.1   GATT rounds and their main results

Year	Round and number of attending countries	Average depth of tariff cuts in percent ad valorem in the industrial sector	Number of tariff concessions exchanged
1947	Geneva 23	19	45,000
1949	Annecy 29	2	5,000
1951	Torquay 32	3	8,700
1956	Geneva 33	2	2,700
1960–62	Dillon 39	8	4,400

Source: data elaborated from Asbeek Brusse, *Tariffs, Trade, and European Integration*, 118 and Hoekman and Kostecki, *The Political Economy of the World Trading System*, 101.

government was modest because of the existence of the escape clause and peril-point procedures. With the clumsy procedure of bilateral item-by-item negotiations and within the modest authority granted by the RTAA, the new round, named after the undersecretary of state for economic affairs, Douglas C. Dillon, started in September 1960. As the Eisenhower administration was coming to an end, it would be up to the Kennedy administration to negotiate it.[23]

Initially, the EEC offered to reduce its common external tariff across the board by 20 percent, subject to reciprocity. Used internally by the Six in reaching their common tariff, this approach of across-the-board tariff cuts on all products in major categories of goods could replace the bulky method of negotiating on each item. Yet the source of the EEC offer was mainly internal, originating from the French and Italian aim of placating Germany, which requested a unilateral reduction in the CET.[24] Under the RTAA, the United States lacked the right to proceed with 20 percent linear reductions. The U.S. offer fell far short of the 20 percent across-the-board figure, and a massive pullback of offers by others was avoided at the last minute when President Kennedy, "at his peril," authorized the American delegation to go beyond the peril points on U.S.$76 million of U.S. imports. As a result of these influences, the average reduction in industrial tariffs was only about 10 percent for the EEC and slightly less for the United States.[25]

---

[23]   On the Dillon round see Alkema, "Regionalism in a Multilateral Framework," 178–86; Ernest H. Preeg, *Traders and Diplomats: An Analysis of the Kennedy Round of Negotiations under the GATT* (Washington, DC, 1970), 40–41 and Thomas W. Zeiler, *American Trade and Power in the 1960s* (New York, 1992), 64–5.

[24]   Andrew Shonfield (ed.), *International Economic Relations of the Western World, 1959–1971*, vol. 1 (London, 1976), 168–74.

[25]   Preeg, *Traders and Diplomats*, 40–41.

Even more difficult were the negotiations in the agricultural sector. By 1961, the Six had started elaborating their CAP, which, with its variable levy system, threatened to reduce imports. Foodstuff-exporting countries such as Denmark, Canada, Australia, and New Zealand had the firm intention of making agriculture the major issue of the Dillon Round. The EEC wanted to withhold concessions on the grounds that it planned to establish a common agricultural policy and could not negotiate before the CAP had been settled. In contrast, the GATT partners wanted concessions from the Six because agriculture represented the sector where trade barriers were expected to rise most as a result of the CAP. It is worth noting that Washington did not choose to oppose the variable levy system on the ground that it was inconsistent with the GATT rules. The CAP was considered the price the United States had to pay for European integration. After all, the EEC was founded on economic integration, which also presupposed a common agricultural policy. After tough negotiations, and after the U.S. Department of Agriculture had suggested suspending the trade talks to signal American displeasure, the stalemate was broken when Washington consented to completing negotiations without resolving the problems created by the emerging CAP. The EEC and the United States formally agreed that Washington had "unsatisfied negotiations rights." The United States had the right to seek satisfactory compensations under GATT Article XXIV. The EEC pledged not to increase protection until the CAP was implemented, and undertook not to implement any restrictive or import-controlling system. Most important, while implementing the CAP, the Six agreed to open negotiations with the United States to discuss the state of American exports.[26] As a result, a major confrontation between the United States and the EEC over agriculture was merely postponed.

The overall results were not wholly fruitless, although the gains in term of trade were modest. Both sides made concessions on manufactured goods, reducing tariffs by 20 percent on average. The Six cut tariffs on transportation equipment, electrical and industrial machinery, and chemicals, the United States on machinery, electrical apparatus, steel, and automobiles, while it excluded chemicals for lack of authority. Agricultural products (excepting a few products covered by tariffs), ECSC products, and List G products—whose CET level had been set in February 1960, and which the Six did not wish to change again—were not included. As a result, the 20 percent reduction concerned only one-third of U.S.–EEC trade, reducing by 7 percent the average protection for all sectors.[27]

In the Dillon Round, the relatively inadequate power of the U.S. executive did not favor major results. The Americans finally became aware of the difficulty of negotiating effectively under the limitation of the RTAA. Moreover, the Dillon Round proved that the utility of the item-by-item method of negotiation had come to an end. With the increase in number of the contracting parties attending the rounds, the method had become too time-consuming. Inadequate results, linked

[26]   Steve Dryden, *Trade Warriors: USTR and the American Crusade for Free Trade* (Oxford, 1995), 40–41.

[27]   Ibid.

to awareness that item-by-item bargaining had outlived its effectiveness and the fact that a new kind of authority was required to negotiate effectively in Geneva, steered Washington to push for a new multilateral conference of a different kind. When in July 1961 British prime minister Harold Macmillan announced that the United Kingdom would apply for EEC membership, the Kennedy administration concluded that the Dillon Round would not be able to deal with the developments taking place in Europe. A bold new start to deal with the EEC and with European integration was necessary.[28]

Kennedy's Initiative for a Sweeping Liberalization of International Trade: Integrating the EEC and Boosting the U.S. Economy

While the Eisenhower administration had to react to the creation of the EEC, the Kennedy administration had to face up to the implementation of the EEC and then the British request, presented in July 1961, to join it.[29] While following the policy of support established by Truman, the Kennedy administration held that new initiatives were necessary to address changes that were taking place in Western Europe. Kennedy feared that the EEC could develop into an inward-looking bloc and that the two sides of the Atlantic could become rivals in the economic, military, and political fields. This concern had also troubled Eisenhower, but with Kennedy it increased because of two factors: the policy of French president Charles de Gaulle and the U.S. deficit in its balance of payments. As for the first aspect, U.S. relations with France were becoming strained, above all because of divergences over the governance of the Atlantic Alliance and monetary issues.[30] As for the second, in 1958 the persistent U.S. deficit began to increase dramatically as a result of domestic economic recession, overseas military spending and investments, and a sharp decrease in the U.S. trade surplus. From 1959 to 1961, the deficit in the U.S. balance of payments averaged U.S.$3.2 billion per year, as compared with an average U.S.$1.1 billion per year between 1952 and 1958. Moreover, from 1950 to 1960 the U.S. gold supply fell from U.S.$22 billion to U.S.$17 billion, the prewar level, and in 1960, for the

---

[28]   Shonfield, *International Economic Relations of the Western World*, 175. Curzon, *Multilateral Commercial Diplomacy*, 100; Zeiler, *American Trade and Power in the 1960s*, 64–5. On the British application see Alan S. Milward, *The United Kingdom and the European Community: The Rise and Fall of a National Strategy* (London, 2002).

[29]   On Kennedy's policy towards European integration see Winand, *Eisenhower, Kennedy and the United States of Europe*, 139–60; Lundestad, *"Empire" by Integration*, 56–78; and Douglas Brinkley and Richard T. Griffiths (eds), *John F. Kennedy and Europe* (Baton Rouge, LA, 1999).

[30]   On de Gaulle and the United States, among the many scholars who have dealt with the issue, see Frédéric Bozo, *Two Strategies for Europe: De Gaulle, the United States and the Atlantic Alliance* (Lanham, MD, 2001); Frank Costigliola, *France and the United States: The Cold War since World War II* (New York, 1992).

first time, foreign dollar reserves exceeded U.S. gold reserves.[31] At the same time, the dollar gap that had characterized the Western European economies in the 1950s became a dollar glut at the end of the decade, and these dollars were increasingly cashed in for gold, contributing to the fall in U.S. holdings. The erosion of gold holdings, combined with the deficit in the balance of payments, undermined the credibility of the U.S. pledge to convert any dollar into gold, causing concern on both sides of the Atlantic over the strength of the exchange-rate system. In this context, the combination of EEC discrimination, the growing competitiveness of European producers, and the capital outflow of U.S. investment in Europe could no longer be considered as favorably as when the U.S. balance of payments did not represent a problem and the gold reserve seemed unlimited.[32]

Solving the deficit remained a priority for Kennedy, as he deemed it a threat to the supremacy of the U.S. dollar and, consequently, to the United States' overall position in the world and its capacity to carry out effective policies in the Cold War. However, building a consensus in this area of policy was not an easy task. Treasury Secretary Douglas Dillon pinned the blame squarely on military expenditures abroad, and in Western Europe in particular, and saw the reduction of military commitments as the easiest way to resolve balance-of-payments problems. Dillon was convinced that the deficit was not caused by the role of the dollar as the main source of liquidity in the growing world economy, and that adjustments and interventions in other fields, such as capital outflows and overseas expenditures, would allow the international monetary system to be preserved. However, the State Department held that the deficit was the result of a flawed international monetary system, called for structural reforms, and strongly rejected the solution of withdrawal of military forces on the ground that it would undermine Western European confidence in NATO and in the United States. Kennedy identified U.S. security commitments to Western Europe as the main cause of the deficit, but was hesitant to reduce the U.S. military presence because of the consequences this move could have for relations with European allies. At the same time, he was reluctant to reform the monetary system because of the impact this adjustment could have on the standing of the dollar. As a result of these conflicting considerations, the response that emerged consisted of a set of less dramatic measures that, considered as a package, were targeted at ending the deficit. Initiatives were taken to reduce capital outflows, stabilize the dollar and

[31]   *Survey on Current Business*, Washington, DC, 1968.

[32]   For an analysis of how the deficits in the balance of payments affected U.S.–Western Europe relations see Francis J. Gavin, *Gold, Dollars, and Power: The Politics of International Monetary Relations, 1958–1971* (Chapel Hill, NC, 2004). The literature on monetary problems for this period is vast. See, among the others, Susan Strange, *International Monetary Relations* (London, 1976); vol. 2 of Andrew Shonfield (ed.), *International Economic Relations of the Western World, 1959–1971* (London, 1976); Harold James, *International Monetary Cooperation since 1945* (Washington, DC, 1996); Barry J. Eichengreen, *Exorbitant Privilege: The Rise and Fall of the Dollar and the Future of the International Monetary System* (Oxford, 2011).

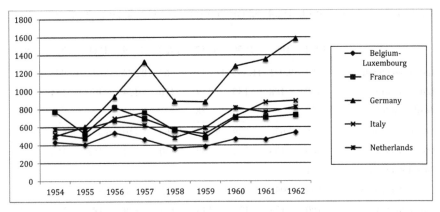

Figure 1.1   U.S. exports to the Six, 1954–62 (in thousands of U.S.$, current prices)

Source: *Direction of Trade Statistics Historical, 1948–1980* (Washington, DC, 2002).

reduce the gold drain, achieve rapid, noninflationary domestic growth, and convince the Europeans, above all Germany, to share the U.S. military burden. Foreign trade policy, too, was intended to play a major role in redressing the deficit.[33]

In order to understand this last aspect and the centrality of the EEC in Kennedy's decision to promote a new round of the GATT negotiations, it is necessary to illustrate the place of the EEC in U.S. trade. As Table 1.2 shows, the EEC was a major and dynamic market for U.S. exports. The implementation of the EEC customs union in 1959 did not prevent the United States from increasing exports to the area from a total value of U.S.$2871 million in 1958 to U.S.$4577 million in 1962. Moreover, together with Japan, the EEC was the area where U.S. exports increased by the fastest rate. In 1962, the EEC was the United States' primary trade partner in terms of volume and percentage of total trade.

As Table 1.3 illustrates, trade with the EEC was also important from the point of view of the U.S. trade balance, as a considerable part of the U.S. surplus stemmed from trade with this area.

Figure 1.1 shows that, among the EEC members, the Federal Republic was the most dynamic market for the United States. Notwithstanding the beginning of

---

[33]   For the debate and the policy of the Kennedy administrations over the balance of payments see Hubert Zimmermann, *Money and Security: Troops and Monetary Policy in Germany's Relations to the United States and Britain, 1950–1971* (Cambridge, 2002); Gavin, *Gold, Dollars, and Power*; Thomas Zoumaras, "Plugging the Dike: The Kennedy Administration Confronts the Balance-of Payments Crisis with Europe," in Brinkley and Griffiths, *John F. Kennedy and Europe*, 168–81; Fred L. Block, *The Origins of International Economic Disorder. A Study of United States International Monetary Policy from World War II to the Present* (Berkeley, CA, 1978), 177–81.

Table 1.2   U.S. exports 1954–62 (in thousands of U.S.$, current prices)

	1954	1955	1956	1957	1958	1959	1960	1961	1962
Industrial countries	8,387	9,021	11,363	11,875	9,763	10,384	12,617	12,928	13,283
Index growth	100	108	135	142	116	124	150	154	158
% of total trade	57			58					61
Western Europe	4,495	4,675	5,989	6,262	4,964	5,110	6,852	6,821	7,152
Index growth	100	104	133	139	110	114	152	152	159
% of total trade	31			30					33
United Kingdom	798	995	969	1,145	905	1,100	1,492	1,212	1,130
Index growth	100	125	121	143	113	138	187	152	142
% of total trade	5			6					5
EEC	2,806	2,597	3,663	3,867	2,871	2,869	3,987	4,170	4,577
Index growth	100	93	131	138	102	102	142	149	163
% of total trade	19			19					21
Canada	2,95	3,383	4,13	4,017	3,540	3,827	3,813	3,838	4,053
Index growth	100	115	140	136	120	130	129	130	137
% of total trade	20			19					19
Asia	1,184	1,427	1,855	2,069	1,907	1,671	2,182	2,232	2,455
Index growth	100	121	157	175	161	141	184	189	207
% of total trade	8			10					11
Japan	691	680	995	1,317	987	1,080	1,451	1,841	1,574
Index growth	100	98	144	191	143	156	210	266	228
% of total trade	47			63					73
Western Hemisphere	3,096	3,021	3,551	4,314	3,892	3,408	3,634	3,817	3,649
Index growth	100	98	115	139	126	110	117	123	118
As % of total trade	21			21					17
Developing countries	5,740	5,814	6,864	7,982	7,525	6,742	7,686	8,009	8,316
Index growth	100	101	120	139	131	117	134	140	145
As % of total trade	39			39					38

Source: Direction of Trade Statistics Historical, 1948–1980 (Washington, DC, 2002).

Table 1.3   U.S. trade balance 1954–62 (thousand of U.S.$, current prices)

	1954	1955	1956	1957	1958	1959	1960	1961	1962
World	4024	3561	5522	6730	3349	789	4362	5218	4092
EEC	1800	1356	2113	2178	1039	266	1530	1767	1929

Source: Direction of Trade Statistics Historical, 1948–1980 (Washington, DC, 2002).

the implementation of the customs union, exports to Germany rose and did so at a faster rate than exports to the other five members of the EEC.

Yet these favorable trade patterns did not reassure Washington. In 1962 the customs union's implementation was only just beginning; it was expected to be fully operational in 1970. The goal of reducing EEC barriers remained paramount in order to permit efficient exports from other countries to enter the EEC at competitive prices. The CET had to be kept low, and, by the same token, other common policies that the EEC was developing could not be permitted to create a protectionist bloc. Among these policies, a prominent position was certainly held by the CAP. Washington feared that it could lead to an economically inefficient degree of EEC self-sufficiency that could work to the detriment of traditional, efficient agricultural exporters, such as the United States, Canada, Australia, and New Zealand, and radically alter world trading patterns.[34] In 1954, U.S. agricultural exports accounted for 10.2 percent of total U.S. farm income, and by 1962 this figure had risen to 15.0 percent. Among the U.S. economic sectors, farmers were the most reliant on exports. In the 1950s both the U.S. Department of Agriculture and American producer organizations became increasingly oriented towards commercial exports sales, as it became clearer that productive capacity exceeded the domestic capacity to absorb production. Among overseas markets the EEC had an important position. In 1961, U.S. exports of agricultural products to the area represented about a quarter of total U.S. agricultural exports, and, most importantly, half of the U.S. trade surplus with the EEC originated from agricultural exports, which ran at the rate of almost five times U.S. imports from the EEC. In the same year, U.S. agricultural exports to the Six represented 32.4 percent of U.S. total exports to the area.[35]

---

[34] *United States and the World Trade in Perspective, Seventh Annual Report of the President of the United States of Trade Programme*, September 1963, 1–7, Administrative History Office of the Special Representative for Trade Negotiations, box 1, LBJL.

[35] United States Bureau of Census, *The Statistical History of the United States: From Colonial Times to the Present* (New York, 1976), Series U, 201–6; *Foreign Trade Related to Various Measures of Production: 1869–1970*, 887; and *Foreign Agricultural Trade of the United States*, U.S. Department of Agriculture, Economic Research Service (March 1970), 18–19. For U.S. agricultural policy see Thorald K. Warley, "Western Trade in Agricultural

Given the importance of the U.S. agricultural sector, negotiations over agriculture that would moderate likely EEC protectionism appeared urgent. Although, in the view of the White House and the State Department, European integration required support for a common agricultural policy, certain protectionist excesses of the CAP should be prevented.[36] In contrast, the U.S. Department of Agriculture (USDA), more interested in supporting the interests of U.S. farmers than in European integration, and facing well-organized lobbies in Congress, was vociferous in opposing the CAP and in asking the U.S. government to protect agricultural exports.[37]

Washington was also worried about the trade preferences extended by the EEC to the member countries' former colonies. These discriminated against Latin America and the other less-developed countries and, consequently, could increase the pressure on the U.S. market, or lead these countries to expand trade with the Soviet bloc.[38]

Through the customs union, the CAP, and the association agreements, the EEC could become a major protectionist trading bloc. Thus, Washington deemed new initiatives urgent. A prominent role in the elaboration of the policy towards Western Europe was played by Undersecretary of State for Economic Affairs George Ball, an advocate of free trade and European integration.[39] Ball suggested providing the U.S. president with greater powers to develop foreign commercial policy. Ball recommended new trade legislation equipping the U.S. president with the authority to reduce duties by 50 percent across the board, that is to say, by a uniform percentage, over a five-year period, so as to launch a new GATT round leading to a sweeping liberalization of international trade. Foreign trade policy would be concentrated on a new and bold initiative aimed at tackling the EEC, an initiative that would be used as "a justification for a major new round of trade negotiations and a precedent for reducing tariffs by percentage cuts across the board rather than the tradition item-by-item haggling."[40]

Products," in Shonfield, *International Economic Relations of the Western World*, vol. 1, 320–22.

[36] FRUS 1961–63, IX, Section 11/230 Memorandum From the Under Secretary of State for Economic Affairs (Ball) to President Kennedy, 23 October 1961.

[37] *Narrative History of the Special Representative for Trade Negotiation*, vol. 1, 2, 1969, Administrative History of the Office of the Special Representative for Trade Negotiations, box 1, LBJL.

[38] FRUS 1961–63, IX, Section 11/227, Paper Prepared by the President's Special Assistant Petersen, Proposal for 1962 United States Foreign Trade and Tariff Legislation, 4 October 1961.

[39] For Ball's central role in the formulation of trade policy see also Eckes, *Revising U.S. Trade Policy*, 31–2.

[40] Report to the Honourable John F. Kennedy, dated 31 December 1960. Pre-presidential papers—Transition files, Task Force reports, box 1073, JFKL; George W. Ball, *The Past Has Another Pattern* (New York, 1984), 159–65.

Two aims were pursued: first, reducing EEC discrimination in order to avoid the fragmentation of the Western economy and the multilateral system into separate trading blocs; and second, increasing U.S. exports, considered crucial to economic growth and, by increasing the trade surplus, to closing the balance-of-payments deficit. Ball also made clear his views on the responsibilities of the Europeans: "any surplus countries accumulating foreign exchange ... should accept a responsibility to take measures to increase its imports of goods and services" from the United States. The burden of military expenses would be shared by augmenting the already favorable trade balance with the Western European countries to a level high enough to compensate for military commitments and investments in Europe.[41] In short, Western Europe had to share military costs by accepting more imports from the United States as a form of compensation to Washington.[42]

The necessity for an initiative on foreign trade policy became urgent with the British decision to seek EEC membership, taken in July 1961. Washington welcomed the British step. The entry of the United Kingdom would strengthen Western Europe, counterbalance de Gaulle's nationalism, and strengthen transatlantic relations. The enlargement of the EEC to include the United Kingdom and other EFTA countries would end the economic division of Western Europe, and a liberal country like the United Kingdom could keep the EEC from becoming too inward-looking. Further, the British rate of GDP growth was inferior to the EEC average. EEC membership could stimulate British growth, and consequently U.S. exports. Nonetheless, enlargement of the EEC created economic concerns for its potential discriminatory impact. Washington looked with apprehension at the prospect of the United Kingdom, the world's largest agricultural product importer, adopting the protectionist system of the CAP and Commonwealth preferences being extended to the enlarged EEC, discriminating against U.S. and Latin American goods. Washington ran the risk of facing the discriminatory effects arising from an EEC regional bloc, with a highly projectionist CAP, with preferential trade arrangements with the British Commonwealth and with the less-developed countries linked to the EEC by association agreements. Initiatives to avoid all the negative consequences of the enlargement and to mutually sustain European integration and the multilateral system appeared necessary to observers in Washington.[43]

---

[41]   Report to the Honourable John F. Kennedy, dated 31 December 1960, Pre-presidential papers-Transition files, Task Force reports, box 1073, JFKL.

[42]   George Ball's memo to Dean Rusk, January 1961. General Correspondence Folder, 48–164, B General, 1 January–31 March 1961, box 12, JFKL.

[43]   NARA 59 Department of State, Central Files, 375.800/8-761, Memorandum by Ball to Kennedy, 7 August 1961; FRUS 1961–63 XIII West Europe and Canada; Economic and Political Integration. 16 Memorandum for the President "UK Adherence to the European Common Market" by George Ball, 23 August 1961; FRUS 1961–63 XIII West Europe and Canada. Economic and Political Integration. 17 Circular Telegram From Department of State to Certain Missions in Europe by Dean Rusk, 5 September 1961; FRUS 1961–63, IX, Section 11/227, Paper Prepared by the President's Special Assistant Petersen, Proposal for

A GATT round aimed at a sweeping liberalization had already been envisaged before the British decision to seek EEC membership. As a matter of fact, the expiration of the RTAA due in 1962 had already given Ball the opportunity to prepare a trade bill with a totally new approach. The British move intensified the urgency of a GATT round.[44] As Ball put it, "The proper road to the defence— and indeed, the advancement—of our trading interests is to pursue liberal trade policies ourselves and to insist that the Common Market do likewise. This means that we must be in a position to reduce our own tariffs on a reciprocal basis."[45] Washington responded to events in the EEC regional trading bloc by invoking freer trade and multilateralism.

The Trade Expansion Act: A Bold New Trade Law with EEC Regionalism in Mind

In October 1961, the internal debate over trade policy intensified. Ball held that the utility of the RTAA had come to an end, and that a new trade bill with a completely new approach was necessary to make significant tariff reduction possible. The U.S. president had to hold a strong starting position calling for broad tariff reduction across the board and inclusion of agriculture and tropical products in the new round. Such goals required a totally new trade bill. As for the timing, Ball's plan was to announce in 1962 the general directions of the new trade policy, but to hold off the introduction of an explicit legislative proposal until 1963, which would not be an election year. Ball also took into account the mixed feelings that existed in the United Kingdom over EEC membership, aiming to avoid the danger that announced tariff reductions in the GATT might complicate Britain's entry. The Macmillan government had justified the decision to seek membership by citing the discriminatory effects of economic exclusion from the EEC. However, if such discriminatory effects could be diminished through a GATT round, justifications for membership would lose sway, or so feared Ball.[46]

1962 United States Foreign Trade and Tariff Legislation, 4 October 1961. FRUS 1961–63 XIII West Europe and Canada. 19 Telegram from the Department of State to the Embassy in the United Kingdom, 17 October 1961.

[44] FRUS 1961–63 XIII West Europe and Canada. Economic and Political Integration. 20 Circular Telegram From Department of State to Certain Missions in Europe by Dean Rusk, 27 October 1961.

[45] FRUS 1961–63 XIII West Europe and Canada. Economic and Political Integration. 16 Memorandum for the President "UK Adherence to the European Common Market," by George Ball, 23 August 1961.

[46] FRUS 1961–63, IX, Section 11/228. Memorandum From the Deputy Assistant Secretary of State for Economic Affairs (Trezise) to the Under Secretary of State for Economic Affairs (Ball) "Comments on Petersen's Trade Legislation Proposals," 10 October 1961; FRUS 1961–63, IX, Section 11/230 Memorandum From Ball to President

Kennedy too had doubts about presenting a trade bill during an electoral year, but events in Geneva and in Brussels convinced him it would not be wise to wait. In Geneva, at the GATT ministerial meeting of November 1961, disaffection was expressed with the cumbersome item-by-item reduction of tariffs, and a linear approach was invoked; developing countries expressed their disapproval of the GATT, seen as unproductive and unreflective of their trade interests, and agriculture and nontariff barriers were identified as areas to be addressed. Pinpointing the lines that the GATT had to follow, the November 1961 meeting provided a major impetus in the direction of a new round.[47] Moreover, the Dillon Round was clearly demonstrating the U.S. government's lack of authority to engage in a major liberalization of trade. In Brussels, the Six were negotiating for the enlargement of their Community. For these reasons, the initiative for the new and audacious trade law had to be taken in 1962, while Washington still had time to influence the EEC developments. The U.S. president followed the advice of White House assistant Howard C. Petersen, who suggested taking the initiative in 1962 so as to anticipate European developments and give little time to protectionist lobbies in Congress to organize against the bill.[48]

In January 1962 the text of the trade bill was sent to Congress. In order to underline the break with the RTAA, the bill was named the Trade Expansion Act (TEA). Kennedy listed five major developments that had made the United States' traditional trade policy obsolete: "the growth of the European Economic Community; the growing pressures of the U.S. balance-of-payments positions; the need to accelerate U.S. economic growth; the Communist aid and trade offensive; the need for new markets for Japan and the developing counties."[49] Extensive new tariff-cutting authority was necessary to promote the implementation of a liberal and multilateral trading system, to foster economic growth through an expansion of exports, and to redress the deficit in the balance of payments and maintain military commitments. Kennedy indicated above all the EEC, with its faster economic growth, as the area to which the United States had to increase exports. The essential condition was that Western Europe must remain open to external trade, and this required that the United States accept a reciprocal reduction in

---

Kennedy, 23 October 1961. William Diebold, Jr and H.L. Stalson, "The Background of the Decisions to be Made." Background paper n. 1 for meeting of 20 November 1961, Council on Foreign Relations, Discussion Group on United States Foreign Policy.

[47]   FRUS 1961–63, IX, Section 11/ 215. Editorial Note; Preeg, *Traders and Diplomats*, 41–2.

[48]   FRUS 1961–63, IX, Section 11/227, Paper Prepared by the President's Special Assistant Petersen, Proposal for 1962 United States Foreign Trade and Tariff Legislation, 4 October 1961. On Kennedy's initiative for a new round see, Zeiler, *American Trade and Power in the 1960s,* 151–4.

[49]   President's message to the Congress, H.R. document no. 314, 87th Congress, 2nd Session; reprinted in Hearings Before the Committee on Ways and Means of the House of Representatives on H.R. 9900.

its own tariffs. As for agriculture, considering the importance of the Western European market for U.S. farmers, increased authority was required to negotiate with the EEC to keep the latter open to U.S. exports.

In October 1962 the Trade Expansion Act was approved with a strong bipartisan majority. In signing the bill, Kennedy stated, "This is the most important international piece of legislation ... affecting economics since the passage of the Marshall Plan. ... By means of agreements authorized by the act, we can move forward to partnership with the nations of the Atlantic Community."[50] Beyond Kennedy's emphasis, the TEA was a totally new type of law in U.S. trade legislation and conferred the mandate to drastically reduce protectionism.[51] As for the tariff-cutting authority, due to expire on June 30, 1967, it gave the president (a) general power to reduce duties by half, and to eliminate duties of 5 percent or less; and (b) special power to eliminate duties in negotiations with the EEC (1) on items where the exports of the United States and the EEC together accounted for 80 percent or more of total free world exports to the free world (the *dominant-supplier clause*); (2) on agricultural commodities, if the agreement maintained or expanded U.S. exports of the same commodity; and (3) on tropical and forest products, if the EEC provided comparable access for such products from the free world and the products were not produced in significant quantities in the United States.

The dominant-supplier clause deserves more attention here for its link with the EEC. Kennedy's decision to look for Congress's approval in 1962 raised in Ball the concern that in the United Kingdom opposition to membership could be strengthened by the prospect of gaining better access to the EEC market merely by attending a GATT round. In order to ensure that Kennedy's decision would not complicate British membership and considering British willingness to reduce tariffs worldwide, Ball drafted the dominant-supplier clause. The U.S. president would have the authority to reduce to zero tariffs on those products for which the United States and the EEC together accounted for more than 80 percent of world trade. The EEC was defined as those countries that had agreed to achieve a common external tariff on the date when the United States started formally preparing negotiations. If the United Kingdom joined the EEC, tariffs could be cut to zero on a large range of items; if it did not, the clause would apply only to aircraft and margarine. The dominant-supplier clause had also the purpose of obtaining maximum advantages from the EEC enlargement by exploiting it to extensively cut tariffs across the Atlantic and enhance U.S. exports. The commodities touched by the clause—chiefly machinery, railway equipment, automobiles, and organic chemicals—were the most advanced technical goods entering world trade, in

---

[50] George M. Taber, *John F. Kennedy and a Uniting Europe: The Politics of Partnership* (Bruges, 1969), 70; and Zeiler, *American Trade and Power in the 1960s*, 152–3. On the approval of the TEA see Zeiler, 64–168; Dryden, *Trade Warriors* 47–9.

[51] This description of the TEA is grounded on Administrative History-Office of the SRTN—Narrative History, box 1, LBJL; and Stanley D. Metzger, *Trade Agreements and the Kennedy Round* (Fairfax, VA,1964).

which the United States held a competitive position. The clause had the advantage of enabling the United States to negotiate down the CET of the enlarged EEC and was well suited to integrating the EEC into the multilateral system. It would have created a kind of Atlantic free trade area between the United States and the EEC, but enlarged to all nations through the MFN rule, thus extending the liberalization of trade to the entire multilateral system.[52]

Actually, it was not clear what expectations the Kennedy administration had of the clause. Since the outset it had been doubtful that, once negotiations for the new round had started, the Americans' zeal for cutting would be so drastic as to exceed the 50 percent general authority. Maybe a more realistic explanation was given by Metzger, one of the drafters of the TEA, who claimed that the clause aimed to demonstrate the U.S. willingness to liberalize trade and steer its partners to follow its lead. It would prove the determination of the United States to adopt a trade program aimed at the free movement of industrial goods, and could encourage the EEC to remain open to world trade during its critical enlargement stage.[53]

With the TEA, the U.S. government clearly stated its intention to include agriculture in the round, for the first time since creation of the GATT. To the establishment of the regional CAP, the United States responded with the request to deal with agriculture at the multilateral level. The aim was not to attack this policy's existence, but rather to influence its formulation before all of its main features were established, in order to moderate its discriminatory aspects. Washington kept the line adopted in 1958 when the Treaty of Rome was presented to the GATT: it did not challenge the existence of the CAP, but rather decided to negotiate pragmatically.[54]

The U.S. government was aware of the difficulty of obtaining meaningful results in agriculture. In the GATT, reduction of protectionism occurred when a reciprocal interest in enhancing exports existed. This was not the case for agriculture. Washington was interested in maintaining exports to the EEC, while the EEC had no exports to enhance. Thus, the United States lacked bargaining power. Moreover, U.S. credibility was undermined by its own protectionism: the U.S. GATT waiver obtained in 1955 to protect agricultural products made it difficult for Washington to present itself as the sponsor of trade liberalization in agriculture. U.S. support for European integration further weakened U.S. bargaining power: Washington

---

[52] Ball, *The Past Has Another Pattern*, 198–9; FRUS 1961–63 XIII West Europe and Canada. 21 Telegram From the Department of State to the Embassy in the United Kingdom, 30 October 1961. Telegram drafted by Schaetzel, approved by Ball and sent by Bowles.

[53] Metzger, *Trade Agreements and the Kennedy Round*, 27. On this issue see also William Diebold, Jr. "A Watershed with Some Dry Sides," in Brinkley and Griffiths, *John F. Kennedy and Europe*, 235–62.

[54] For the U.S. stance on the CAP see Components of a Strategy for the Kennedy Round written by George Ball, Preliminary Draft, December 10, 1963, Herter Papers, box 7 JFKL. This document written in 1963 summarizes the aims of the Kennedy administration with the passing of the TEA.

supported the CAP as an instrument to give unity to the EEC and, as a result, under the lead of the State Department, never challenged this common policy by, for example, questioning the compatibility of the CAP variable-levy system with the GATT. To put pressure on the Europeans and under the insistence of the USDA, the U.S. government affirmed that it would not conclude the GATT talks in the industrial sector unless meaningful results were achieved in agriculture. Yet, the White House and the State Department had no intention of putting at risk the industrial bargain, where lay the biggest gains, for the sake of agriculture.[55]

The TEA introduced those changes necessary to reduce trade barriers in the new context where the EEC was emerging as powerful trading bloc. The crucial role of the European actor is shown by the fact that the U.S. law clearly spelled out the EEC. Moreover, the dominant-supplier clause and the provisions for agriculture and for tropical products showed that the TEA was framed bearing in mind that the EEC and all its elements that could affect international trade, notably the CET, the CAP, the association agreements with the former colonies, and potential enlargement with the entrance of the United Kingdom. Equally important, the broad authority to cut tariffs provided for in the TEA made possible a major innovation in U.S. trade policy, notably the ability to reduce tariffs across the board. The EEC represented an opportunity to ask Congress for the authority to reduce tariffs multilaterally and maintain a relatively open global system. The very existence of a regional trading area on the other side of the Atlantic encouraged the United States to adopt a bold policy to liberalize international trade. Without a strong European counterpart capable of credibly offering reciprocal concessions thanks to the size of its market, the U.S. offer of a comprehensive tariff cut could hardly have been suggested.

A final aspect of this context should be considered here. As noted, Kennedy presented the trade bill as a tool to establish a partnership to guarantee the strength and cohesion of the Atlantic Alliance. To assess the full importance of the TEA and grasp the link between trade and security issues in Kennedy's foreign policy, it is necessary to place the economic reasons leading to the TEA in the wider political context of the Atlantic "interdependence" referred to by President Kennedy and the prospects for what came to be called the *Atlantic partnership*. Against the developments taking place in Western Europe, the Kennedy administration wanted to strengthen the Atlantic Alliance and keep it united under U.S. leadership. The enlarged EEC had to be fitted into the wider Atlantic framework of NATO and of the GATT. Only in such a framework could the United States support European integration. The answer to this objective was the *grand design for an Atlantic partnership between equals*. The whole idea of partnership sprang from the existence of a new actor and the economic and political interdependence between the two sides of the Atlantic. The partnership was considered an instrument to

---

[55]   On the divergences the State Department and the Department of Agriculture see Components of a Strategy for the Kennedy Round, written by George Ball, Preliminary Draft, December 10, 1963, Herter Papers, box 7, JFKL.

establish a framework for the long-run development of economic and political transatlantic relations, and to contain changes in the Atlantic Alliance brought about by the existence of the EEC. The ultimate goal was to bring together two separate but equal entities in order to adjust differences and then combine their force to hold communism at bay, and to develop the global south, as Kennedy put it.

In concrete terms, the Atlantic partnership would be built on three pillars. The first was represented by the multilateral nuclear force (MLF), suggested in 1962 by Kennedy to promote U.S. control of European developments in the military and nuclear fields. The second was British entrance into the EEC, which would strengthen transatlantic ties.[56] The third pillar was the TEA. The partnership concept, as applied to trade, consisted in linking the two sides of the Atlantic in a low-tariff trade area, strengthening their unity through greater economic interdependence. A drastic liberalization would build the economic foundation of the Atlantic partnership. Toward that end, the TEA with its dominant-supplier clause had to launch the Atlantic partnership by diminishing trade discrimination between the two sides and establishing a firm economic basis for partnership. The TEA must be viewed not merely as an instrument for reducing trade barriers, but also as the commercial tool of Kennedy's grand design to shape relations with Western Europe. As Ball put it, "The TEA was conceived as an instrument by which the United States—through the encouragement of trans-Atlantic trade—could bring about a greater a degree of common economic interest and policy within the Atlantic framework, and as a further step toward the creation of the Atlantic partnership."[57]

In truth, contradictions existed in this partnership between equals. As Winand notes, the Kennedy administration, while "insisting that the partnership should be equal, continued to speak of the indispensable leadership role of the United States."[58] Washington said "Atlantic framework" but meant, as Lundestad puts it, a U.S.-dominated framework.[59] Furthermore, the United States seemed willing to share the burdens of being a superpower, but unwilling to share the power. It asked the EEC to accept more U.S. exports as recompense for the military costs of defending Europe and as a way of decreasing the deficit in the American balance of payments, but it insisted on the necessity of U.S. leadership. As a result, the partnership-between-equals initiative resembled a cosmetic cover to keep the EEC firmly within the Atlantic framework, to make the Europeans pay more, and to maintain U.S. leadership.

---

[56]   Kennedy's grand design and the MLF have been analyzed by many scholars. Among them see Winand, *Eisenhower, Kennedy and the United States of Europe*, 160–203.

[57]   Components of a Strategy for the Kennedy Round written by George Ball, Preliminary Draft, December 10, 1963, Herter Papers, box 7, JFKL; Narrative History of the Special Representative for Trade Negotiation, vol. 1, 2, 1969, Administrative History of the Office of the Special Representative for Trade Negotiations, box 1, LBJL.

[58]   Winand, *Eisenhower, Kennedy and the United States of Europe*, 191.

[59]   Lundestad, *"Empire" by Integration*, 40.

Kennedy's initiatives towards Western Europe were elaborated in the framework of the policy on European integration established by Truman and continued by Eisenhower. Kennedy responded to the developments taking place in Western Europe by continuing U.S. support for European integration, while calling for a new GATT round to reduce world protectionism and foster links across the Atlantic. The TEA was a way to mutually sustain EEC regionalism and GATT multilateralism and to ensure that the development of regionalism in Europe would be conciliated with U.S. support for an open and nondiscriminatory economic system. Kennedy's trade program set the direction and the tone of the U.S. response to European developments: it favored an outward-looking EEC with a strong American connection propelled by a new GATT round that had both political and economic implications. Equally important, the new round represented an ambitious effort to liberalize world trade and was intended to set the tone for future world trade.

Chapter 2

The EEC's Answer to the U.S. Proposal: Accepting the Round While Defending its Regionalism

Trade Regionalism and Economic Growth in the Economic Policy of EEC Members

This section provides background information needed to understand the reaction of the EEC member states to the U.S. proposal. It illustrates the political economy of the Western European countries after 1945 and emphasizes the importance the EEC members attached to the regional dimension of their Community as a means to stimulate economic growth. The reconstruction of the Western European economy after World War II was grounded on the double aim of favoring economic growth with full employment—in order to achieve social and political stability—while giving a new role to Germany, which had been in the past a major engine of European growth, but also the source of two world wars. On the domestic side, corporatist arrangements were intended to facilitate high investment returns. On the international side, regional institutions—the OEEC and the EPU—were established to ensure the stability of supply and outlet markets, give credibility to the decision to reduce trade barriers, and guarantee that governments would not withdraw their commitment to liberalize. Investment and export-led economic growth were the objectives. As Eichengreen has noted, investments and exports were "two sides of the same coin."[1]

The driving force of the economic policy of Western European countries was a combination of state intervention and measures to increase the exposure of the domestic economy to international market forces. In this context trade liberalization was supposed to have a major relevance, as it would favor economic growth through an expansion of exports. Any effort to increase investment would have not led to sustained, high investment levels without two indispensable conditions: a constant flow of the necessary inputs, and stable outlets, whether domestic or external. The guarantee of foreign supplies and outlets became paramount in European economic policy. Only constant flows of the necessary imports and assurance of stable outlets

---

[1]   Eichengreen, *The European Economy since 1945*, 39. For an analysis of international institutions in the reconstruction of Western Europe see Barry J. Eichengreen, "Institutions and Economic Growth. Europe after World War II," in Nicholas Crafts and Gianni Toniolo (eds), *Economic Growth in Europe since 1945* (Cambridge, 1996) 38–72.

for excess production would permit national industry to work at full capacity, provide full employment, and finance welfare programs. In addition, social cohesion would fuel the politics of productivity that lay at the base of corporatist arrangement. Only high economic growth, tighter social cohesion, and greater political stability would provide a stable basis for democratic consolidation at a continental scale. The war had changed the role of the state in economic policy. Governments had assumed new policy goals that went beyond the task of recovery and aimed at promoting economic growth, full employment, and social welfare. State intervention progressively became the new orthodoxy of economic policy. Trade barriers became part of a wider political economy employed for ever broader policy objectives. It is against the backdrop of this framework and, in particular, the link between investment and trade that the political economy of trade liberalization and the commercial policies of Western European countries should be considered.[2]

Equally important, it is against this backdrop that the establishment of the EEC with a customs union at its basis should be understood. The customs union was expected to have a fundamental role, as it would favor export-led economic growth through liberalization of trade on a regional basis. As Milward has noted, the customs union would sustain the boom in exports that had occurred since 1953 to an area the hub of which was the Federal Republic of Germany, by means of a regional trading area protected from international competition. Trade with Germany was considered indispensable to industrialization, modernization, and, consequently, economic growth. This framework of postwar economic policy led the Six to choose to face the internationalization and multilateralization of trade, promoted by the United States, with a regional agreement and with a new form of international cooperation, notably integration. The creation of the EEC embodied the solution to the problems of how to guarantee the expansion of intra-European trade, and how to integrate the key German market in a European regional market. European economic security and prosperity depended on the German market in such a crucial way that a commercial policy to guarantee access to that market became an essential element of any policy to integrate the Federal Republic into Western Europe. Moreover, well before the formation of the EEC, the Six had already established a trading network. From 1954 onwards, foreign trade between them grew faster than foreign trade elsewhere in Europe. The regional dimension of trade between the Six had already appeared before 1957 and represented a fundamental aspect of the decision to establish the EEC. The customs union aimed at continuing a trend established previously.[3]

---

[2]   On the reconstruction of the Western European economy see Milward, *The Reconstruction of Western Europe*. For an analysis of the economic policy of the Western European states see Crafts and Toniolo (eds), *Economic Growth in Europe since 1945*.

[3]   Alan S. Milward, *The European Rescue of the Nation-state* (London, 2000), chap. 4, "Foreign Trade, Economic and Social Advance, and the Origins of the European Economic Community," 119–223. On the negotiations leading to the Treaty of Rome see Enrico Serra (ed.), *Il Rilancio dell'Europa e i Trattati di Roma* (Brussels, 1989).

To understand the reaction of each of the Six to the U.S. proposal, it is also worth analysing their stances towards the establishment of the EEC and its regionalism. As for the Federal Republic, as noted by Milward, while its markets had an essential function for most Western European countries, it had a more variegated trade network. From 1951 to 1959 its exports to the rest of the world increased faster than those to Western Europe, and, after 1956, North America was the market to which German exports grew at the strongest rate. Thus, the hub of Western Europe trade also had major trade interests outside Europe.[4] This aspect of German trade became crucial in the German domestic debate on the EEC. For security reasons Chancellor Adenauer opted for the "small Europe" of the Six, rejecting the British proposal for a broader and weaker free trade area (FTA) among OEEC members. Adenauer had to resist the opposition of the German minister of economy, Ludwig Erhard, who supported the FTA initiative. Erhard feared that the Six's customs union was too small and could hurt German exports elsewhere, was unhappy about the dirigiste and protectionist features of the Treaty of Rome, and worried about the effects of the trade division of Western Europe. Support for the FTA came also from German industry, represented by the Federation of German Industry, the Bundesverband der Deutschen Industrie (BDI), which favored the Treaty of Rome for its bigger export opportunities to France and Italy, but as a first step towards an FTA. At the same time, a number of German economic sectors—textile, pulp and paper, and nonferrous metal industries—fully supported the Treaty of Rome for the protection it gave against other European competitors. It was on these sectors that Adenauer could count in getting the Treaty of Rome approved and the FTA rejected. Erhard and the BDI remained the strongest advocates of the FTA, and after its failure they looked with apprehension at the establishment of the EFTA in 1959 and the trade division of Western Europe. They feared it could cause a reduction in German exports and hinder liberalization at European and world levels. In spite of the fact that aggregate trade patterns showed that in 1959–63 none of the major industrial sectors suffered from the creation of the EEC or, then, of the EFTA, Erhard and the BDI managed to keep the issue of Western Europe's division high on the German political agenda.[5]

In France, after the initial reticence that pushed the other five negotiators to succumb to Paris' demands so as to ensure its participation in the Treaty of Rome, the regional dimension of the EEC was fully embraced. As Lynch claims, between 1944 and 1958

---

4   Milward, *The European Rescue of the Nation-state*, 196–8.

5   Markus Schulte, "Industrial Interest in West Germany's Decision Against the Enlargement of the EEC: The Quantitative Evidence up to 1964," *Journal of European Integration History* 3, 1 (1997), 35–61; Markus Schulte, "Challenging the Common Market Project: Germany Industry, Britain and the Europe, 1957–1963," in Ann Deighton and Alan S. Milward (eds), *Widening, Deepening and Acceleration: The European Economic Community 1957–1963* (Baden-Baden, 1999), 167–83. See also Gerold Ambrosius, "The Federal Republic of Germany and the Common Market in Industrial Goods in the 1960s," in Régine Perron (ed.), *The Stability of Europe: The Common Market. Towards European Integration of Industrial and Financial Markets? (1958–1968)* (Paris, 2004), 47–61.

France transitioned from a highly protected and controlled imperial economy to an economy linked to "neighbouring states at similar levels of economic development in a set of legally binding arrangements under the Treaty of Rome." The treaty well reflected French interests. It implemented a customs union for industrial products, in which French goods could compete in a framework smaller than the multilateral one established by the GATT. It implemented a common agricultural policy thanks to which French farmers could be subsidized and French goods enjoyed protected outlets. It contained provisions allowing France to retain links with the French Union and the setting up of association agreements. With foreign trade playing a growing role in the French economy, the Treaty of Rome gave France the opportunity to modernize its economy within a regional area protected from international competition. It represented an excellent intermediate solution to French economic problems that could not be solved at the national level. The strategy was to confront the French economy with a limited degree of competition within the EEC and share the costs of modernizing its agriculture and empire with its partners.[6] Although de Gaulle had throughout the 1950s stated his opposition to any loss of sovereignty, when he returned power in 1958 he did not reject the treaty. On the contrary, he approved the devaluation of the Franc, the return to convertibility, and the Rueff plan, which allowed France to cope with the increased competition derived from entering the EEC. De Gaulle continued the Fourth Republic's policy of strengthening the French economy through the EEC.[7]

As for the other four members of the EEC, Italy fully shared France's idea of liberalization of trade on a regional basis. It appreciated the market opportunities provided by the Treaty of Rome, and wished to open its market in a framework smaller than that established by the GATT or the British-proposed FTA.[8] The Benelux countries were traditionally liberal. They supported the Treaty of Rome as a means of ensuring a market for their exports, but wished to keep the EEC open to world trade. The government in The Hague, in particular, after having promoted tariff liberalization in the wider contexts of the GATT and OEEC until the mid-1950s with no results, embraced the smaller EEC. However, some Dutch circles believed that the Dutch idea of a liberal EEC had been watered down in the Treaty

---

[6]   Francis M. B. Lynch, *France and the International Economy: From Vichy to the Treaty of Rome* (London, 1996), 211–15.

[7]   On de Gaulle's acceptance of the Treaty of Rome and rejection of the British FTA see Francis M. B. Lynch, "De Gaulle's First Veto: France, the Rueff Plan and the Free Trade Area," *Contemporary European History* 9, 1 (2000), 111–35.

[8]   For Italy and European integration see the many works of Fauri, Ranieri and Varsori. Francesca Fauri, *L'Italia e l'integrazione economica europea 1947–2000* (Bologna, 2001); Ruggero Ranieri, "Italian Industry and the EEC," in Deighton and Milward, *Widening, Deepening and Acceleration*, 185–98; Antonio Varsori, *L'Italia nelle relazioni internazionali dal 1943 al 1992* (Rome, 1998); Federico Romero and Antonio Varsori, *Nazione, Interdipendenza, Integrazione. Le relazione internazionali dell'Italia (1917–1989)* (Rome, 2006). For an account of the reaction of the Italian industry to the EEC see Francesco Petrini, *Il liberismo a una dimensione: la Confindustria e l'integrazione europea, 1947–1957* (Milan, 2005).

of Rome. The Hague was aware that the structure of Dutch imports—mainly semimanufactured goods and end products from non-EEC countries—made it essential to have an EEC open to international trade in order to avoid a shift in the source of imports from third countries to more expensive EEC goods. Following this logic, The Hague favored a liberal EEC policy towards nonmembers.[9]

The Treaty of Rome provided for exclusive Community competence in the trade field. This implied that the six members that until 1957 had had national and different commercial policies now had to define and implement a common commercial policy, finding the necessary compromises to set aside their differences over how open to world trade their Community had to be. One critical concern is worth underlining. For all of the Six, the regional dimension of the EEC was essential because of the market opportunities it gave and the protection it provided against third countries. This was true for Italy and France, and for the Federal Republic and the Netherlands countries as well. For sure, Bonn and The Hague favored an outward-looking EEC and wanted to protect trade with third countries. Notwithstanding differences on how open to trade with third countries the EEC had to be, all members fully agreed upon the relevance of the regional dimension of the EEC in fostering economic and income growth.

The implementation of the customs union required the removal of all trade barriers between member states and the setting up of CET and a common commercial policy towards third countries. From 1959 the Six started dismantling intra-EEC trade barriers and setting the CET according to a three-phase calendar that required the full establishment of the customs union by the end of the transitional period (December 31, 1969). The dismantling process was based on across-the-board cuts, with the exception of some products for which other methods were retained. As for the CET, the Treaty of Rome established the general rule of the arithmetic average of duties applied in 1958 in the four customs unions of the EEC. The CET was formed by averaging the high tariffs of France and Italy with the much lower tariffs of the Federal Republic and Benelux (see Table 2.1). Certain products, representing 15.7 percent of imports from third countries, were excluded from this general rule and put on a list—List G—for which the CET was negotiated among the Six by March 1960.[10] Following the provisions of the

---

[9]   For the position of the Benelux countries see Milward, *The European Rescue of the Nation-state*, 173–96; Richard T. Griffiths, "The Common Market," in Richard T. Griffiths, *The Netherlands and the Integration of Europe 1945–1957* (Amsterdam, 1990), 183–208; Anjo G. Harryvan, *In Pursuit of Influence: The Netherland's European Policy during the Formative Years of the European Union, 1952–1973* (Brussels, 2009).

[10]   The pace of elimination of intra-EEC duties and of the definition and implementation of the CET is described, with useful tables, by Colette Nême and Jacques Nême, *Economié Européenne* (Paris, 1970), 48–86. For an account of the implementation of the customs unions through the 1960s see Ruggero Ranieri, "The Origins and Achievements of the EEC Customs Union (1958–1968)," in Antonio Varsori (ed.), *Inside the European Community: Actors and Policies in the European Integration, 1957–1972* (Baden-Baden, 2006), 257–81.

Table 2.1   Average ad valorem percentage incidence of import duties of the Six in 1958

SITC	Product	Benelux	France	Germany	Italy	CET
5	All chemicals	7	16	8	17	12
61	Leather manufactured goods	11	11	12	18	12
62	Rubber manufactured goods	17	17	10	19	18
63	Wood and cork manufactured goods, except furniture	11	19	7	22	16
64	Paper and board manufactured goods	14	16	8	18	15
65	Textiles, except clothing	14	19	11	20	16
66	Nonmetallic mineral manufactured goods	12	16	6	21	13
67	Silver, platinum, gems, jewellery	5	13	3	7	6
681	Iron and steel	5	13	7	17	10
6841	Primary aluminum	0	20	0	25	9
691	Ordnance	9	14	7	17	11
699	Manufactured metal goods	11	20	10	23	16
71	Machinery other than electric	8	18	5	20	13
72	Electric machinery	11	19	6	21	15
73	Transport equipment	17	29	12	34	22
81	Building parts and fittings	15	19	8	25	17
821	Furniture	13	23	8	21	17
84	Clothing	20	26	13	25	21
851	Footwear	20	21	10	21	19
86	Instruments	13	25	8	20	16

Note: SITC, Standard International Trade Classification.

Source: Data taken from different tables reproduced in *Political and Economic Planning: Atlantic Tariffs and Trade* (London, 1962).

Treaty of Rome, France and Italy had to reduce their national duties in order to join the CET, while Germany and the Benelux countries had to raise theirs, as Table 2.1 shows. This circumstance should be kept in mind in order to understand the reactions by EEC members to the U.S. initiative for further reductions of duties at the multilateral level.

    To understand the reaction of the Six to the U.S. initiative and then their stance in the GATT talks, it necessary to illustrate a last element, notably trade patterns since 1954. Table 2.2 highlights how important trade at the regional level of the

Table 2.2   EEC member states' exports 1954–63 by destination (in millions of U.S.$ at current prices)

	1954	1958	1963		1954	1958	1963
The Federal Republic of Germany				*The Netherlands*			
EFTA	1.524	2.649	3.967	EFTA	584	847	1.036
% of total	29.2	27.1	27.2	% of total	24.8	23.7	21
Index growth	100	174	260	Increase	100	145	177
EEC	1.534	2.731	5.455	EEC	862	1.597	2.646
% of total	29.3	27.9	37.4	% of total	37	44.6	53.6
Index growth	100	178	356	Increase	100	185	306
USA	295	913	1.051	USA	158	209	203
% of total	5.6	9.3	7.2	% of total	6.7	5.8	4.1
Index growth	100	309	356	Increase	100	132	128
Rest of the world	1.873	3.463	4.112	Rest of the world	747	926	1.049
% of total	35.9	37.7	28.2	% of total	31.5	25.9	21.3
Index growth	100	185	220	Increase	100	124	140
France				*BLEU[a]*			
EFTA	616	760	1.313	EFTA	423	524	674
% of total	17	14.2	16.3	% of total	18.6	16	14
Increase	134	123	213	Increase	100	154	297
EEC	907	1.527	3.093	EEC	991	1.522	2.941
% of total	25	28.5	38.3	% of total	43.5	46.4	61
Increase	100	168	341	Increase	100	154	297
USA	156	470	421	USA	191	444	411
% of total	4.3	8.7	5.2	% of total	8.3	13.5	8.5
Increase	100	301	270	Increase	100	232	215
Rest of the world	1.952	2.593	3.238	Rest of the world	673	789	798
% of total	53.7	48.6	40.2	% of total	29.6	24.1	16.5
Increase	100	133	166	Increase	100	117	119
Italy							
EFTA	398	642	959				
% of total	24.6	22.3	19				
Increase	100	161	241				
EEC	356	792	1.799				
% of total	22	27.5	35.7				
Increase	100	222	505				
USA	129	345	480				
% of total	8	12	9.5				
Increase	100	267	372				
Rest of the world	732	1.097	1.801				
% of total	45.4	38.3	35.8				
Increase	100	150	246				

Note: [a] Belgium and Luxembourg.

Source: *Direction of Trade Statistics Historical, 1948–1980* (Washington, DC, 2002).

EEC was for the Six and how dramatically intra-EEC trade increased in the period from 1958, the year before the implementation of the customs union began, to 1962. It also shows that the dramatic increase in intra-EEC exports was accompanied by a reduction in exports to the rest of the world. At the same time, differences existed among the member states. The Federal Republic had relevant trade interests outside the EEC: EFTA took a considerable share of its exports, a share that continued to rise in value after 1958, while the United States took a valuable 7.2 percent of German exports in 1963. Compared with Germany, France had a large proportion of exports going to the EEC and a lower percentage of exports going to the EFTA countries and to the United States. Belgium–Luxembourg had relevant exports to the EFTA, but also to the United States. As was the case with the Federal Republic, the EFTA markets took a considerable share of Dutch exports. Ranking the EEC members' interests in trade with the EFTA measured by share of exports to the area, the Netherlands were second only to Germany. By contrast, exports to the United States were less significant and rather instable. Italy had major interests in exports to EFTA, and, at the same time, a considerable share of exports went to the United States.

Figures 2.1 and 2.2 give an idea of EEC trade patterns as a whole. Figure 2.1 concerns the destination of EEC exports. From 1958 to 1962 the exports of the Six to the EEC increased from 30.1 to 39.7 percent of EEC total exports. The share of exports to the United States and EFTA remained more or less stable, while the share to the rest of the world decreased from 40.8 to 31.1 percent.

Figure 2.2 concerns the source of imports of the EEC as a share of the total. In 1958, 29.6 percent of EEC imports came from the EEC itself. This share increased to 37.5 percent by 1962. The share of imports from the United States was stable, while the share from the EFTA decreased slightly. Along with exports, imports from the rest of the world also dramatically decreased: while in 1958 they represented 42.5 percent, by 1962 they had decreased to 34.6 percent.

De Gaulle, the United Kingdom, and the GATT

Previous accounts of the Kennedy Round, grounded on U.S. sources, have described the French government as primarily busy in opposing all American initiatives—the TEA included. An analysis of the French reaction grounded on the French archives reveals that the French did not oppose the U.S. initiative and sheds new light on French trade policy.

In elaborating his policy towards Europe, President Kennedy had to deal with the charismatic figure of Charles de Gaulle, who, unfortunately for Washington, had a different conception of the Atlantic Alliance and its policies, and of the position of the EEC and France in the Alliance. As has been described by the many scholars who have written on Franco-U.S. relations in the 1960s, along with the critical issue of decision-sharing within the Alliance, "Kennedy and de Gaulle disagreed over the governance and structure of the West's nuclear deterrent, the

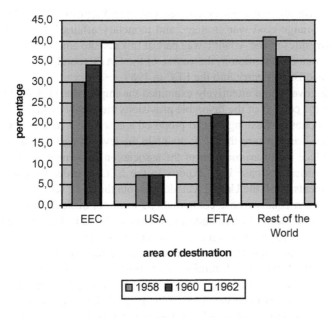

Figure 2.1   EEC exports by area of destination as a percentage of the total
Source: *Direction of Trade Statistics Historical, 1948–1980* (Washington, DC, 2002).

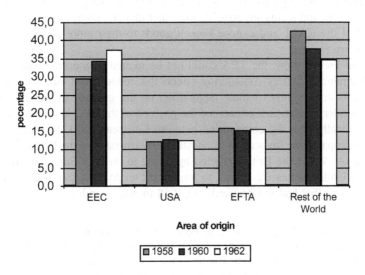

Figure 2.2   EEC imports by area of origin as a percentage of the total
Source: *Direction of Trade Statistics Historical, 1948–1980* (Washington, DC, 2002).

response to the Berlin crisis, policy on Germany and Vietnam, the nuclear test ban treaty, long-range cold war strategy, and monetary affairs."[11] Trade policy between the two sides of the Atlantic was part of this dispute and influenced U.S. perception of France's intention in the course of the GATT round, above all after the French vetoed British entry into the EEC in 1963.

The French government attentively examined the impact the TEA could have on the EEC. In the context of the favorable provisions the Treaty of Rome granted to the French economy, Washington had proposed a new GATT round in order to decrease or even bring to zero the CET; maintain the level of agricultural exports to the EEC; reduce the discrimination of the association agreement against other developing countries; increase U.S. exports to the EEC in order to redress the balance of payments; push the United Kingdom to join the EEC; set up an Atlantic partnership between equals whose contradictions were not difficult to identify in Paris; and, finally, implement a free trade area across the Atlantic. Paris looked with suspicion at the Kennedy trade program and had every intention, by one means or another, of limiting the impact the new conference could have on the EEC.

In February 1962, the French minister of foreign affairs, Maurice Couve de Murville, claimed that the EEC would be unwilling to drastically reduce its tariffs for an important range of manufactured goods. Even if the EEC had to be open to the outside world and avoid autarky, it had to preserve its essential European character and therefore needed a common external tariff against the outside world to maintain its unity.[12] By the same token, the minister of finance, Valéry Giscard d'Estaing, held that the U.S. initiative was "précipitée," dictated by developments in Europe and wrongly timed. France was already reducing barriers at the EEC regional level, and it was not possible to further increase competition in the wider context of the GATT and expose French goods to their more competitive U.S. counterparts.[13]

In the French view, the TEA could not be treated as a normal proposal for tariff bargaining, merely considering effects that reduction of duties could have on imports and exports. A trade negotiation on the grounds of the TEA had a much broader impact, as it concerned the position of the EEC in world trade, and could radically alter the competition between European and U.S. products. The French compared the invocation of an Atlantic partnership to the British initiative for an FTA. While the British reacted by trying to create a European free trade area, the United States was trying to implement an Atlantic free trade area. The same reasons that had led de Gaulle in 1958 to put an end to FTA negotiations

---

[11]   Frank Costigliola, "Kennedy, de Gaulle, and the Challenge of Consultation," in Robert O. Paxton and Nicholas Wahl (eds), *De Gaulle and the United States: A Centennial Reappraisal* (Oxford, 1994), 169. For de Gaulle's foreign policy, see also Bozo, *Two Strategies for Europe*; Costigliola, *France and the United States*.

[12]   *New York Times*, February, 21 1962, "Common Market Held Cool to Kennedy Tariff View," 9.

[13]   Interview of the author with Valéry Giscard d'Estaing, Florence, October 27, 2004.

pushed him in 1962 to categorically refuse an Atlantic free trade area. The regional dimension of the EEC would be watered down, and French products would have to struggle with more competitive U.S. goods.[14]

Paris doubted that, under the pressure of domestic economic sectors, the U.S. government could really propose such drastic tariff cuts. It was likely that the plan for tariff disarmament, just as with other U.S. initiatives launched with the same solemnity—Alliance for Progress, Years of the United Nations for development— would be considerably reduced in practice. However, for the time being the TEA had to be considered for what it purported to be, a "revolutionary" answer to the "challenge" to the United States represented by the success of the EEC.[15]

No one in the French government thought of rejecting altogether the U.S. initiative, even if it had reasons to do so. After all, France was already reducing its trade barriers in the framework of the EEC, while the eventual entrance of the British into the EEC would further increase competition. However, a French refusal would have increased strain with the United States. Most importantly, it would trouble relations with the Federal Republic and the Netherlands, which supported the U.S. initiative, thereby provoking a serious crisis in Brussels. At the same time, if the new round could be reduced in its scope, Paris had every reason to attend in order to boost exports to EFTA countries and to the United States, above all after the years 1959–62 had proved that French products could compete in a context wider than the national one.

In accepting participation, the French tried to reshape the U.S. initiative by setting conditions that widened the scope of the round, making it more complex and articulated. First, the French categorically opposed the dominant-supplier clause and the consequent implementation of an Atlantic free trade area.[16] Second, the French noted that the liberal provisions of the TEA—general authority to reduce tariffs by 50 percent, the dominant-supplier clause, elimination of duties for tropical products and of duties inferior to 5 percent—were part of a more protectionist framework characterized by the safeguard measures of the peril

---

[14]   NARA State Department CDF 1960–63, box 720, Memorandum of Conversation between Ball, Schaetzel and Giscard d'Estaing, March 30, 1962, and ibid. Telegram no. 4599 from Paris to State Department, March 30, 1962; MAEF GATT 930, Note du Quai D'Orsay "Kennedy Round," undated document but written after April 1 and before May 8 1963. The document illustrates the reaction of the French government to the U.S. initiative in 1962.

[15]   MAEF, DE/CE 1961–66 GATT 930, Direction des Affaires Economiques et Financière, Note 217/CE, November 19, 1962.

[16]   This reconstruction of the French position is grounded on the following documents: MAEF, DE/CE 1961–66 GATT 949 Direction des Affaires Economiques et Financières, Note 174/CE, Loi américaine sur le commerce et les futures négociations tarifaires, October 17, 1962; ibid., GATT 949 Direction des Affaires Economiques et Financières, Note 238/ CE, Les Etats-Unis et la Communauté Economique Européenne, December 10, 1962; ibid., GATT 930 Aide-mémoire à l'attention de M. le Secrétaire Général 1962; ibid., GATT 930, Direction des Affaires Economiques et Financières—Service de Coopération Economique, Note 14/CE, Offre américaine de négociations tarifaires, January 18, 1963.

point and escape clause provisions. This framework caused uncertainty over reductions of duties by the Americans. Moreover nontariff barriers such as the customs valuations system of the American Selling Price (ASP), which allowed the U.S. government to considerably raise duties on a given product, further reduced the meaningfulness of tariff cuts. According to the French, the TEA was not a balanced act. It would cause a reduction of CET while leaving intact most U.S. protectionist tools, with the result that the United States would increase its exports to the EEC, while the Six would continue to face NTBs in the United States. Hence, the new round had to be an opportunity to harmonize commercial rules at the international level so as to give all countries the same advantages. The French government also underlined the necessity of harmonization of competitive conditions, as drastic tariff reductions could not be achieved unless accompanied by a certain degree of coordination of economic and social policies across the Atlantic. The example of the EEC and the failure of the British FTA illustrated that this request for coordination reflected a genuinely fundamental principle of French policy, rather than dubious or phony argumentation.

The French identified another issue that would take center-stage in the Kennedy round, the *disparity problem*. In the U.S. tariffs structure, there were some very low duties and others that were extremely elevated, even prohibitive ad valorem duties of 100 and 200 percent. By contrast, the CET, being already an average, was more uniform and moderate. A reduction of duties by a uniform percentage, as suggested by Washington, would have different effects on low and high duties. A cut of 50 percent on a duty of 200 percent or 100 percent would maintain a high duty, while it would meaningfully reduce a moderate one, and bring almost to zero a low duty. A solution had to be devised to lop off the peaks in the U.S. tariffs and to harmonize tariffs across the Atlantic.

As for agriculture, a basic point was clear in Paris. One of the France's aims in signing the Treaty of Rome had been to ensure regional outlets for its agricultural products. Hence no negotiation in Geneva could be allowed to impede this fundamental goal. Therefore, it was unsafe to negotiate on agriculture in Geneva while the CAP was not yet fully agreed in Brussels. Once the CAP had been fully approved, negotiations in Geneva could begin. With this fundamental position in mind, the French did not oppose the inclusion of agriculture in the round, which constituted an opportunity to deal with problems affecting world trade in the agricultural sector and the impact on world trade of the domestic policies of the big exporting countries.

The last aspect to be considered was the link between the new round and the Brussels negotiations over British EEC membership. The question was not merely how to respond to the U.S. initiative, but also how to respond to two contemporary requests that would increase competition: the U.S. proposal for multilateral reduction of tariffs and the British query about membership. The extent to which the GATT negotiations would be economically and politically desirable would be determined by the result of talks with the British. One thing was certain in Paris: either a GATT round or British membership would be accepted, but not both.

France would not undertake a meaningful reduction of protection multilaterally if it accepted British membership, which would drastically increase competition within the EEC. Thus the French stance on the new round would be conditioned by the result of the Brussels negotiations. Paris anticipated that, in the case of failure of the latter, a broad tariff disarmament would become an indispensable replacement. For that reason, Paris questioned the usefulness of discussing a new round without knowing whether the GATT tariff cuts would replace membership or accompany it. According to Paris, the timing of the U.S. proposal was in this respect unfortunate, and it seemed reasonable not to further complicate the membership talks with an early start to the new round. The conclusions of the Brussels talks should be known first.

Paris did not oppose the American move for a new GATT round, but it wanted negotiations on French terms, not simply a round following the lines of the TEA, which, after all, was an American law. The round had to be brought into precise limits that would make the reductions of trade barriers more bearable. The regionalism of the EEC had to be protected, and implementation of an Atlantic free trade area was out of the question. Hence, the dominant-supplier clause had to be made harmless, in one way or another. Then, once the results of negotiations with the British were known, a new round could begin.

The EEC Reaction in the Industrial Sector: Accepting the Round, with Some Qualifications

When the TEA was presented to Congress in January 1962, the Six were busy negotiating on the issues that had pushed Washington to launch a new round: the enlargement of the EEC, the implementation of the customs union, the association agreements, and the CAP. In so doing, the EEC was defining its common commercial policy and establishing the pattern of its world relations. The U.S. proposal implied that liberalization of trade at the regional level would be accompanied by liberalization at the multilateral level. At this point, the ball arrived in the court of the Europeans. Now it was up to them to respond, deciding whether and how they intended to attend the round, and to what extent they would support Washington's declared intention to drastically reduce, or even eliminate, duties. In so doing, the Six would choose how their Community was to fit into the multilateral trading system and how trade integration at the regional level would be accompanied by increased trade integration at the multilateral level. Their answer had decisive importance: the EEC's position in world trade was dependent on its stance in the prospective negotiations, and so, therefore, was the future of world trade itself. The U.S. initiative put the EEC in the position of having to delineate its stance on world trade and the pattern of its regional and multilateral integration. The EEC had to continue to delineate its international trade policy, a fundamental step that would affect the patterns of its trade integration at regional and multilateral levels. In this sense, taking a position on the U.S. initiative implied a further decision in the definition of the EEC's common commercial policy.

The reaction of the EEC member states varied from enthusiasm to caution. In January 1962, Erhard met Kennedy and Ball in Washington and conveyed his full support for the U.S. trade program, which he described as "well designed to cope with the dangers of discriminatory actions such as threaten to grow out of, for instance, UK membership in the Common Market." Moreover, liberalization of international trade at the multilateral level would be the only way to keep the EEC from becoming inbred. With the EEC setting up its customs union, there would be "bickering with third nations who feel discriminated against," claimed Erhard, and the only way to improve the situation "was to follow the lead indicated by President Kennedy by adopting an extremely liberal policy which would place the entire non-Communist world on one and the same footing," concluded the German minister.[17] In September 1962 Erhard again expressed his support for Kennedy's trade policy, calling it "a fine development," and advocated a rapid start for the new round.[18] Erhard's complete endorsement of the U.S. initiative, which seemed to include support for the dominant-supplier clause, came as no surprise. The German minister was a convinced free trader who liked to point out that his government had reduced tariffs unilaterally in the 1950s. He had opposed the Treaty of Rome, had supported the British initiative for an FTA, and, after the creation of the EFTA, had favored a wider trade arrangement between the EEC and the EFTA to reduce discrimination in Europe. Then, in 1961, Erhard fully supported British membership, considered a means to achieve a more open EEC.[19]

However, despite Erhard's enthusiasm, a general hesitation existed in the Federal Republic about the effects that a GATT round along TEA lines could have on the German economy and on the EEC. Chancellor Adenauer looked with apprehension at the dominant-supplier clause and maintained a reserved stance on the whole Kennedy trade program, which seemed to have as a goal the invasion of Western Europe by more competitive U.S. goods. Adenauer's fears were shared by German industry, which, by 1962, came to appreciate the EEC both for the protection it provided against other European competitors and for the increased export opportunities to France and Italy.[20] The negative effects on trade between

---

[17]   FRUS 1961–63, XIII, Section Economic and Political Integration, 26. Memorandum of Conversation. Meeting at the White House Between President Kennedy and Professor Erhard, German Minster for Economic Affairs, January 8, 1962.

[18]   FRUS 1961–63, XIII, Section Economic and Political Integration, 49. Memorandum of Conversation. Meeting with Vice Chancellor Erhard, October 14, 1962.

[19]   The economic policy of Erhard is described in Ulrich Lappenkueper, "'Ein Europa der Freien und der Gleichen': La politique européenne de Ludwig Erhard (1963–1966)," in Wilfried Loth (ed.), Crisis and Compromises: The European Project, 1963–1969 (Baden-Baden, 2001), 65–91.

[20]   Schulte, "Industrial Interest in West Germany's Decision against the Enlargement of the EEC," 36–7.

Germany and EFTA counties had failed to materialize, as German exports to EFTA were increasing. What is more, the same industrial sectors that had opposed the FTA also opposed a drastic reduction of duties across the Atlantic. Therefore, even if the goals of keeping the EEC open to world trade and solving the economic divisions of Western Europe were still pursued, the regional dimension of the EEC had come to be appreciated by German industry, and the idea of an Atlantic free trade area raised distrust. It was one thing was to alleviate the effects of the division of Europe and to create opportunities to boost German exports, but to achieve these objectives by such a radical solution as drastic reduction of tariffs worldwide was quite another.[21] Apart from Erhard, no one backed the far-reaching elimination of tariffs envisaged by the TEA, which would lead to the dilution of the regional dimension of the EEC, a structure that was clearly bringing trade advantages.

The stance of the Benelux countries was similar. They were quick to convey their support for the TEA and hoped that the U.S. law could contribute to reducing the duties of developed countries and keep the EEC open to world trade. However, together with this support, there also remained certain worries regarding the most radical provision of the TEA. Not even the traditionally liberal Dutch wanted to see their Community disappear in an Atlantic free trade area. They wished to keep a liberal EEC, which was in conformity with their trade structure, but their desire for free trade did not extend to the point of dissolving the EEC. For that reason, it is overly simple to think that it was only de Gaulle who rejected a drastic liberalization. The Dutch and the Germans, traditionally more liberal than France, did not favor it either. The Italians fully shared the French stance. Italy was the least developed economy of the EEC, was traditionally a protectionist country, and was opening its trade barriers at the EEC regional level, thus increasing competition. Therefore, it favored only moderate reduction of trade barriers for fear of weakening the EEC.[22]

Following approval of the TEA, the first significant discussion between the Six took place in November 1962, when the Committee of Permanent Representatives (Comité des représentants permanents, COREPER) sent to the EEC Council of Ministers a note that clearly stated four concerns. First, it highlighted the inopportuneness of opening a new front of trade negotiations before knowing the result of membership talks with the British. The Six were unable to accept a drastic liberalization while they were negotiating British entrance, which, if successful, would have an even larger economic impact than the GATT round. The negotiations with the British were already a GATT round on a European basis, and the Six could not accept conducting two rounds at the same time. Second, the

---

[21] "Problems and Trends in Atlantic Partnership II," Staff Study prepared for the use of the Committee on Foreign Relations, United States Senate (Washington, DC, 1968), 41–5.

[22] MAEF, DE/CE, 1961–66, GATT 930 Direction des Affaires Economiques et Financières, Note 183/CE Déclaration du Conseil sur le Trade Expansion Act, October 22, 1962. PRO T 312/621 Telegram no. 3, from United Kingdom Delegation in Brussels to Foreign Office, January 21, 1963.

note commented that the maintenance of a liberal common commercial policy was in the interest of the EEC members in order to enhance exports to Western Europe and the United States. However, trade negotiation along the lines of the TEA would hamper the regional dimension of the EEC. The economic and financial potential of the EEC and its natural resources was not equal to that of the United States. The EEC would weaken its position in the industrialized world if the potential of its internal market could not be achieved because of a drastic reduction in tariffs. Equally important, tariff protection did not have the same meaning on the two sides of the Atlantic, since the CET constituted an important element of cohesion for the Six. Third, the note warned that a drastic reduction in tariffs could also hinder the development of the less developed regions of the Six. Lastly, the TEA gave the Americans advantages over the EEC, such as financial support to firms hit by foreign competition, nontariff barriers, and the escape clause, while the existence of disparities in current rates implied that a linear reduction would yield unbalanced tariff cuts.[23]

Despite the uncertainty of the outcome of the Brussels negotiations with the British, which prevented a definitive stance on the U.S. proposal, certain basic positions were clear. The Six agreed to a GATT round to further liberalize international trade on a multilateral basis and seize the opportunity to enhance their exports. In their political economy, a reduction of tariffs was seen as an opportunity to sustain the ongoing growth of industrial exports to the United States and the EFTA countries. To do so, they were ready to reduce the CET so as to obtain the reciprocal reduction of U.S. and EFTA duties. Improvements in competitiveness made liberalization on the multilateral plan bearable to countries like France and Italy that were traditionally more protectionist. Moreover, negotiating with the EEC's single voice provided the bargaining power to question U.S. tariff policy, change the U.S. tariff structure characterized by high duties, attack U.S. nontariff barriers, and push Washington to make large tariff cuts. Negotiating as a trading unit gave that power to bargain with the United States which the Europeans had lacked in the 1950s. In the early 1960s, from behind the protection of the CET, the EEC was ready to start competing with the United States and reduce tariffs multilaterally.

However, the Six, and by no means only the French, had no intention of drastically reducing the CET, which had to be preserved to defend European industry and to give an identity to the EEC. Moreover, they proposed certain

---

[23]   CM2/1963 946 Note S/628/62 and annex 2 "Eléments qui pourraient faire l'objet d'études ultérieures au sein de la Communauté," November 30, 1962. On the link between the TEA and the negotiations with the British see also HAEC-CEAB 5/1169 Lettre de Wehrer, de la Direction des Relations Extérieurs, à Van Kleffens, de la Délégation de la Haute Autorité auprès du Gouvernement du Royaume-Uni, March 4, 1963; MAEF DE/CE GATT 930 Direction des Affaires Economiques et Financières—Coopération Economique, Note 113/CE The Trade Expansion Act, April 26, 1963. The note reassumed the situation before the French vetoed the British membership.

conditions to ensure a quantum of balance in the negotiations. The disparity issue
had to be resolved, and U.S. nontariff barriers that hampered exports had to be
eliminated. On these two fundamental aspects there existed a unity in Brussels.[24]

Setting up a balanced set of negotiations was particularly considered by the
Six. As Table 2.3 shows, each of them imported from the United States more than
it exported in the other direction.

Table 2.3   Trade of the Six with the United States, 1954–63 (millions of U.S.$,
current prices)

		1954	1955	1956	1957	1958	1959	1960	1961	1962	1963
	Exports	295	387	498	601	643	913	897	870	966	1051
Germany	Imports	532	764	952	1351	1005	1094	1423	1516	1758	1988
	Balance	−237	−377	−454	−750	−362	−181	−526	−646	−792	−937
	Exports	129	160	202	231	255	345	387	383	441	480
Italy	Imports	299	405	522	684	526	373	668	863	884	1028
	Balance	−170	−245	−320	−453	−271	−28	−281	−480	−443	−548
	Exports	156	210	226	246	304	470	401	417	426	421
France	Imports	381	458	682	831	563	429	746	737	775	901
	Balance	−225	−248	−456	−585	−259	41	−345	−320	−349	−480
	Exports	158	159	179	159	181	209	196	192	200	203
The Netherlands	Imports	336	435	521	540	410	435	599	566	607	649
	Balance	−178	−276	−342	−381	−229	−226	−403	−374	−407	−446
	Exports	191	246	304	267	287	444	358	371	414	411
BLEU	Imports	263	314	409	426	310	325	391	375	451	471
	Balance	−72	−68	−105	−159	−23	119	−33	−4	−37	−60

Source: *Direction of Trade Statistics Historical, 1948–1980* (Washington, DC, 2002).

The question of the EEC trade deficit with the United States was linked to the
critical issue of the burden-sharing emphasized by Kennedy. The Six, not only the
French but also the Atlanticist governments of the Hague and Bonn, refused to
undertake a sweeping liberalization of international trade to receive more imports

---

[24]   CM2 1963/946 Note Introductive S/24/63. Premières conclusions du Comité
spécial de l'Article 111, January 14, 1963.

from the other side of the Atlantic in order to rectify the U.S. balance of payments, caused, Kennedy claimed, by U.S. investments and military commitments in Europe. While the U.S. president held that responsibility was to be shared, the Europeans believed that they were already helping and sharing enough. The United States already enjoyed a favorable trade balance, and U.S. exports to the EEC were growing at a faster rate than U.S. imports from it. Moreover, claimed the Europeans, the U.S. balance of payments was not caused by European trade policy, but had a U.S. domestic origin; hence solutions had to sought elsewhere and, more specifically, in the internal economic policy of the United States and in the monetary system. The TEA's dominant-supplier clause came under particular suspicion. The Six did not wish to see the total elimination of tariffs, considered "an integral and essential part of the structure of the Community," and "did not wish to see their Community dissolved in an Atlantic free trade area, the purpose of which would be to enable the Americans to rectify the deficit in their balance of payments at the expense of Europe."[25]

The Six were undoubtedly taken by surprise by the dominant-supplier clause. They questioned the feasibility of an Atlantic free trade area without implementing harmonizing measures and safeguard clauses, like those applied by the Six in establishing the CET. Above all, however, they deemed it a challenge to the existence of EEC, as it would dilute the regional dimension of the EEC, considered essential for their economic growth. The point was not merely that U.S. products were more competitive than European ones, that the categories of products that met the world-exports value were the categories where, to a very large extent, the United States exported more than it imported from the EEC, and that a drastic reduction or even elimination of tariffs could harm European industry. The CET was seen as one of the elements of European identity and a fundamental and necessary part of the Community, still not sufficiently developed to afford the loss of such an important feature. A drastic reduction of the CET would damage the cohesion of the EEC, chipping away the cement that bound it together at a critical period of its development. The EEC was grounded on the CET, a solid tie giving endurance and strength to the EEC itself, much like a constitution that usually identifies nation-states.[26]

The clause raised doubts about Kennedy's support for European integration and deepened the suspicions the Six had about the Atlantic partnership to be built up through the new round. The partnership seemed to hide an American economic hegemonic design to be implemented through the dismantling of tariffs and the maintenance of other trade barriers that were more effective than customs duties

---

[25]   PRO T 312/621 Telegram no. 3, from United Kingdom Delegation in Brussels to Foreign Office, January 21, 1963. See also HAEC, MAEF Secrétariat Général, Entretiens et Messages, vol. 19, Rencontre entre Pompidou et Erhard, November 21, 1963.

[26]   For this function of tariffs see Alan S. Milward, "Tariffs as Constitutions," in Susan Strange and Roger Tooze (eds), *The International Politics of Surplus Capacity: Competition for Market Shares in the World Recession* (London, 1981), 57–66.

in preventing European exports to the United States. The TEA was judged to be a mercantilist law to increase U.S. exports more than a law to liberalize international trade. Doubts regarding Kennedy's aims in putting forward the TEA engendered doubts about the notion of an Atlantic partnership between equals.[27]

However, differences also existed among the Six. The Federal Republic and the Benelux countries, even if with the exclusion of some sectors, approved of a general reduction of 50 percent across the board. In joining the CET they increased their national duties; therefore for them the reduction of 50 percent in the GATT simply meant regaining the 1958 levels. By contrast, France and Italy supported more moderate reductions, as they had to withstand the cumulative reductions of joining the CET and those stemming from the GATT. However, this was not the only element that caused differences. Bonn aimed to use the reduction of the CET as a bargaining chip to reduce third countries' duties and enhance German exports. Paris and Rome, however, were opening their economy at the EEC regional level, were profiting from preferential access to the German market and, while interested in increasing their exports to third countries, had a more cautious position. As shown in the following chapters, in the course of the negotiations the Six would have to reconcile these different stances in a common position—and thus in a common commercial policy—to negotiate in Geneva as a trading unit.

Whereas all the six member states accepted a reduction of duties in the industrial sector, it would be misguided to think that they—and the Western governments in general—moved from the extreme protectionism of the 1930s to free trade in the 1960s. As noted by Milward, they were constrained by the fact that a decision to move toward trade liberalization could provoke a negative reaction in those sectors that aimed for protection. Moreover, while governments held that liberalization of foreign trade encouraged the growth of productivity and incomes while satisfying consumer demands, they also judged protectionism necessary to foster technological modernization and more sophisticated manufacturing sectors. The tariff policy was made by governments that were reorganizing industries and, although with different intensity, intervening to actively promote long-term economic and social welfare. This circumstance influenced their tariff policy. The link between industrial and commercial policies, between investment and trade, led to the assumption that trade liberalization was not a question of tariff reductions alone. The situation gave the trade policies of the period their peculiar mixture of liberalism and protectionism, and, as shown in the following chapters, it deeply influenced decisions over tariff cuts.[28]

---

[27]   HAEC-CEAB 5/1169, Lettre de Wehrer, de la Direction des Relations Extérieurs, à Van Kleffens, de la Délégation de la Haute Autorité auprès du Gouvernement du Royaume-Uni, March 4, 1963.
[28]   Milward, *The European Rescue of the Nation-state*, 121–32.

The EEC Reaction in the Agricultural Sector: Accepting the Round While Implementing the CAP

While in the industrial sector the EEC accepted a liberal policy, the tone of its reaction to the U.S. request to deal with agriculture in the GATT was completely different. Washington's suggestion touched upon the CAP that the EEC had started elaborating in 1958. An account of this elaboration is outside the scope of this book; however, as the CAP and the new GATT round came to interfere with each other, it is necessary to recall some basic aspects of this policy in order to understand this nexus.

The preservation of an adequate level of income in agriculture was an essential policy goal of all the European governments. They pursued interventionist policies aimed at improving the living standard of farmers through instruments that protected them against competition and world price instability. Support for agricultural income also meant support for agricultural output, which, consequently, led to food surpluses and prices higher than those outside Europe. At the beginning of the 1950s, attempts were already being made to create a common European framework to regulate agriculture. In view of the conclusion of the Treaty of Rome, there was no possibility that the regulation of agriculture would remain outside the scope of the EEC. Agricultural exports were crucial to Dutch export earnings, and to a lesser extent to Italian earnings. France had made expensive efforts since 1945 to favor agricultural exports, for which it wanted a guaranteed outlet in 1957, and aimed at sharing the financial burden of supporting its farmers. The establishment of a common market for farm and food products and of a common agricultural policy was among the aims of the Treaty of Rome. These were considered a measure to improve incomes in the agricultural sector or, as Milward notes, a kind of "extended public welfare."[29] Moreover, the political economy of trade liberalization consisted of freeing the most dynamic part of world trade while giving shelter to less competitive sectors or those considered strategic. While implementing a customs union for the free circulation of industrial products and establishing a liberal CET, the EEC planned to protect some sectors strictly, among which were agriculture, steel, and textiles.

Among the Six, the stronger supporters of the CAP were the two exporting countries of the Netherlands and France. The Dutch, with an efficient agricultural sector, above all for dairy and livestock products, aimed at liberalizing intra-EEC exchanges, and wanted low support prices and moderate external protection, to

[29]   Milward, *The Reconstruction of Western Europe*, 229. For a description of the attempts made at European level to organize agriculture and the origin of CAP see Milward, *The European Rescue of the Nation-state*, 224–315. On the attempts made to organize agriculture before the 1957 see also Richard T. Griffiths and Brian Girvin (eds), *The Green Pool and the Origins of the Common Agricultural Policy* (London, 1995). The most recent account of the negotiations leading to CAP from 1958 to 1964 is Ann-Christina L. Knudsen, *Farmers on Welfare. The Making of Europe's Common Agricultural Policy* (Ithaca, NY, 2009).

avoid altering trade with markets outside the EEC. France, a larger and more efficient producer of most agricultural products than the other five member states, aimed at moderate prices and high protection from overseas exporters. France had entered the EEC with the goal of getting preferential advantages for its agricultural products and for cereals—wheat and feed grains—in particular. French cereals were competitive at the EEC regional level but were uncompetitive at the world level, given the cheaper U.S., Canadian, Australian, and Argentinian prices. The level of world prices represented an obstacle to French agricultural exports of cereals—particularly soft wheat—and France needed the Six to purchase its agricultural surpluses and to finance its uncompetitive exports outside the EEC. France hoped to shift to the greatest extent possible the financial burden of surplus disposal to its partners. To reinforce its requests, France stressed that, having opened its industrial market to the exports of the five members, it had to be recompensed with outlets in the EEC.[30]

Italy was a relatively efficient producer of fruit and vegetables and hoped to increase exports to the EEC and gain access to EEC funds to support its agriculture. At the same time it desired a CAP that allowed it to maintain its cheap imports of meat and grains from outside the EEC, and in particular from Argentina.[31] With a highly protected and inefficient agricultural industry, Bonn wanted to maintain its high prices and the bilateral arrangements it had with its five partners and with third countries, and hoped to maintain its cheap food imports from outside the EEC. Thus, Bonn was never particularly enthusiastic about the establishment of a comprehensive common agricultural policy that could run contrary to its commercial interests outside the EEC. In the end, it reluctantly accepted the setting up of this policy in order to avoid problems within the EEC and in relations with France, the country whose participation in the EEC was essential. However, Germany soon started to challenge the CAP.[32]

Since the beginning of the negotiations leading to the Treaty of Rome, it had been clear that formulating an agricultural policy acceptable to all of the six member nations would be a formidable task. The Six had rival and diverging interests that had to be conciliated within a common policy. Creating a common market for farm products was much more difficult than creating one for manufactured goods. It was not a question of liberalizing internal exchanges, but of setting up a mechanism to protect agriculture, while reconciling conflicting interests inside and outside the EEC, different views on how to organize this common policy, and varied relations with third countries. The Treaty of Rome set only the basic aims of this common policy and stated that the full elaboration of the policy was due by the end of the transitional period. By 1962, the main features of the CAP had been approved,

---

[30]   On the French and Dutch agricultural policy see Milward, *The European Rescue of the Nation-state*, 224–315.

[31]   On Italy and CAP see Rosemary Galli and Saverio Torcasio, *La partecpazione italiana alla politica agricola comunitaria* (Rome, 1976).

[32]   Knudsen, *Farmers on Welfare*, 57–121.

despite the reluctance of the Federal Republic, which was displaying its recalcitrance in implementing the kind of CAP that stemmed from the 1960–62 negotiations.[33]

The common policy would be characterized by free circulation of products; central market organization for products with common prices to be progressively unified and guaranteed in order to stabilize the agricultural market at the EEC level and regulate imports; a variable levy system to protect European products from competition from third countries to replace the old system of tariff and quota protection; and a financial support system. The Council of Ministers adopted the first regulations for cereals, pork, eggs, and poultry. A schedule was agreed upon for regulations for dairy products, meat, and sugar, and the European Agricultural Guidance and Guarantee Fund, with financial regulation valid until June 1965, was established. Farm incomes were to be ensured by a price support policy; excess of supply above demand would be bought by Community agents, and a preferential system of levies protecting products of the Six at the EEC frontiers would be established. Third countries' products entering the EEC were subjected to a variable levy system meant to guarantee that they would enter at a price level higher than the prices set for EEC products. By the same token, when EEC products were exported, the gap between lower world market and artificially higher EEC prices was filled by subsidies. In this way price stability could be guaranteed, competition from third countries was undercut, and EEC products could compete in the international markets thanks to subsidies. However, no decision on common prices was taken. It was merely agreed that, for the time being, prices would be frozen at their current level and harmonization of prices would begin in 1963. Another part of the CAP had been added. Yet the regulations for other products, the definitive financing system, and the level of common prices, starting with grains, had still to be agreed.[34]

Since 1962 the focus of the negotiations had become the common price of grains, a particularly thorny issue that would trouble the GATT negotiations. France, the largest and most efficient producer among the Six, had the lowest prices, the Federal Republic had the highest, while the other four were somewhere in the middle. The Federal Republic maintained an inefficient and greatly protected agricultural sector and argued that it would be difficult to agree on a common price level within a short time if this implied lowering the grain price and consequently, claimed the Germans, the income of farmers. Bonn wanted common prices set at the high German level. This position was categorically refused by France, which indicated that only an agreement moving the price about one-quarter of the way towards the German level would be acceptable. This level could encourage French agriculture to develop unexploited capacity, thus enabling France to increase production. However, if the common price was set at too high a level, other less efficient EEC farmers would have an incentive to increase their production, thus

---

[33]   Ibid., 122–206.

[34]   For a description of the CAP protectionist mechanism see Richard Baldwin and Charles Wyplosz, *The Economics of European Integration* (London, 2009), 201–28.

operating against French interests. High prices would also generate inflation, creating a burden on French industry's competitiveness.[35] As the following chapters show, this unsettled part of the CAP interfered with the Geneva talks.

The CAP was developed in tension with international trade. The Six were setting up an EEC market for food and farm products, the cost of which was passed on to third countries' suppliers. For mercantilistic reasons, the Dutch and the Germans claimed that the CAP had to take into account the consequences for third countries. They had bilateral quota agreements with third countries to import cheaper food and hoped to retain them. Guaranteeing quantitative assurance to third countries was categorically opposed by France on the stated grounds that doing so conflicted with the entire CAP system of protection based on prices, although in reality French opposition arose because such assurances would retain third-country competition that the French wanted to exclude. The Netherlands claimed that the price policy of the EEC had to take into account third countries and be lowered in case of disruptive consequences, but this option was opposed by Bonn, which had the highest prices among the Six.[36] As a result, the CAP promised to be more protectionist than the six national policies of the EEC member states because it represented the sum of all the protectionist requirements of the Six.

It was against this background that the U.S. proposal to include agriculture in the new GATT round was made. The Six agreed to include agriculture. They held that they could not refuse outright such a request and considered the new round an opportunity to organize agriculture at a multilateral level.[37] Apart from this basic agreement, deep differences existed in Brussels. As long as GATT talks would not endanger the CAP, France had a positive interest in attending the Geneva negotiations, which represented an opportunity to reorganize and stabilize the markets of basic commodities and question the agricultural policy of the big exporting countries, notably the United States, Australia, and Canada. Moreover, the negotiations represented an instrument to put pressure on Germany to approve the CAP. The U.S. request to negotiate in Geneva and not to conclude the round unless meaningful results were achieved in agriculture played into the French hands. Bonn had a major interest in attending the negotiations in the industrial sector in order to enhance German exports. If Bonn wanted to successfully conclude the GATT negotiations in the industrial sector, it had to implement the CAP, because without the CAP, the EEC could not negotiate as a unit in Geneva. By contrast, the Germans, the Dutch, and the Italians aimed to use the Geneva talks to reach an agreement between the EEC and third countries to ensure that

---

[35]   Knudsen, *Farmers on Welfare*, 207–65.

[36]   CM2 1963/540 PV de la 117ème session du Conseil de la CEE, December 2–3, 1963.

[37]   CM2/1963 946 Note S/628/62 and annex 2, "Eléments qui pourraient faire l'objet d'études ulterieures au sein de la Communauté," November 30, 1962.

they could continue to import cheap food from outside the Community, a goal in opposition to French interests.[38]

Thus if the EEC members wanted to negotiate as a unit in Geneva, they needed a common policy in Brussels. Participating in the agricultural part of the negotiations implied the preliminary establishment of a common policy in Brussels and an agreement on how protectionist this policy would be. Because of German reluctance and the differences among the EEC members on some critical aspects of this policy—such as the impact on third countries—the achievement of such an agreement would not be an easy task.

Despite these differences, the Six shared at least one basic view. None of them was interested in increasing exports outside the EEC and, therefore, none was motivated to reduce its trade barriers to obtain the reciprocal reduction of other countries' barriers. Even if they approached it in different ways, they were all concerned with maintaining their protectionism. As shown in the rest of the book, it was exactly this stance that would make reductions of trade barriers in Geneva almost impossible. In the GATT, reductions of barriers took place where a reciprocal interest in enhancing exports and, consequently, reducing protection existed. This was not the case for agriculture.

The EEC was setting up its regional organization of agriculture, and the negotiations in Geneva would show the place that the Six wanted the EEC to have in world trade for farm products. From the beginning, the direction the EEC took seemed to be clear. While agreeing to attend the suggested negotiations, EEC members had no interest in reducing trade barriers to enhance their exports outside the EEC. Although they had to patch up their conflicting interests in the impact the CAP would have on imports from outside the EEC, and although tension over the formulation of the CAP had already appeared, all of EEC members had the priority aim of protecting their farmers. From the very beginning it was evident that the EEC was not heading for a reduction of protectionism in this sector.

The European Commission and the EEC Trade Policymaking for GATT negotiations

Trade policy was the first field where the original members of the European Community pooled sovereignty. The delegation of the authority to the supranational level required the establishment of an institutional framework to conduct the trade policymaking. Article 111 of the Treaty of Rome required the Commission to submit proposals to the Council of Ministers for "a common action and [...] a uniform commercial policy." Thus, it gave the Commission the task of preparing proposals to be presented to the Council of Ministers that would then adopt a mandate or directives on the basis of which the Commission would negotiate in

---

[38]   CM2 1963/947 PV de la 101ème session du Conseil de la CEE, Bruxelles, May 8–10, 1963.

the GATT. For the transitional period, Article 111 assigned the Commission the exclusive right to negotiate over tariffs, but it did not assign the same right over NTBs. This meant that, for sectors regulated by the latter, such as textiles and agriculture, the Commission lacked authority.

The Commission was to be assisted by a special Committee, named the Article 111 Committee or simply the 111 Committee. However, the article did not specify of what nature the assistance should be, and did not prescribe the structure of the Committee. It did not state who should sit on the Committee, whether the Council collectively should nominate the people to serve on it, or whether this should be left to the individual member states. Unsurprisingly, the latter course was followed. As a result, the 111 Committee consisted of senior national civil servants appointed by the national governments. Moreover, the article did not deal in detail with the relations between the Commission and the member states' representatives in the Committee, the procedures for the Commission's consultation with it, and what matters should be referred to it. In 1958, the 111 Committee was established. Member states appointed their most senior trade policy officials in order to effectively defend their trade interests. The first and decisive battle took place over who should take the chair. Starting from its legal role as negotiator, the Commission wanted to treat the Committee as an ordinary advisory committee or working group. This meant that the Commission would chair it, provide a secretariat and dictate the agenda. The member states, led by the inaugural Belgian Presidency, insisted that, under the terms of the Treaty, the Committee was an organ of the Council. Consequently the Presidency should take the chair. The Commission tried to seize the initiative by sending Commissioner for External Affairs, the Belgian Jean Rey, to early meetings of the committee. Its expectation was that member states' representatives, being officials, would defer to his political status. Unfortunately for the Commission, this did not happen. Member states seized the Presidency and consolidated their grip on the chairmanship. As a result, the 111 Committee became the Committee where the representatives of the members controlled the Commission.[39]

The Commission was aware that the new round would test its capacity to generate proposals and mediate for a common stance in Brussels, as well as its negotiating skills in Geneva. It therefore set out to demonstrate its ability to perform these tasks. However, its aims went beyond this. In the first place, it saw the GATT talks as an opportunity to affirm its role as the sole negotiating agent on behalf of the EEC. In the previous and first GATT round attended, the Dillon Round, member states had maintained a very active role. They had joined the negotiations with third countries and enjoyed speaking rights. They had curtailed the Commission's room for maneuver through strict negotiating directives and close supervision.[40] In the new

---

[39] Michael Johnson, *European Community Trade Policy and the Article 113 Committee* (London, 1998).

[40] Frans A.M. Alting von Geusau, *Economic Relations after the Kennedy Round* (Leyden, 1969), 445.

round, the Commission had every intention of eliminating the presence of national governments and affirming its role as sole negotiator both for the industrial sector, for which it had legal competence, and the agricultural sector, for which it did not. As shown below, this was a difficult task for the Commission, as member states were reluctant to renounce an active role in the GATT.[41]

Moreover, the Commission did not see its role as that of a honest broker in Brussels or as a carrier of messages from the Council of Ministers in Geneva. It had its preferences—which in some cases differed from those of the Member states— and was intent on structuring its proposals in such a way as to enhance them. In the industrial sector, it favored moderate reductions of duties in order to foster exports without weakening the regionalism of the EEC. The question of tariff disparity was pointed out, and qualms were raised regarding the possibility that a simple linear reduction could lead to a balanced reduction of tariffs, especially if the United States retained their discriminatory regulations. It doubted that a drastic reduction of tariffs could take place without parallel measures dealing with competition, economic cooperation, social and transport issues, just as the French had claimed. Equally important, it sought to use the new GATT negotiations to sway member states to implement a common commercial policy that also covered NTBs and was grounded on a common industrial policy.[42] This was rather remarkable considering that none of the Member states shared these priorities.[43]

As for the agricultural sector, the Commission—in particular Sicco Mansholt, the Dutch Commissioner responsible for agriculture—saw the round as a lever to foster the elaboration of the CAP in Brussels and the acceptance of this policy in Geneva. The Commission considered the CAP as one of the most important features of the EEC and European integration. Thus, agriculture could be included in the Geneva talks, but without putting the common policy at risk, rather enhancing its final elaboration. Moreover, the new round was also seen as an opportunity to regulate this sector at a multilateral level, harmonize the domestic agricultural policies of the developed countries and moderate the protectionism of the CAP. It was with these objectives in mind that the Commission prepared itself for the new round.[44]

---

[41]   AECB BAC 118/83 845, Commission—CPC/I/4/62 rev. May 8, 1962.

[42]   AECB BAC BAC 62/1980 49 DG Note de la DG des Relations Extérieurs, October 22, 1962. AECB BAC 62/1980 49 DG Rélations Extérieurs, Comité de la politique commerciale, PV de la 12ème réunion, November 12, 1962.

[43]   AECB BAC 118/83 845 EEC Commission—direction Générale des Relations Extérieurs CPC/I/4/62 rev. May 8, 1962; ibid., BAC 62/1980 49 DG Note de la DG des Relations Extérieurs, October 22, 1962. AECB BAC 62/1980 49 DG Rélations Extérieurs, Comité de la politique commerciale, PV de la 12ème reunion, December 12, 1962.

[44]   AECB, PV 224, April 3, 1963 and ibid., "Participation de l'agriculture aux négociations à entreprendre dans le cadre du TEA," April 9, 1963 and AECB, PV 227, April 30, 1963.

Chapter 3
Devising the Rule of the Kennedy Round

From the French Veto to German Synchronization

After World War II, the drift towards protectionism that had intensified with the Great Depression continued unabated. The only countries that did not follow this trend were the northern Atlantic economies of Western Europe and North America. In these regions, under the U.S. leadership, governments slowly started to liberalize trade within the framework of the GATT and of regional institutions. The opening of the most advanced economies constituted an important exception to the generally protectionist pattern.[1] The U.S. decision to propose a new round of GATT negotiations and the EEC's agreement to join it confirmed the policy of trade liberalization in the Atlantic economies. Despite this basic agreement, differences existed on how to make trade more free, and the EEC and the United States had to reconcile their opposed positions in order to start the new round of talks.

This agreement had to be elaborated while the EEC was going through a complicated phase. When the Treaty of Rome was negotiated between 1955 and 1957, the six governments were aware that, as implementation of the customs union advanced and common policies were set up, tensions and conflict between them would grow. The deeper integration that would result required further coordination of national economic policies, a definition of the economic structure of the EEC, and determination of the patterns of trade relations with third countries. The EEC's members, therefore, needed to overcome predicable divergences caused by their differing economic structures and traditional trade relations with nonmember states. These anticipated tensions were exacerbated by the decision by President de Gaulle in January 1963 to veto the British request for membership in the Community.

While the United States moved quickly to set up the new round, an event external to the GATT discussions had significant consequences for Kennedy's program of freer trade. After almost 15 months of bargaining in Brussels, on January 14, 1963 de Gaulle rebuffed the United Kingdom's bid for EEC membership. Further, he turned down Kennedy's MLF initiative. The reasons that led the French president to reject two major elements of Kennedy's grand design have been considered by many scholars and are not discussed here. What matters here is that Kennedy's trade program was one of the casualties of the French veto. Although the Trade Expansion Act passed by Congress contained many liberal provisions, de Gaulle's

---

[1]   Ronald Findlay and Kevin O'Rourke, *Power and Plenty. Trade, War and the World Economy in the Second Millennium* (Princeton, NJ, 2007), 392.

decision reduced the extent to which tariffs could be eliminated and international trade liberalized. Without British membership in the EEC, the dominant supplier clause could be applied only to aircraft and margarine. The French veto in effect represented the first stage of the not yet started round because it limited how much liberalization could be achieved. In addition, the veto added a European dimension to the bargaining in Geneva. With Western Europe's commercial division confirmed, the GATT remained the only framework through which to facilitate the expansion of trade between the EEC and the EFTA.

When the GATT contracting parties gathered in Geneva in May 1963 for the ministerial meeting that had to make the decision to launch the new round, the United Kingdom was not a member of the EEC, while the Atlantic alliance and the EEC were under considerable strain created by the French move. De Gaulle's move influenced how the United States, the United Kingdom, and the other EEC members perceived Paris's stance towards the round. They suspected that a veto of the trade negotiations could be on the General's agenda. After all, he had already turned down two important elements of Kennedy's program. As a result, during the talks other delegations were often unable to discern whether the French were placing conditions on negotiations in order to deadlock the round or were simply trying to enhance their position.[2] As will be shown in the following chapters, the French in fact had no interest in casting a veto on the GATT round. However, they fully exploited their opportunity to extract concessions in the intra-EEC bargaining and in Geneva.

The French rejection of British membership and the manner in which it was handled created a crisis in the EEC. The enlargement of the Community had been indefinitely postponed by a single member, showing that a fundamental issue could be decided by French unilateralism rather than by collective decision-making. The mutual confidence upon which the very existence of the EEC depended was badly shaken. Moreover, de Gaulle's rejection of the Atlantic partnership and the signing of the Franco-German Treaty in January 1963 seemed to show that the French president had every intention of imposing his own vision on the EEC and its relations with the United States. Yet the economic and political reasons that had led to the signing of the Treaty of Rome were still very relevant. Notwithstanding the bitterness caused by de Gaulle's move, no one wished to sacrifice the EEC for the sake of the British. These common interests prompted the other five members of the Community (the Five) to overcome the crisis and set the Community back in motion.[3]

---

[2]   See, for example, PRO FO 371/172314 Ramsbotham from British Embassy in Paris to Barnes in Foreign Office, November 15, 1963.

[3]   AECB PV 218, February 20, 1963 and PV 221, March 13, 1963 reporting the meetings between the Commission and the governments of the Five in the aftermath of the veto. PRO T 312/621 Telegram no. 3 From UK Delegation in Brussels to Foreign Office, January 21, 1963. See also Ludlow, *The European Community and the Crises of the 1960s*, 11–39.

In putting the French veto behind them and getting ready to attend the new round, the Five faced the problem of how to prevent further unilateral decisions by the French. The question was how to bring them along to the TEA negotiations while making sure they would not cast a veto at the last moment. The Five had to ensure that, after concessions had been made to the French in the CAP or in the association agreements with former colonies, Paris would not jeopardize talks in Geneva. For the Five, the EEC's participation in the round remained of foremost importance for two reasons: they aimed to reduce trade discrimination in Western Europe and across the Atlantic, and equally important, they intended to show themselves to be loyal allies to Washington, not minor partners led by the anti-American French.[4]

Germany was particularly determined to conclude the GATT negotiations successfully. With 27.2 percent of its exports going to EFTA countries in 1963, and with growing export rates to the United States in the years 1959–63, the Federal Republic had to defend its trade interests outside the EEC.[5] Moreover, after the resentment created in the other capitals by the bilateral Franco-German Treaty of January 1963, the Germans had to demonstrate their commitment to European integration and their loyalty to U.S. Atlanticism.[6]

As for de Gaulle, with the liberalizing potential of TEA hampered, there was no reason to sabotage the negotiations in Geneva. France too was interested in decreasing discrimination in Western Europe and in attacking U.S. barriers. However, French acquiescence to the new round was conditional on approval of the association agreements and, above all, on full elaboration of the CAP.[7] The French stance was strengthened by evidence that the Six could not negotiate over agriculture in Geneva as a trading unit if they failed to establish a common policy in Brussels. Thus, U.S. insistence on including agriculture in the GATT round played into the hands of the French. Paris could reasonably require elaboration of the CAP as a condition for attending the round and put pressure on the recalcitrant Germans to accelerate implementation of this policy. Moreover, Paris was resolute in exploiting fear of a new veto in order to extract concessions from the Five on other EEC matters. The French wanted to be compensated for letting the EEC attend a negotiation in which they were interested in any case. The TEA was

---

[4]   AECB PV 221, March 13, 1963; NARA 59 State Department Central file subject numeric 59 box 3489, FT 4 US/TEA, Memorandum from Stanley Cleveland to Schaetzel, February 27, 1963.

[5]   The figures are taken from the previous chapter.

[6]   HAEC MAEF, OW 50 Rapport envoyé le 1er Mars, a Bonn, par M. Hankort and PRO FO 371/172307. Note of a meeting between the president of the Board of Trade and the United States State Department, March 4, 1963. Oliver Bange, "Picking Up the Pieces" (PhD dissertation, London University, 1997), 191–3.

[7]   AECB PV 218, February 20, 1963 reporting conversation between Hallstein, Couve de Murville and Giscard d'Estaing in Paris.

thus not another element of the grand design to be rejected, but an opportunity to reduce trade barriers and to extract concessions from partners, Bonn in particular.[8]

It was against this backdrop that at the meeting of the Council of Ministers of April 1–2, 1963, German foreign affairs minister Gerhard Schröder presented his synchronization plan. His aim consisted of setting up a working agenda for the Community and in synchronizing the compromises that the Six would make in different areas. Concessions to the French would not be made until they agreed to specific steps in trade negotiations and other areas of interest to the Five. The German synchronization plan was well received by the other five partners as a way to prepare for Geneva, and as a means of advancing the EEC in an equitable way.[9]

Yet acceptance of the plan did not remove all hurdles. Giscard d'Estaing expressed full support for the prospective GATT negotiations and underlined the EEC's interest in following a liberal policy. However, the French minister stated that is was impossible to carry on negotiations over the agricultural sector in Geneva if the CAP was not defined in Brussels. Giscard d'Estaing made clear that his government wanted full approval of the CAP before negotiating over agriculture in the GATT round. Here lay the French answer to German synchronization. Ultimately, the Six compromised by declaring themselves in favor of attending the round "in the framework of a harmonious development of its external and internal activities."[10] The nexus between the GATT round and the CAP had, for the moment, been resolved with this vague formula.

Quarreling over the Disparities in Tariffs and Getting Ready for the GATT Ministerial Meeting

It is against this background that the beginning of the new round should be analyzed. At the GATT session of February 1963, the date of the ministerial meeting was hurriedly set for May 16–21, 1963. The Kennedy administration needed to demonstrate its firm intention to set up the round in order to put pressure

---

[8] MAEF, DE/CE, 1961–66 GATT 930, Direction des Affaires Economiques et Financière—Service de Coopération Economique, Note 92/CE, Nouvelles négociations tarifaires multilatérales, April 1, 1963; ibid., Note du Quai D'Orsay "Kennedy Round", undated document written between April 1 and May 8, 1963.

[9] AAPD 1963, document 134, Aufzeichnung des Staatssekretärs Lahr, March 28, 1963; CM2 1963 PV de la 100ème session du Conseil de la CEE, April 1–2, 1963; AECB PV 224, April 3, 1963; PRO FO 371/172307 Telegram no. 82 from Brussels to Foreign Office, April 3, 1963. For a more detailed description of the syncronization plan and of how the Germans elaborated it, see Ludlow, *The European Community and the Crises of the 1960s*, 11–39.

[10] "dans le cadre d'un développement harmonieux de ses activités internes et externes" my translation from the document CM2 1963 PV de la 100ème session du Conseil de la CEE, April 1–2, 1963.

on the EEC to come to Geneva.[11] On the other side of the Atlantic, the Five had to reassure Washington about their willingness to attend the round, while the French judged it wise not to anger their partners by opposing the hasty fixing of the date.[12] Equally important, looming beyond the GATT ministerial meeting was the United Nations conference on trade and development of May 22, 1963. Here the Soviet Union would take every opportunity to challenge the GATT and to spark a rift between the LDCs and the industrialized countries. The latter therefore intended to anticipate the United Nations meeting in order to show that the GATT was actively dealing with the LDCs' commercial problems.[13]

The ministerial meeting would adopt the agenda for the negotiations and the process for reducing barriers to exchange. Establishing the process was of particular importance. For the first time in GATT history, a round was to achieve across-the-board tariff cuts, deal with agriculture, and address the problems of LDCs. Since the rules for playing the game were as important as the game itself, governments spent almost two years bargaining over them, eventually resorting to pragmatic solutions.

In this phase leading to the GATT ministerial meeting, the attention of the industrial countries focused on the rules for reducing tariffs on manufacturers, the part of international trade they were most interested in. The EEC pointed to the disparities in rates as the first problem to be resolved. As Table 3.1 shows, the CET had a narrower spread between the highest and lowest levels, and was more moderate and homogeneous than the tariff structures of the United States and the United Kingdom.

The EEC feared that it would be in a disadvantageous position if all duties were cut by 50 percent, as this would still leave some U.S. duties at a high level. Because of the lower rates of its duties, in future negotiations the EEC would be unable to use the CET as a bargaining tool to bring down other countries' tariffs. It was in this round that maximum concessions had to be obtained. Therefore the rates had to be harmonized in order to lop off the peaks in the American tariffs. This objective was promoted by all members of the Six and, in particular, by the Federal Republic. Reinhardt, the German member of the 111 Committee, proposed negotiating the target duties for the product categories of all industrialized countries. Under the German suggestion, the 111 Committee elaborated the écrêtement plan, which advocated greater reductions for very high duties and more moderate reductions for relatively low ones. In this way, the duties of the most industrialized countries would be moved towards target duties for raw material, semimanufactured goods, and finished products.[14] The suggestion resembled a

[11] PRO FO 371/172307, Note of a meeting between the president of the Board of Trade and the United States State Department, March 4, 1963.

[12] CM2 1963/949 PV de la 207ème réunion du Comité des Représentantes permanents, Bruxelles, April 13–14, 1963.

[13] PRO T 312/621, "The Kennedy Round," February 1963.

[14] CM2 1963/304 PV de la 40ème réunion du Comité 111, January 10, 1963; CM2 1963/949, Etat Actuel des Travaux préparatoires du Comité Spécial de l'article 111, March

Table 3.1   Comparison of EEC, U.S., and UK Tariff Rates

	EEC	U.S.	UK	EEC	U.S.	UK
Rates of duties	No.	No.	No.	%	%	%
Free	298	364	316	7.9	9.7	8.4
1–5%	214	237	17	5.7	6.3	0.5
6–10%	1031	729	1113	27.4	19.5	29.6
11–15%	1290	870	239	34.3	23.1	6.3
16–20%	771	508	920	20.5	13.5	24.5
21–25%	146	275	206	3.9	7.3	5.5
26–30%	6	276	154	0.2	7.3	4.1
31–35%	2	107	725	0.05	2.9	19.3
36–40%	2	69	8	0.05	1.8	0.2
41–45%	0	120	31	0	3.2	0.8
46–50%	0	91	27	0	2.4	0.7
51–55%	0	43	0	0	1.1	0
56–60%	0	8	0	0	0.2	0
<61%	0	63	4	0	1.7	0.1
Total	3760	3760	3760	100	100	100
Average	11.7%	17.8%	18.4%			

Source: AECB BAC 845 118/83 Comparaison statistique du Tarif Douanier Commun de la CEE, du Tarif des Etats-Unis et du Tarif du Royaume-Uni, Office Statistique des Communautés européennes, 1963.

proposal to the OEEC already put on the table by Ludwig Erhard in 1953 and was also the result of the discussions that had taken place on a similar plan presented to the GATT by the French minister Pierre Pfimlin in 1954. These proposals had been nurtured by the so-called "low-tariff country club"—the Scandinavian and Benelux countries—that had lower levels of duties and asked for harmonization. Hence the écrêtement plan was not a French maneuver to sabotage the round, as Washington would later claim. Rather, it was born out of a German initiative and was the result of discussions that had been ongoing since the 1950s.[15]

At the end of April 1963 Theodorus Hijzen, the Dutch head of the EEC Commission delegation to the GATT, put forward in Geneva the écrêtement plan,

---

21, 1963.

[15]   On the debate taking place in the 1950s see Asbeek Brusse, *Tariffs, Trade, and European Integration, 1947–1957*, 115–42 and Ynze Alkema, "European–American Trade Policies, 1961–1963," in Brinkley and Griffiths (eds) *John F. Kennedy and Europe*, 212–33.

suggesting duties of 0 percent for raw material, 5 percent for semimanufactured goods, and 10 percent on manufactured products.[16] The écrêtement plan met categorical U.S. objection. As the head of the U.S. delegation, W. Michael Blumenthal, made clear, in the Dillon Round the EEC had criticized the United States for blocking trade liberalization because its delegation lacked authority to reduce tariffs across the board. With congressional approval of the TEA, the U.S. intent to make equal cuts had been widely supported by other countries. In this environment, for political, legislative, and practical reasons, Washington could accept only a linear reduction to be uniformly applied to all duties, with limited exceptions. Behind the scenes, Blumenthal admitted that the TEA did not legally prevent the United States from agreeing to unequal concessions. Yet they were politically impossible, as such a deal would be unacceptable to Congress.[17]

The basic dispute arose because the EEC, having lower and more compact tariffs, aimed at harmonizing duties worldwide. In contrast, the United States refused the écrêtement because, having higher duties, it would have to implement larger reductions to reach the target rates. The differing stances of the EEC and the United States were thus dictated by their trade-respective interests. From a theoretical point of view, however, both positions were questionable. They did not consider that the protective incidence of a duty is bound to the price elasticity of supply and demand and not only to its level. Moreover, the average of tariffs can be a misleading figure, as it does not consider the commercial importance of the product, while the weighting of each tariff according to the country's total imports overlooks the incidence of high duties that hamper trade.[18]

Leaving aside this technical consideration, it is worth remarking that the écrêtement plan lacked credibility in U.S. eyes. As it had nothing to do with equal linear reduction and the United States would have to cut duties by a higher percentage, Washington questioned whether the EEC intended to constructively attend the round. Furthermore, U.S. mistrust of the French worked against the plan. The Americans were convinced, mistakenly, that the écrêtement was a French proposal and, therefore, an attempt to put roadblocks in the way of the round without having to formally veto it. In Washington's understanding, the French were maneuvering to wreck another element of Kennedy's grand design, and the Five were naive enough to follow Paris's lead. In assessing U.S. strategy for the Kennedy Round, the White House and the State Department had counted

---

[16]   HAEC BAC 506 026/1969, Rapport du Comité 111 sur l'attitude de la CEE, April 30, 1963; PRO FO 371/172308, Telegram no. 40 from Cohen to Foreign Office, April 27, 1963; PRO BT 303/168 Note, "French Proposal on Reductions in High and Low Tariffs in the Kennedy Round," undated.

[17]   Telegram from the Department of State written by George Ball to Certain Diplomatic Missions, May 4, 1963, Herter's papers, box 11, JFKL; PRO FO 371/172328 Letter from Chadwick to Reilly, May 14, 1963.

[18]   Evans, The Kennedy Round in American Trade Policy, 190. On the issue see also Preeg, Traders and Diplomats, 60–66.

on the Germans to bring the French onboard. If the Germans were toeing the French line, this strategy would collapse.[19] Washington failed to see that the Five shared trade interests with the French and that this mutuality led them to side with Paris. Wariness about de Gaulle was not enough to cause them to forget their own interests and ally themselves with the Americans.

The meager results that the Americans believed écrêtement would bring, the perception that it was a French obstructionist move, and irritation over the Five's support of the proposal led a strong reaction from Washington. The U.S. negotiators toughened their attitude towards the Six, pushing them to drop the plan. Secretary of State Rusk and his undersecretary, George Ball, brought the question of the formula for cutting tariffs to the political level in order to push the EEC to give up its position. Washington counted on its influence in Bonn and The Hague, and on the desire of these two governments to find a genuine solution so as to move ahead the negotiations. Thus the United States placed particular pressures on these two governments to abandon the écrêtement plan.[20]

The forceful U.S. opposition could not be ignored by the EEC Council of Ministers during the 8–9 May 1963 meeting that had to approve a common stance prior to the GATT ministerial meeting. In light of the U.S. response, Bonn and The Hague softened their backing of the écrêtement plan and turned toward a compromise. Even the Quai D'Orsay realized that it had to insert some flexibility into its position to avoid a deadlock. The German state secretary, Alfred Müller-Armack, proposed a compromise on tariff reductions. The EEC would state its willingness to attend the round based on a linear and automatic system of reduction of tariffs in order to substantially reduce duties and disparities. It would suggest setting up a working group to study the tariff structure of the participants and a process through which to eliminate disparities. The key to the agreement, the price for French acquiescence to giving up the écrêtement plan as the EEC's formal stance, consisted of leaving open the rules of the negotiations and in proposing the establishment of the working group.[21]

More problematic for the ministers was finding a common position on agriculture, as it touched upon the pace of the elaboration of the CAP. Giscard d'Estaing and

---

[19]   Memorandum from the Special Trade Representative Christian Herter to President Kennedy, May 1, 1963, Herter's papers box 1 JFKL.

[20]   NARA 59, State Department Central file subject numeric box 3489, FT 4 US/ TEA, Memorandum of Conversation between the Dutch Ambassador Spierenburg and the American Ambassador Tuthill, April 29, 1963 and ibid., Telegram from the U.S. mission to the European Communities in Brussels to Department of State, May 2, 1963.

[21]   On the Council meeting see CM2 1963/947 PV de la 101ème session du Conseil de la CEE, May 8–10, 1963; CM2 1963/947 CEE Conseil, Directives arrêtées par le Conseil lors de la session des 8 et 9 mai 1963 en ce qui concerne l'attitude de la Communauté à la réunion ministérielle du GATT. See also HAEC MAEF, OW 50, Telegram no. 768/782 de Boegner au Quai d'Orsay, May 10, 1963; AAPD 1963, documents 161, May 9, 1963 and 164, Botschafter Harkort, Brussel (EWG/EAG), an Bundesminister Schröder, May 11, 1963.

Couve de Murville suggested inserting into the mandate to the EEC representatives a statement affirming that the EEC would agree to include agriculture in the round as soon as the CAP was defined. The French proposals provoked a tough response from Schröder and State Secretary Rolph Lahr. While recognizing that the EEC could not negotiate over agriculture in Geneva if an agreement between the Six had not been reached in Brussels, the Germans refused to approve in advance the entire CAP. After all, Lahr pointed out, under the Treaty of Rome such approval was required only by the end of the transitional period. The Dutch prime minister, Victor Marijnen, agreed that international negotiations over agriculture would be difficult to carry out if the Six had different agricultural policies. However, he too refused to link the opening of the Geneva negotiations to the preliminary adoption of the entire CAP. The other members displayed a softer stance. They were caught between their unwillingness to isolate the Germans and back the French, and evidence that without a common policy the EEC could not negotiate in Geneva. Sicco Mansholt reaffirmed that the EEC could not bargain in Geneva over agricultural products if its own policy was not established. Like France, he considered the GATT round an instrument by which to put pressure on the Germans.

A compromise was elaborated by the president of the Council of Ministers, the Luxembourger Eugène Schaus, and was linked to a parallel consensus on the timetable to approve the next set of agreements for the CAP. The Council of Ministers agreed to take part in the GATT agricultural negotiations, recognizing that these talks could occur only if the EEC adopted a common policy in this sector. However, adopting such a policy did not mean that the entire CAP had to be defined. At the same time, the Six agreed to adopt the next agreements for the CAP by December 31 1963, but to elaborate a mandate to negotiate in the round before this date. The Five clearly wanted the mandate to be adopted before the CAP agreements in order to prevent a French maneuver in this sector.[22] The synchronization between the CAP and the GATT round was thus reaffirmed.

The last issue to be settled concerned EEC representation at the GATT ministerial meeting. The Commission wanted to be the sole negotiator on agriculture, for which it lacked authority under the Treaty of Rome. It grounded its request on the impossibility of separating tariffs from other barriers to trade when negotiating with third countries. Member states had often remarked the Commission's lack of authority in agriculture, but none of them formally questioned it. For the GATT ministerial meeting, they agreed that the EEC would be represented by the delegation of the country holding the presidency of the Council, Luxembourg, and Jean Rey, Robert Marjolin, and Sicco Mansholt for the Commission. Coordinating meetings between the EEC negotiating team and the six governments would take place in Geneva so that fresh instructions could be given to the negotiators. Member states would be represented in Geneva by high-

---

[22]   HAEC EM 16, MAE Appunto per il sottosegretario, May 20, 1963.

ranking ministers, showing the political importance that they assigned to the round but also their desire to control EEC trade policymaking.[23]

The session of the Council of Ministers in May was a sort of convalescence in which the EEC returned to an almost normal working situation. Member states were aware of the political and economic importance of the GATT negotiations, and that their outcome would affect EEC trade policy, U.S.–EEC relations, and the multilateral trading system. The need to elaborate a common position for the GATT ministerial meeting helped the Six to get the EEC back to work in a climate that, as Erhard recounted, was not excessively conflictual.[24]

The GATT Ministerial Meeting of May 16–21, 1963: Launching the Kennedy Round

Between 16 and 21 May 1963, the representatives of the contracting parties gathered in Geneva for the GATT ministerial meeting. The meeting was intended to focus on reducing tariffs in the industrial sector, on reducing protectionism in agriculture, and on trade and development. However, the bargaining centered on the rules to reduce tariffs, the issue considered most urgent by the United States, the EEC, and the other developed countries. The meeting was dominated by the diplomatic skirmish between Brussels and Washington, with the result that the plenary session was soon abandoned, and the bargaining continued bilaterally between them with the mediation of Eric Wyndham White, the GATT director general. The United Kingdom, the small EFTA countries, and Japan were relegated to the sidelines while the two big players hammered out their differences.

The U.S. delegation was led by the U.S. trade representative, Christian Herter, the former secretary of state under President Eisenhower, and by Michael Blumenthal, the head of the U.S. delegation in Geneva. George Ball was present as well to supervise the negotiations, showing the political relevance Washington attached to the round. To advance their point of view, Herter, Blumenthal, and Ball pressured GATT members to adopt the U.S. position and isolate the EEC from the outset. This strategy, however, led nowhere, as the EEC did not budge from its opposition to across-the-board cuts in tariffs.[25]

In the first U.S.–EEC bilateral meeting, Herter suggested retaining the equal cut as the only principle; then in a second phase the EEC's worries over disparities in rates, a subsidiary problem, would be considered.[26] Given that the EEC

---

[23] HAEC MK23 Conversation avec M. Emile Noel, April 26, 1963; CM2 1963/948 CEE Conseil Aide-mémoire (Secret) à l'attention de M. le Secrétaire Général, May 22, 1963.

[24] Telegram no. 294 from Cunningham of the American Embassy in Luxembourg to Secretary of State, May 11, 1963.

[25] On the GATT ministerial meeting see Preeg, *Traders and Diplomats*, 60–64.

[26] Telegram no. 3045 from Morris of the American Embassy in Bonn to the Secretary of States, May 13, 1963, Herter paper, box 11, JFKL; NARA 59 Department of State,

representatives, led by the Belgian minister Maurice Brasseur, lacked authority to decide on the U.S. proposal, a coordination meeting took place among member states' representatives. The EEC Commission and Giscard d'Estaing found the U.S. proposal unacceptable, for it did not consider the EEC stance, and wanted to stick to the May 8–9 mandate. By contrast, the other members were inclined to amend the EEC's original stance so as to facilitate an agreement.[27] The Dutch and the Germans were particularly active in pressuring for a compromise and asking other delegations to be flexible. They had advised the U.S. negotiators to be sufficiently open to the disparities problem, while they would mediate within the EEC. In addition to this complex set of distinct interests, the bargaining between the United States and the EEC took place in nervous and frayed atmosphere that made an agreement more difficult to reach. With Washington and Paris pulling in opposite directions and with acrimony between the EEC and U.S. delegations, Erhard considered it essential to play the role of mediator. The German minister was convinced that it was possible to modify what he considered an intransigent French attitude. Behind the scenes, he urged Herter to act in a spirit of compromise, while in the EEC coordinating meetings, he kept playing his mediating role.[28]

To reach a final agreement, seven U.S.–EEC bilateral meetings and six EEC coordinating meetings were necessary. Each time that Herter brought a new proposal to the table or an EEC counterproposal was dismissed by the Americans, the session had to be interrupted to allow the EEC delegation to get fresh instructions from the ministers present in Geneva. No doubt the EEC shuttle diplomacy slowed the negotiations. Rey showed reluctance to be flexible. He held that the EEC had already made considerable concessions and that no more yielding was possible; otherwise the EEC would lose its credibility. Moreover, for the first time in five years, noted Rey, the Commission was bargaining "devant une position américaine particulièrement intransigeante et désagréable." Rey noted the effort made by the U.S. delegation to isolate the EEC in Geneva, an attempt that had nothing to do with fostering an Atlantic partnership. The Commission was backed by Giscard d'Estaing. Yet, while calling for a firm EEC stance, the French minister was ready to consider compromises. The Germans and the Dutch held that the Commission was overdramatizing the difficulty of the negotiations, and again called for flexibility.[29]

Central Files, FT 4 US/TEA Telegram from Secretary of State Rusk to the Mission to the European Communities, May 17, 1963.

[27] CM2 1963/947 CEE Conseil, Troisième Réunion de Coordination, May 18, 1963.

[28] Telegram no. 1211 from Herter in Geneva to Secretary of States, May 18, 1963, Herter papers box 11, JFKL.

[29] CM2 1963/948 CEE Conseil, Cinquième Réunion de Coordination, May 20, 1963; the tensions between the U.S. and EEC delegations are reported also in HAEC EM 16, MAE Svolgimento dei lavori presso il GATT. A tutto il May 21, 1963 (allegato 6). MAEF Cabinet de Couve de Murville 1961–66, no. 160 Télex 170 de la délégation française a MM. Decarbonnel, Clappier, Ortoli, Matignon, May 20, 1963.

At the sixth EEC coordinating meeting, Erhard suggested the compromise that was subsequently accepted by the United States. The linear tariff cut of 50 percent across the board would be retained as a working hypothesis. In the case of disparities in tariffs, reductions would be based on special and automatic rules for their elimination. A working group would be established to identify such disparities and elaborate these rules. Thus, the wide variations in duties and the equal linear cut were placed on the same formal basis. After the compromise had been achieved within the EEC, Erhard—with Dutch support—hinted that member states' representatives should be present at the last meeting with Herter. In this way, the bargaining could continue until an agreement was reached and the EEC shuttle diplomacy that had slowed the negotiations would be avoided. The suggestion highlighted the frictions that existed with the Commission. Rey predictably rejected it and underlined the skills of the Commissions' representatives. To reinforce his point of view, the commissioner emphasized that, if member states attended the session, the differences among them would be exploited by the Americans to weaken the EEC. To the rescue of the Commission came Giscard d'Estaing, who announced his refusal to attend. The French minister did not want the member states most susceptible to U.S. pressure to attend the negotiations. Because of this unmovable French opposition, the proposal was eventually dropped.[30]

Eventually the GATT ministers agreed that a significant liberalization of world trade was desirable and that a multilateral trade conference would begin in Geneva on May 4, 1964. Both industrial and agricultural sectors would be considered, and both tariff and nontariff barriers would be dealt with. Equal and substantial linear tariff cuts would be made, with limited exceptions submitted to justification and formal processes of dispute. In case of significant disparities, tariff reductions would be set on the basis of special rules of automatic and general application. A Committee for Trade Negotiations (TNC) made up of representatives of contracting parties was charged with agreeing on a negotiating plan to reduce tariffs and to deal with NTBs. As for the agricultural sector, the EEC and the United States could not agree on a broad goal for negotiations. The final formula—promoting an expansion of trade in foodstuffs—was rather vague. Special attention would be given to the problems of the LDCs, which would be exempted from the rule of reciprocity of concessions. Under this arrangement, rules remained to be elaborated and the confrontation between the two sides of the Atlantic was shifted to the TNC.[31]

Despite all the quarrels and the ambiguity of the agreement reached, the United States and the EEC were able to achieve the major result of launching

---

[30] CM2 1963/948 CEE Conseil, Cinquième Réunion de Coordination, May 20, 1963; ibid., CEE Conseil, Sixième Réunion de Coordination, May 21, 1963; MAEF Cabinet Couve de Murville 1961–66, no. 160, Note "Réunion ministérielle du GATT," May 21, 1963.

[31] Conclusion and resolutions adopted on May 21, 1963 in GATT BISD, 12th Supplement, Geneva, 1964 and PRO FO 371/172309 GATT—Restricted Min (63) 9, May 22, 1963. Telegram no. 1468 from Herter in Geneva to President Kennedy, May 22, 1963, Herter papers box 11, JFKL.

a far-reaching round of negotiations. They shared the common aim of reducing tariffs, and this led them to compromise. Despite the mutual mistrust a new round began auspiciously, as it set out from a broader starting point than the previous GATT round. Willingness to liberalize trade was therefore a fundamental shared objective. The GATT ministerial meeting highlighted the areas on which the negotiations would concentrate, notably in the industrial sector. Thus from the very beginning the new round appeared to be heading toward the reduction of tariffs in the area of major concern to the developed countries. The vague formula reached on agriculture and the disappointment of the LDCs, which had hoped to obtain more concrete concessions from the industrialized countries, did not prevent the EEC and the United States from launching the new round.

The need to attend the GATT conference helped the Six to find a quantum of unity after the crisis provoked by de Gaulle's veto of British entry into the EEC. Internal differences existed, but did not prevent a common position. The Six were able to attend the negotiations as a single unit, capable of defending their point of view and obtaining concessions from Washington. Despite internal tensions, the EEC was working effectively and had the ability to bargain as an equal partner with the United States. In spite of internal tension and acrimony, the EEC member states were able to elaborate a common stance and participate in the negotiations. Their primary interest in taking part in the round in Geneva as a trading unit motivated them to overcome the tensions caused by the French veto.

As for the EEC's trade policymaking, the ministerial meeting demonstrated that negotiations within the EEC presented challenging technical problems. The Six were working toward a common outlook and had endowed the Commission with negotiating authority. This was a cumbersome process, since decisions were hammered out only after prolonged discussions, and tended to come very late in the day. The EEC decision-making machinery slowed progress and made the negotiations in Geneva even more complex.

The Commission was having problems in establishing its role. As broker it had failed to mediate between member states. Rey and Marjolin stuck to their rigid stances and did not attempt to reconcile various agendas so as to achieve a common position. The role of mediator was instead taken by Erhard. An agreement was reached without the Commission's brokering, showing that member states were able to do so on their own and thus sidelining this institution. As for the Commission's role of negotiator, the Dutch and the German requests to be present at the talks with Herter showed that challenges could also come from member states that overtly supported the supranational aspects of the Treaty of Rome. As a matter of fact, the Germans were traditionally seen as more supportive of supranationality than the French. National positions on the delegation of power to the Commission were thus not driven by ideological support for supranationalism. Rather, they reflected the need to promote national trade interests in specific circumstances.

The first GATT ministerial meeting of what was to become the era of Atlantic partnership took place in a difficult atmosphere. The U.S. tactics surprised the Six. The Americans conducted a tough campaign against the EEC—above all against the French, claimed Paris—in an attempt to isolate it.[32] The U.S. position towards the EEC had evolved since the GATT Article XXIV negotiations in 1958. Now the aim was not to defend the EEC, but to press it to reduce tariffs. Equally important, U.S. firmness was created by the "de Gaulle factor." Washington feared that Paris was trying to deadlock or delay the round, and that the Five might bow to what were essentially French interests in order to keep the Community intact. American intransigence was therefore created by the determination to push the Five to oppose the French.[33]

Kennedy believed that his program was being impeded by the attitude of the EEC in Geneva. His worries went hand in hand with dismay over the fact that the British and the Germans had started referring to the negotiations as the Kennedy Round. When he met with the French and the Germans in the aftermath of the GATT session, the U.S. president felt the need to lecture them on the importance of the round and the link between trade, security, and monetary issues. Meeting with French foreign minister Couve de Murville in Washington at the end of May 1963, Kennedy noted that the U.S. deficit in the balance of payments was caused by military and foreign aid programs. Therefore, trade had to be liberalized so that Washington could enhance its exports and balance the military and foreign aid program. However, Couve saw things differently. Washington was dealing with "the problem of the balance of payments piecemeal," while the Western countries needed "to have sound monetary policy." In any case, the United States did not have a genuine deficit; it was enjoying a foreign trade surplus and exporting too much U.S. capital abroad.[34]

The meeting with the Germans was no more positive. With Chancellor Adenauer and Erhard in June 1963 in Bonn, the U.S. president wondered "why this was called the Kennedy Round and why it should not be called the Adenauer Round or the de Gaulle Round." Kennedy hinted that economic relations "including such matters as monetary policy, offset arrangements and the Kennedy Round of trade negotiations … were possibly even more important to us now than nuclear matters." The West was strong enough to deter any attack, Kennedy believed, while huge unresolved problems remained in the economic field. It was foreign trade that enabled the United States to earn enough to maintain overseas commitments. Thus, bargaining over trade was to be conducted at the highest level, involving heads of governments and not left to technical specialists.

---

[32]   Telegram no. 4931 from Paris to Secretary of State, May 29, 1963, Herter papers, box 10, JFKL; CM2 1963/948 CEE Conseil Aide-mémoire à l'attention de M. le Secrétaire Général, May 22, 1963.

[33]   Memorandum of telephone conversation between Herter and Tuthill, May 29, 1963, Herter papers box 1, JFKL; PRO FO 371/172309 "The Kennedy Round" Brief by the Board of Trade in view of the talks with President Kennedy, June 20, 1963.

[34]   NARA Department of States Files, Presidential Memoranda of Conversation: Lot 66 D 149, April–June 1963, Memorandum of Conversation between Kennedy and Couve de Murville, Washington, May 25, 1963.

"We must conduct these negotiations at the top level—otherwise we'll be ruined by bookkeepers," claimed Kennedy. Adenauer did not seem to be impressed with Kennedy's remarks. In his view, Germany had economic problems too and its "export balances were gone."[35] Unsurprisingly, after the stormy GATT ministerial session and meetings with the Europeans, Kennedy's irritation that this fraught round of talks bore his name grew.[36]

Hard Times for the EEC Commission

A series of meetings occurred in Geneva between June and November 1963 to set the rules for the upcoming negotiations. However, because of the fundamental differences between the United States and the EEC, no compromise could be reached. Discussion of the tariff-cutting formula was complicated by disagreement over how to identify a disparity. The EEC suggested a broad formula, whereas the United States preferred a restrictive one in order to avoid watering down the principle of a large linear cut to all tariffs. In discussions with its trading partners the EEC discovered that in the large majority of cases the disparities concerned products imported from EFTA countries. The EEC thus risked retaining discrimination against the EFTA countries because of rates set by the United States. Hard, confused, and prolonged bargaining followed, with both the EEC and the United States sticking to prior positions and the British and the Japanese seeking to mediate by putting different formulas on the table.[37]

For the Dutch, the Germans and the Italians, the EEC had to quickly adopt a new stance on negotiations so as not be blamed for any delay. The Commission, the French, and the Belgians, by contrast, believed that the EEC should take all the time necessary to elaborate new proposals corresponding to its interests.[38] In light of Paris's refusal to rapidly find a solution, Bonn believed that the French had "reverted to their normal delaying tactics" and speculated that this reflected a desire to postpone decisions on the round until the end of the year, or to wreck it altogether.[39] In truth, the French were not preparing to torpedo the negotiations.

---

[35] FRUS 1961–63, IX Foreign Economic Policy, 72. Memorandum of Conversation between Kennedy, Rusk, Adenauer and Erhard, June 24, 1963.

[36] Kennedy's discomfort is mentioned in Ted Sorensen, *Kennedy* (New York, 1965), 412.

[37] CM2 1964/305 PV de la 49ème reunion du Comité 111, July 19, 1963; PRO FO 371/172311 Telegram no. 124 from Cohen to Foreign Office, September 20, 1963 reporting a conversation between Denman and Horn, the German Delegate to GATT.

[38] CM2 1963/305 PV de la 53ème réunion du Comité 111, November 5, 1963; CM2 1963/539 PV de la 114ème session du Conseil de la CEE, November 4–5, 1963.

[39] PRO 241/840 Telegram no. 314 from Roberts of the British Embassy in Bonn to Foreign Office, September 25, 1963, reporting a conversation between Horn and Denman; PRO 241/840 Telegram no. 175 from Cohen to Foreign Office, November 26, 1963.

Instead, they aimed to elaborate a formula that would effectively defend their trade interests. Moreover, with the Germans dragging their feet on the CAP, the French felt no hurry to reach an agreement in Geneva. In effect, persistent disagreement over the EEC's agenda prevented the formulation of a common stance. By the end of November, talks in Geneva had reached at an impasse. With the EEC lacking a negotiating position and the attention of the Six focusing squarely on their internal wrangling, GATT discussions were adjourned to 1964.[40]

In this phase, the Commission faced major challenges in playing its role of negotiator. Because of internal disagreements, member states were not giving instructions, and yet they strictly controlled the Commission in Geneva. As the British noted, in negotiating sessions Hijzen "was flanked by the French and the German delegates" … and "from time to time the French Delegate [whispered] fiercely in Hijzen's ear."[41] Franco-German surveillance of Hijzen, the very fact that he attended discussions with third countries flanked by member states' representatives, showed a willingness to supervise the Commission during this period of uncertainty.

Problems for the Commission came also from the direction of the United States. The Americans had counted on the Commission's liberalism and willingness to attend the round to counter French obstructionism. After the ministerial meeting they felt aggrieved by the actions of the Brussels institution. Ball felt that its previous enthusiasm for the Kennedy Round was dissipating. However, what most annoyed the undersecretary was his perception that the Commission was more protectionist than some of the member states. As Ball put it to Walter Hallstein, its president, the "Commission was [not] playing its proper role, and … it appeared all too often to be siding with the most restrictive French view in any showdown."[42] Moreover, according to the U.S. negotiators, who received the full backing of the British, Brussels was inadequately represented in Geneva and lacked a clear stance. The EEC needed a senior and adequate representative, possibly Rey or Marjolin. In these circumstances, the Americans were becoming impatient about the EEC's trade policymaking.[43]

---

[40]   PRO 241/840 Telegram no. 175 from Cohen to Foreign Office, November 26, 1963; PRO FO 371/172316, Note on the Kennedy Round by Mason, December 16, 1963.

[41]   PRO FO 172311 Telegram no. 129 from Cohen to Foreign Office, September 27, 1963. See also NARA 59 Central Files Subject numeric 1963, box 3491, Telegram no. 1446 from Blumenthal to Herter, October 2, 1963.

[42]   HAEC, JMAS 95 Letter from Hinton, Director of Atlantic Political-Economic Affairs Office in State Department, to Tuthill, June 26, 1963, reporting a conversation between Hallstein, Narjes, Ball, and Blumenthal. See also HAEC, JMAS 95, Memorandum of Conversation between Hallstein and Tuthill, May 20, 1963.

[43]   PRO BT 241/389 Telegram no. 85 from Cohen to Foreign Office, July 3, 1963; PRO FO 371/172310 Letter from Cohen to O'Neill of the UK delegation to the EEC, August 7, 1963; PRO FO 172311 Telegram no. 129 from Cohen to Foreign Office, September 27, 1963; NARA 59 Central Files Subject numeric 1963, box 3491, Telegram no. 1446

In spite of the Americans' disappointment with the Commission, Washington had no intention of writing it off. In Ball's opinion, American policy required that the supranational institution be built up in order to strengthen European integration. Yet the political objective of strengthening the Commission had to be achieved while at the same time concluding the talks successfully. Washington had to continue to maintain contact with the national governments, while also insisting on the involvement of the Commission. This perspective contrasts with Erhard's suggestion to Herter that the United States negotiate with the member states and "play down" the Commission, going over its head.[44]

Anglo-American unhappiness with the EEC's trade policymaking led Eric Wyndham White to take an astonishing initiative. At the end of November 1963, the French member of the 111 Committee, Jean Wahl, informed his colleagues and the Commission that White had suggested to the French the implementation of an informal committee to discuss the major issues of the Kennedy Round and speed it up. The most pertinent aspect of the proposal was the composition of the committee, which would be made up of France, Germany, the United States, and the United Kingdom, with the clear aim of leaving the Commission out of the talks. The French government resolutely rejected the suggestion. It had no reason to weaken the unity of the EEC, which gave strength to the Six as a whole that they lacked individually. It had no interest in sitting alongside the Germans, too receptive to American pressure for French liking, as they negotiated in Geneva. Moreover, the French had no reason to speed up the Kennedy Round. Predictably, the Benelux countries and Italy rebuffed White's proposal, as it cast doubt on their own decision-making power and the unity of the EEC. Together with France they decided that an immediate answer was to be given by the Commission itself, requesting that White withdraw his suggestion. What was remarkable was the German reaction. German 111 Committee representative Reinhardt fully agreed with the stance of his colleagues. However, he could not take a formal position, because White's idea was still being discussed in Bonn. As a result, Reinhardt could not sign the response to be given to the GATT director general.[45] Once more, challenges to the negotiating role of the Commission did not come solely from governments that overtly questioned supranationalism, such as France, but also from those that professed to support it, such as the Federal Republic. The need to promote their trade interests determined the position the member states took on their negotiating agent.

---

from Blumenthal to Herter, October 2, 1963; HAEC, JMAS 95, Letter of Ball to Tuthill, November 8, 1963.

[44] NA 59 State Department Central file subject numeric box 3488, ECIN 3 EEC, Telegram ECOBUS 140 from Tuthill to Secretary of State, August 1, 1963. Letter from Blumenthal to Herter, October 16, 1963, Herter Papers box 1, JFKL. Preliminary Draft of the report "Components of a Strategy for the Kennedy Round" by Ball, December 10, 1963, Herter's papers, box 2, JFKL.

[45] AECB BAC 122/1991 17 Note pour Monsieur le Ministre Rey (from Hijzen), November 19, 1963.

The EEC Mandate of December 1963

As noted, the EEC demonstrated a manifest unreadiness to negotiate in Geneva because of internal quarrels over its agenda. In response to German foot-dragging on unified grain prices (UGPs), de Gaulle threatened to dissolve the EEC.[46] The Germans did not deem the threat credible. They surveyed the advantages the French enjoyed under the Treaty of Rome and concluded that the threat would not be implemented. Hence they remained reluctant to move ahead with approval of the CAP.[47] The German stance, however, did not lack its own contradictions. On the one hand, Bonn yearned for synchronization between the CAP and the GATT round in order to prevent any French unilateral decision on the trade negotiations. On the other, it desired a slower pace in development of the CAP, thereby putting in doubt the synchronization plan it itself had elaborated. The Germans, rather than the French, ran the risk of being the stumbling block that would keep the round from reaching a successful conclusion.

German dissatisfaction with the CAP also concerned the effect of this policy on the EEC's imports, and Bonn called for modifications in order to maintain German imports from outside the Community. To this aim, it suggested making the CAP negotiable in Geneva and giving quantitative assurances to GATT partners. In particular, the Germans wanted an agreement that the EEC would keep importing 12–13 million tons of cereals a year. The need to protect imports from outside the EEC was shared by the Netherlands, but no solid alliance was built between the two members. The Dutch aimed to keep access for third countries through low unified prices, a solution categorically rejected by Bonn, which, with the highest prices in the EEC, preferred to give third countries quantitative assurances.[48]

Preparation of the EEC mandate for the Kennedy Round got caught up in this dispute over these two aspects of the CAP. First, the pace with which the policy

---

[46]   HAEC- MAEF 17 reel 208, Secrétariat General, Entretiens et Message, Réunion du 4 juillet et Réunion du 5 juillet, De Gaulle, Pompidou, Couve de Murville Giscard d'Estaing , Pisani, Erhard, Schröder, Dahlgrun, Schwarz, Bonn, July 4–5, 1963 and AAPD 1963, documents 218/219, Deutsch-franzosische Regierungsbesprechung, July 4–5, 1963. HAEC-MAEF, Secrétariat General, Entretiens et Message, 17 reel 208, Encontre entre Couve de Murville et Schröder, September 17, 1963 and AAPD Runderlass des Staatssekretars Lahr, September 18, 1963.

[47]   PRO FO 371/172312 Telegram no. 316, from O'Neill in Brussels to Foreign Office, October 4, 1963.

[48]   HAEC-MAEF 17 reel 208, Secrétariat General, Entretiens et Message, Réunion du 4 juillet 1963, Pompidou, Couve de Murville Giscard d'Estaing , Pisani, Erhard, Schröder, Dahlgrun, Schwarz; and AAPD 1963, documents 218/219, Deutsch-franzosische Regierungsbesprechung, July 4–5, 1963. HAEC MK 25 Conversation avec Spierenburg (Duth PERMDEL), October 2, 1963; CM2/1963 539, PV de la 112ème session du Conseil de la CEE, October 15, 1963; AAPD, document 395, Aufzeichnung des Botschafters Blankenhorn, Paris, October 21, 1963; HAEC-MAEF, Secrétariat General, Entretiens et Message, 19 reel 209, Telegram, Ministère Affaires Etrangères, October 28, 1963.

was being defined and implemented, too hasty for the Germans, was not hasty enough for the French.[49] Second was the impact of the CAP on third countries and therefore on the EEC's external trade relations. Different commercial interests within the EEC complicated preparations for the Kennedy Round. Yet it was the GATT negotiations themselves that obliged the Six to adopt a common position.

At the Franco-German meeting at the end of November, French prime minister Georges Pompidou and the newly appointed Chancellor Erhard were able to reach a basic agreement. The chancellor asserted his willingness to adopt the next part of the CAP by the end of the year but avowed that, because of internal difficulties, Bonn could not fix UGPs. This general agreement was sufficient to get French approval of the mandate for the Kennedy Round, albeit the crucial question of cereals prices remained unsolved.[50]

It was against the backdrop of this internal dispute that the Commission formulated its proposals to the Council of Ministers, which would approve the EEC mandate for the GATT negotiations. For the industrial sector, it put forward a brand-new formula, named *double écart*, which, according to the Commission, had the advantage of identifying relevant disparities without hurting the EFTA countries.[51]

Moreover, the Commission put on the table its proposals for agriculture. First, it suggested setting unified prices for grains during 1964–65 half way between the French and the German levels. According to Mansholt's calculation, this level would maintain the EEC imports requirement at 10 million tons a year.[52] Then the Commission elaborated the EEC's negotiating stance for Geneva. Mansholt looked to the Kennedy Round as a major opportunity to regulate agriculture at the world level and, equally important, as a way of controlling and moderating the protectionist effects of the CAP on international trade. The commissioner refused the approach of exporters, for whom it was up to importers to create conditions to ensure market access. This conception left the importers only the duty to compromise between the exigencies of national farmers and external trade. The EEC had to put forward proposals foreseeing obligations for exporters and importers—and also to escape too defensive a position in Geneva—and deal with the national regulations of both importers and exporters. Mansholt's plan consisted of identifying the support received by each item, defined by the difference between the world price—an international reference to be established—and the remuneration obtained by national producers— which would correspond to the domestic price—and to consolidate, that is to say to

[49]   On this aspect see also Ludlow, *The European Community and the Crises of the 1960s*, 11–39.

[50]   HAEC-MAEF, Secrétariat General, Entretiens et Message, 19 reel 209, Tête-à-tête entre le General de Gaulle et le Chancelier Erhard, November 21, 1963; ibid., Rencontre à l'Hôtel Matignon entre le Premier Ministre et le Chancelier Fédéral, November 21, 1963.

[51]   AECB BAC 1 122/1991, Négociations Tarifaires dans le cadre du GATT (Communication de la Commission au Conseil), November 11, 1963.

[52]   HAEC BAC 9 9/1967, Mesures en vue d'établissement d'un niveau commun des prix des céréales, VI/COM(63) 430, November 20, 1963.

bind, this margin of support, or *montant de soutien* (MDS). The contracting parties would engage in talks respecting the level of support, and then every three years, mandatory meetings would take place in the GATT to adapt the engagements to the evolution of trade. According to Mansholt, the EEC could only consolidate the level of protection that would arise out of the establishment of the CAP and its common prices. However, given the growing production of member states' agricultural sectors, and the lower level of income of farmers, the consolidation was a concession from the EEC, or so claimed Mansholt.[53]

The Commission proposals were a breakthrough. They would shatter the habits of the GATT, where, until that moment, negotiations had taken place only on tariffs and, exceptionally, on contingents. They represented a major attempt to organize agriculture at the world level and moved negotiations from measures applied at the border to all provisions having a protectionist effect, including domestic direct and indirect support of all kinds. Moreover, the MDS plan was fully compatible with the CAP. Within the EEC, the degree of protection depended on the level of support prices. Coherently, the Commission suggested a plan that was also based on prices. The EEC could negotiate in the GATT without having to face requests for quantitative assurances and could terminate the round with a general acceptance of the CAP. To implement this plan, UPGs needed to be approved, as they determined the level of EEC protection. Thus, the link between cereal prices and the Kennedy Round was reaffirmed and became a lever to get Bonn's agreement.

The EEC Council of Ministers marathon from December 19 to 23 adopted a mandate for the Kennedy Round on the basis of the Commission's proposals. Elaboration of a common position for the industrial sector was a long process because of its technicalities, but was not particularly difficult as the positions of the Six were relatively close and they all possessed a manifest desire to succeed. Italy, France, Belgium and Luxembourg promptly supported the Commission's suggestion, whereas Germany and the Netherlands had a more confrontational attitude. They questioned the Commission's positions and tended to push for measures that would be easily accepted in Geneva by the United States. Marjolin and Rey mastered all the technical details and, ultimately, saw their points of view prevail.[54]

The adoption of the mandate for agriculture was more difficult, as it touched upon the UGPs. The Italians, the French, and the Benelux countries accepted the MDS plan as a way to give the EEC a negotiating position in Geneva, rather than because they were fully convinced of its feasibility. Furthermore, the French, unenthusiastic about a plan that touched upon their domestic support regime, endorsed it because it required the fixing of UGPs and, therefore, pressured the Germans. In Paris the view was

---

[53]   AECB PV 247, October 30, 1963, "Préparation des négociations agricoles prévues dans le cadre de 'Négociation au GATT'," Communication de la Commission au Conseil, October 30, 1963; CM2 1963 539 PV de la 114ème session du Conseil de la CEE, November 4–5, 1963.

[54]   HAEC BAC 506 026/1969, Compte-Rendu des travaux du Comité 111, December 12, 1963.

that there was no risk in accepting it, since Washington would never back a proposal that rewrote domestic support policies in the GATT. The French thus exploited the Commission's preferences in order to implement their own.[55] In contrast, the Netherlands and Germany had objections to the agricultural plan. The Dutch minister of agriculture, Barend Biesheuvel, wanted the MDS plan to be complemented by a EEC formal guarantee that, in the case of strong increases in the EEC level of cereal production, and if its imports fell below 90 percent of imports in a given period, the EEC would lower its UGPs.[56] The Dutch proposal was ruled out by the other five governments on the grounds that it was unwise to insert into the negotiating mandate clauses in favor of third countries. Moreover, France had no intention of giving such an assurance, whereas Germany had no intention of reducing UGPs.[57]

The toughest opposition to the MDS plan came from Bonn. Although Lahr broadly endorsed it, he suggested that for products for which unified prices had not yet been approved—grains—the EEC would grant quantitative assurances. In this way, Bonn hoped it would not be forced to set UGPs to negotiate in Geneva. A prolonged confrontation between Mansholt and the Germans took place, with the other five members, and notably the French, leaving to the Commission the task of confronting the Germans. The commissioner ruled out quantitative assurances—which he considered inconsistent with the CAP system of protection grounded on prices—and pointed to the need to establish reasonable UGPs to shelter third countries' interests. He also reminded the Germans that, without a sufficiently elaborated CAP, the EEC would not be able to specify the concessions it was willing to make in Geneva. Moreover, there was a risk that the CAP would be determined by the concessions that the EEC would make in the GATT. Fundamental decisions had to be made before the start of the round, concluded the commissioner. To counter German resistance, Mansholt suggested that, for products still lacking common prices, the EEC would negotiate on a fictitious margin of support, established on the ground of fictitious common prices. As shown in the next chapter, this clause did not save the Germans from pressure to adopt UGPs. As a matter of fact, in

---

[55] MAEF DE/CE, 1961–66, GATT 931 Note de la Direction des Relations Economiques Extérieurs (DREE) du Ministère des Finance "Les Accords du 23 décembre 1963," January 8, 1964.

[56] CM2/1963 541, Déclaration de M. Le Ministre Biesheuvel concernant les négociations relatives à l'agriculture dans le cadre de la négociation "Kennedy"; December 19, 1963. On the ambivalent Dutch attitude towards CAP and the problems it created third countries see Anjo G. Harryvan and Jan van der Harst, "For Once a United Front. The Netherlands and the 'Empty Chair' Crisis of the Mid-1960s," in Wilfried Loth (ed.), *Crises and Compromises: the European Project 1963–1969* (Baden-Baden, 2001), 167–91.

[57] CM2 1963/76 PV de la 117ème session du Conseil de la CEE, December 2–3, 1963; CM2/1963 541, Note introductive, Avis du Comité 111 sur la négociation en ce qui concerne les produits agricoles, December 19, 1963; MAEF DE/CE, 1961–66, GATT 931, Note de la Direction des Relations Economiques Extérieurs (DREE) du Ministère des Finance "Les Accords du 23 décembre 1963," January 8, 1964.

order to negotiate in Geneva over this basic commodity, the EEC had to show its level of actual protection by setting UGPs. In any case, the Germans were satisfied. Formally speaking, the adoption of the MDS plan as the EEC's bargaining position did not require UGPs, and they had escaped unwanted decisions. Moreover, the Council of Ministers recognized the need to consider the promotion of world trade and the principle of continuing access for imports from third countries, although no special clause addressing this issue was adopted. Regulations for meat, rice, and dairy products were also adopted. Despite the disappointment of the Commission, the Council of Ministers postponed to April 1964 the approval of UGPs.[58]

After the crisis caused by the French veto, the Six were again able to make substantial and important decisions in the two crucial fields of the CAP and the common commercial policy. Their desire to reach a final compromise pushed them to make concessions and reconcile their different commercial interests. Moreover, the decisions the EEC had to make to attend the round obliged member states to deal with such crucial issues as the impact of the EEC on world trade, above all in the agricultural field. Equally important, the round obliged the EEC to define its CAP.

The Commission played an important role in setting the mandate. It was the source of key proposals and it proved to have the expertise necessary to engage in technical debate and structure the negotiations. The mandate for the industrial sector and, above all, for the agricultural sector owed at least as much to the Commission as to national governments. Thus, the Commission was able to inscribe its preferences on the final outcome, and it emerged from the negotiations with considerably enhanced prestige. National governments showed confidence in the Commission's technical skills and capacity to produce compromise. More significantly, they demonstrated a readiness to exploit and manipulate the preferences of this institution in order to foster their own interests.

The Chicken War

Before moving ahead with this narrative of the Kennedy Round, it is worth pausing to deal with the so-called Chicken War, the commercial war between the EEC and the United States that came to an end as the trade talks were getting started. As is often the case with trade wars, behind an apparently minor and arcane issue lay important political and commercial questions.[59]

---

[58]   AECB PV 254, December 17, 1963; CM2/1963 541 PV de la 119ème session du Conseil de la CEE, December 16–23, 1963. For the EEC Council of Ministers mandate AECB BAC 1 122/1991, Négociations Commerciales dans le cadre du GATT, NCG/15/63, December 21, 1963 and AECB BAC 38/194, 308 Mansholt cabinet papers, "Dispositions prises par le Conseil lors de sa session des 16, 21 et 23 Décembre 1963," January 31, 1964.

[59]   The best account of the Poultry War remains Ross B. Talbot, *The Chicken War. An International Trade Conflict between the United States and the European Economic Community, 1961–1964* (Ames, IA, 1978).

These are the facts. Thanks to technological and managerial developments, U.S. production of frozen broilers increased from 1.2 to 6.8 billion pounds between 1948 and 1962. Consequently, producers looked to markets abroad, in particular, to Western Europe. Germany, with its rising rate of consumption, was the most attractive market, and indeed, U.S. exports to Germany jumped from 3.5 million pounds in 1956 to 122 million pounds in June 1962. In the year from June 1961 to June 1962, Germany received 56% of U.S. exports of frozen broilers to the EEC countries. In the meantime, EEC producers were also increasing their production, thanks to the same technological advancements that had appeared in the 1950s in the United States.[60]

In January 1962, the Six adopted regulation 22, establishing a common market for poultry with a variable levy to operate from July 1 of the same year. Washington looked with apprehension at the negative effects that the regulation could have on U.S. exports, fearing that the CAP would make the EEC self-sufficient in agriculture, beginning with chicken. Until July 1962, the United States could only forecast the effects of the CAP, but after that date it started to see the practical consequences. U.S. exports of broilers dropped drastically when the variable levy was introduced. The GATT-bound duty of 15% doubled and was to increase by 70% in the following years, pricing U.S. poultry out of the EEC's markets. In the first nine months under the levy system, U.S. exports of broilers to Germany plummeted by 40% from the previous year, whereas German imports from France and the Netherlands increased rapidly.[61]

U.S. Secretary for Agriculture Orville Freeman was under considerable pressure from the American poultry industry. In a meeting with the EEC ministers for agriculture, Freeman expressed his disapproval of the CAP and warned that his government would act to protect its exports. On the ground that the levy on poultry was inconsistent with the GATT-bound duty, Freeman asked the EEC to reduce it and to limit its own production. The message that Washington wanted the Six to receive was that they could not apply their variable levy system without considering the negative impact on other countries and recognizing that they would have a strong reaction.[62] The problem at hand, therefore, was the entire agricultural policy of the EEC and its effect on world agriculture. The destiny of American poultry exports to the EEC became a test of the impact that the CAP could have and of Washington's willingness to protect its economic interests. For the American agricultural sectors in particular, poultry became the measure of the U.S. government's willingness to protect the interests of American farmers.

---

[60]   Ibid., 24–6.

[61]   Ibid.

[62]   FRUS 1961–63, XIII, Section Economic and Political Integration, 53. Memorandum from Secretary of Agriculture Freeman to President Kennedy, November 26, 1962 and Memorandum from D. Gale Johnson to Governor Herter on "Trade Negotiations Issues Involving Agriculture—Some Preliminary Comments and Questions," January 17, 1963, Herter's papers, box 2, JFKL.

The EEC refused to follow the plan Freeman had drawn up. Particularly outspoken in opposing the Americans was the French minister for agriculture, Edgar Pisani. He declared that he "wished le *père* Freeman would stop claiming a divine right to dispose of American food surplus in an area which, with the French technological revolution in full swing, was rapidly acquiring surplus on its own."[63] Escalating the quarrel, Pisani claimed that the United States was trying to undermine the EEC. With this clean refusal to take into account U.S. complaints, the Chicken War broke out.[64]

In April 1963, Mansholt visited Washington to discuss with the Kennedy administration the state of transatlantic relations. On the poultry issue, the commissioner presented the view that, in light of the increased production in the United States and in Europe, Washington could not expect to find increased markets in the EEC. The Six had their own surpluses to be disposed of and could not be expected to make absorbing American production a priority. The EEC pointed out that the U.S. government put disproportionate emphasis on chicken for domestic reasons that were not the EEC's affair. Moreover, the U.S. surplus in agricultural trade with the Six proved that American irritation was selective and unwarranted. Herter argued that if the tactics the EEC employed with poultry were to be applied across the board, there would be *no* international trade. He therefore asked the EEC to reduce the levy or to offer compensation to offset damages to U.S. poultry exports.[65] Herter and Ball warned Rey and Marjolin that the United States would retaliate if the EEC maintained the present tariff, while the U.S. Embassy in Bonn exerted pressure on the German government to support a settlement.[66]

Thus, as the U.S. government was ready to propose the new round, a trade war across the Atlantic had just broken out. By mid-1963, with the GATT ministerial meeting looming, the issue had become the subject of newspaper headlines. The Americans seemed convinced that behind this war lay a desire on de Gaulle's part to drive American agricultural products out of the EEC, which could then become an inward-looking region.[67] In this context it came as no surprise that

---

[63]   Cited in Taber, *John F. Kennedy and a Uniting Europe*, 143.

[64]   FRUS 1961–63, XIII, Section Economic and Political Integration, 53. Memorandum from Secretary of Agriculture Freeman to President Kennedy, November 26, 1962. Freeman reported to Kennedy that the French were intractable.

[65]   Memorandum of Conversation. Participants: Herter, Tuthill, Gosset and Mansholt, Washington, April 8, 1963, Herter papers, box 10, JFKL and Memorandum for the President from Herter on Herter's meeting with Mansholt on April 8, 1963, Herter's papers, box 10, JFKL. FRUS, 1961–63, vol. XIII Economic and Political Integration, 75. Memorandum of Conversation between Kennedy, Ball, Freeman, Tuthill, Kaysen, Mansholt and Mozer, April 9, 1963.

[66]   Office of the SRTN Rey-Marjolin talks, May 2–3, 1963, Principal issue in trade negotiations, Herter papers, box 8A, JFKL; HAEC JMAS/95 Aide-Mémoire, July 5, 1963 from the U.S. Embassy in Bonn to the German government.

[67]   Eckes, *Revisiting U.S. Trade Policy. Decisions in Perspective*, 68.

chicken increased in political significance, and that the very future of the Atlantic alliance seemed to depend on poultry: "'Is the Grand Alliance going to founder on chickens?' [Kennedy] asked one day in mock despair."[68]

At this point, the Commission suggested to the EEC Council of Ministers that the levy on poultry be reduced by 1.2 cents per pound. Hallstein, Mansholt, and Rey urged member states to give the United States some relief and reduce the hostilities that the issue was causing in transatlantic relations. However, Couve de Murville and Lahr argued that the Commission was overdramatizing the issue and exaggerating the importance Washington actually gave it. They decided that little needed to be done. Notwithstanding Hallstein's warning that the subject of the levy had been raised with him by high U.S. officials—all the way up to Kennedy himself—the French and Germans were not ready to compromise.[69]

With the refusal of the Council to follow the advice of the Commission, at the beginning of August Washington notified the EEC that it would raise tariffs on EEC imports to the value of U.S.$46 million if by October 16, 1963 the EEC had not reduced the levy or granted adequate compensation.[70] It turned out that the EEC had underestimated U.S. determination to see its trade rights respected. As Tuthill wrote, "The Europeans had been mistaken not to take us [the United States] seriously from the beginning and realize that we were neither bluffing nor trying to make a mountain out of the mole hill."[71] However, by now the Chicken War had become such a hot issue that both sides deemed it wise to turn down the heat. The EEC concluded that further tensions over poultry would risk an explosive debate in Geneva on the legality of the entire CAP system. For this reason, the war had to brought to an end.[72] The EEC decided to grant the United States compensation of U.S.$19 million, which was, however, far from the amount requested.

Following the suggestion of the United States, an impartial GATT panel was set up to elaborate an advisory opinion on the retaliatory measures Washington could take. In November 1963, the panel calculated that they should total U.S.$26 million. Because of the willingness of both sides to quickly conclude the trade war, the EEC accepted this figure. It was then up to President Johnson to indicate which EEC products would suffer reprisals. Products were carefully chosen in order to hit the EEC countries involved: France, Germany, and the Netherlands. On December 4, Johnson announced that his administration would increase duties

---

[68]   Quoted in Sorensen, *Kennedy*, 412.

[69]   CM2 1963/40 PV de la 107éme session du Conseil de la CEE, July 10–11, 1963. HAEC JMAS/95, Memorandum of conversation between Hallstein and Tuthill, July 13, 1963.

[70]   FRUS 1961–63, XIII, Economic and Political Integration, 77. Telegram from the Department of State to the Mission of the European Communities, signed by Rusk, June 12, 1963; and ibid., Telegram from the Department of State to Certain Missions, August 3, 1963.

[71]   HAEC JMAS/95, Tuthill to Ball "Discussion with Hallstein," November 8, 1963.

[72]   Ibid.

on light panels, dextrin, and trucks to punish Germany, potato starch to punish the Netherlands, and brandy to punish France. The Chicken War was now over.[73]

The struggle had demonstrated that there was little the United States could do, apart from retaliate, to prevent the implementation of a CAP it did not like. Yet the State Department had no intention of challenging the existence of this policy, as it held that effective unity within the EEC implied a common agricultural policy.[74] This attitude was also shown by the fact that, despite appealing to the GATT over poultry, the Americans never questioned the legality of CAP. Thus, the poultry affair anticipated the struggle over agriculture that would occur in Geneva, but also the difficult position faced by Washington, which did not wish to question the CAP's existence.

The GATT Ministerial Meeting of May 1964

After Kennedy's assassination in November 1963, the task of negotiating the Kennedy Round shifted to President Lyndon B. Johnson. The new president pledged to maintain the Kennedy administration's policy towards Western Europe and to support trade negotiations. This stance corresponded to Johnson's backing of freer trade as a means to pursue security and economic growth domestically and internationally. Preparations for the round also stayed on course because the officials responsible for the trade negotiations remained in place both in Washington and in Geneva.[75] In sum, Johnson's taking over the presidency went almost unnoticed in the GATT.

The United States, the United Kingdom, and the other EFTA countries gave a hostile response to the EEC's December 1963 mandate, which they perceived as inspired by a combination of French and Commission interests. As for the EEC's *double écart* proposal, they pointed out that it maximized the number of disparity cases, threatening the American's preferred cut of 50 percent across the board, and created problems for other European countries.[76] The United States and the EEC eventually realized that the issue was too complex to be resolved through an automatic rule and pragmatically decided to stop discussing the question. As for agriculture, the EEC partners deemed that the MDS plan would not facilitate the establishment of acceptable conditions for access to world markets and would not

[73] Talbot, *The Chicken War*, 112–14.

[74] FRUS, 1961–63, vol. XIII, Economic and Political Integration, 85 Memorandum of conversation between Ball, Bohlen, Schaetzel, Couve de Murville, and Alphand, October 18, 1963.

[75] Zeiler, *American Trade and Power in the 1960s*, 177–9. On the Johnson administration and Europe, see Thomas A. Schwartz, *Lyndon Johnson and Europe: in the Shadow of Vietnam* (Cambridge, MA, 2003).

[76] AECB BAC 2-122/1991, Rapport no. 6 de la délégation de la Commission pour les négociations du GATT, February 4, 1964.

provide any guarantees to exporters. Equally important, the MDS plan would not reduce the EEC's level of protection, but simply bind it. Moreover, it was difficult to implement because of the complexities in measuring the support governments provided to each product. Since much of the Community's system of supports was grounded on unified prices, Washington saw the plan as tailored to the EEC's goals of extending the CAP to world trade, wiping out all existing GATT rules, and giving international acceptance to the variable levy system. Even worse, from the U.S. point of view, was the fact that it extended negotiations from frontier protection to the agricultural policies of the contracting parties, with the result that domestic policies were subjected to international negotiations.[77]

At the Geneva ministerial meeting held from 4 to 6 May 1964, the Kennedy Round was formally inaugurated. After almost a year of strenuous negotiations, no final decision on the rules had been reached. However, the political willingness to start a new round was strong on both sides of the Atlantic and this led to pragmatic solutions. Blumenthal and Herter tried to commit the EEC to accept the 50 percent linear cut as the formal basis of the negotiations, rather than as a working hypothesis; moreover, they suggested that exceptions to the linear cut could be put on the table on September 10 1964, but under the condition that progress on agriculture had also been achieved.[78]

Lacking a mandate to discuss the new proposals, Rey and Marjolin were compelled to report to the 111 Committee in Geneva. The Dutch and the Germans were ready to accept the Americans' conditions in order to move the round ahead. By contrast, the other four delegations rejected them on the ground that they did not reflect the EEC's trade interests. The French even claimed that they would stop negotiating if the Dutch and the Germans kept on abandoning the EEC's positions. The Commission's officials opposed the U.S. proposals, but were not quick enough in presenting counterproposals. Once more, the role of mediator was played by a national government, this time France, showing that the Commission's ideas and brokering were not necessary to reach a compromise. For the British, the Commission was closely guided by the French officials who attended the meeting in force and possessed remarkable technical skills.[79] In effect, the French delegation, composed of such high-ranking officials as Jean Wahl and Olivier Wormser from the Quai d'Orsay, was able to quickly put forward a compromise. The 50 percent

---

[77]   Memorandum for Herter from Irwin R. Hedges "Background for EEC Discussion on Agriculture," March 5, 1964, Herter papers, box 8A, JFKL. NARA 59, 1964–66, box 460 Telegram no. 1830 from Blumenthal to Herter, February 21, 1964; and ibid., Telegram no. 1985 from Geneva to Secretary of State, April 29, 1964.

[78]   Memorandum to the President from Herter, April 29, 1964, NSF Subject Files: Trade General vol. 1, box 48, LBJL; PRO BT 241/842 Intel no. 69 From Foreign Office to certain of Her Majesty's Representatives, "GATT Ministerial Meeting on the Kennedy Round, Geneva, May 4–6," May 14, 1964.

[79]   PRO FO 371/178092, Note "Ministerial Meeting of Trade Negotiations Committee of the GATT: May 4–6" by Marjoribanks, May 11, 1964.

reduction was defined as a working hypothesis, dependent on solutions for the other problems in the negotiations—nontariff barriers, agriculture, and disparities in tariffs. Moreover, 10 September 1964 was accepted as an unconditional date, not depending on progress made in agriculture. With the French proposal, the EEC would cease to insist on an agreement for generally applicable rules for the treatment of disparities before detailed negotiations could began. The proposal suggested getting negotiations started by putting on the table the various countries' exceptions lists so that the U.S. exception list could be seen, and the EEC could press on other issues, trying to exploit the wider opportunities of a package deal, notably regarding nontariff barriers, agriculture, and disparities.[80]

The Americans fought hard over the EEC drafting, but failed to secure amendments on the main points of substance. They had wanted the GATT ministerial meeting to maintain pressure on the EEC to make concessions, but were unable to oblige it to accept any particular changes. By presenting a package deal, and insisting on parallel progress on other matters, such as nontariff barriers, where the Americans were most vulnerable, the EEC was able to turn the tables on them. Herter and Blumenthal did not receive the support of the British, who found the EEC draft an acceptable basis for starting negotiations and, in any case, did not want to engage in a showdown with the Six.[81] Facing the firm stance of the EEC and with little British support, Herter accepted the EEC draft. This, in any case, contained the positive elements of establishing a date for exceptions lists and the basic position of the 50 percent linear cut. Ministers also called for rules on agriculture to be established at an early date, instructed the TNC to draw up the procedures necessary to negotiate on nontariff barriers, and reaffirmed that every effort be made to reduce barriers to exports by the LDCs. At this point, the Kennedy Round was formally opened.[82]

---

[80]   AECB BAC38/194 309, Mansholt cabinet papers, Aide-mémoire, "Conclusions adoptées par le Comité 111 lors de sa réunion du 4 Mai," May 4, 1964, and CM2 1964/389 PV de la 59ème réunion du Comité 111, May 4, 1964.

[81]   PRO FO 371/178091, Confidential note on the GATT Ministerial meeting 4–6 May 1964 by Marjoribanks, May 7, 1964. See also PRO FO 371/178091, Cabinet—GATT Policy Committee, Meeting of May 21, 1964 on the Kennedy Round, note by Mason, May 20, 1964.

[82]   HAEC BAC 26/1969 511, Note d'information du Conseil, S/360/64 (Cos 45), May 13, 1963; CM2 1964/389, PV de la 60ème réunion du Comité 111, May 6, 1964; AAPD document 122 Ministerialdirigent Stedfeld Z. Genf, an das Auswärtige Amt, May 6, 1964. AECB-BAC 122/1991 2, 1964, Rapport no. 13 de la délégation de la Commission pour les négociations du GATT, May 22, 1964. Telegram no. 2007 from Herter to State Department 6 May 1964, NSF—Subject files, Trade: Kennedy Round, box 48, LBJL; Telegram no. 2004 for Bundy from Herter, May 7, 1964, Bator Papers, box 12, LBJL. PRO FO 371/178091 Confidential note on the GATT Ministerial meeting, 4–6 May 1964 by Marjoribanks, May 7, 1964.

Chapter 4
The Regional Crisis in a Multilateral Context

An Intricate Cereals Puzzle across the Atlantic

As described in the previous chapter, at the GATT ministerial meeting of May 1964 it was agreed to place lists of exceptions on the table in September 1964. The date was postponed until after the U.S. presidential election and set on November 16, 1964. Yet in the aftermath of the meeting, Herter, taking a unilateral position, stated that the U.S. government would not present its exceptions list unless further progress was made on agriculture by that date. By establishing a link between agriculture and the exceptions lists, Herter hoped to push the EEC to agree to rules for this sector and prevent agriculture from being left behind in the negotiations.[1]

The EEC rejected the American effort to tie agriculture to exceptions lists on the grounds that the GATT ministerial meeting had set the date unconditionally.[2] Nonetheless, the U.S. move created an intricate problem for members of the EEC and complicated the EEC's internal discussions about the treatment of agriculture in the GATT and the elaboration of the CAP. The French had made it clear that they would not negotiate on agriculture in Geneva unless UGPs were set in Brussels. Erhard, in turn, refused to agree on UGPs before the German election of September 1965. Washington refused to put exceptions lists for the industrial sector on the table unless progress was made on agriculture. As a result, a complicated transatlantic puzzle involving grain had to be solved, and the nexus between the GATT talks and the CAP was confirmed.

After the deadline of April 15, 1964 for setting UGPs had passed, the EEC deferred a decision until December 15, 1964. However, the German government had so firmly declined to discuss UGPs that doubts increased over whether the new deadline would be respected. Erhard assured EEC members and the Americans that he would not let the GATT round fail because of the German attitude on UGPs. Yet, Erhard saw UGPs as an internal EEC issue with no direct connection with the GATT talks, as an agreement on prices would not remove all agricultural hurdles. Germany would not agree to a price level lower than that suggested by the Commission. This

---

[1]   Telegram no. 2167 from Tubby to Secretary of State reporting Blumenthal's statement to the July 13 TNC meeting, July 15, 1964, NSF—Subject files, Trade General vol. 1, box 47, LBJL.

[2]   AECB BAC38/194 309 Mansholt cabinet papers, Note personnelle de Rabot à Mansholt, June 17, 1964.

level was 60 percent higher than world prices and, therefore, was unacceptable to the Americans, as it would increase production within the EEC and close the gap between consumption and production. The Germans wanted to resolve the contradiction between high EEC prices and their request for a CAP open to world imports by granting quantitative assurances to third countries.[3] However, given that this option was considered in Brussels a "sin against the Holy Ghost," as the Germans put it, Bonn would have to wait, hoping that pressures from Geneva would drive the EEC in the right direction.[4] This stance demonstrated the ambivalence of the Germans' support for the MDS plan. Formally, they had approved it, but in practice they often questioned it by suggesting bargaining on quantitative assurances. They had not, in reality, accepted the implications of the plan, and conducted the bargaining as if much more was still open to discussion than was really the case. To be sure, this corresponded to German commercial interests in importing from outside the EEC, but made Bonn's position wavering and incoherent.

Paris ruled out quantitative assurances, labeling them incompatible with the CAP system based on common prices. In truth Paris was not concerned about incompatibility. Negotiating in the GATT on the basis of quantitative assurances would remove the pressure to get down to approval of the UGPs. The Kennedy Round had to be used to convince the Germans that either they agreed to UGPs or they would watch the round fail. Thus, the American move increased pressure on the Germans and played into the hands of the French.[5]

Like France, the Commission held that quantitative assurances were inconsistent with the CAP and pressed for approval of the UGPs. The latter were a fundamental step in establishing the CAP, the policy that Mansholt believed would ensure the supranational aspect of the EEC. Moreover, without UGPs the EEC could not negotiate along the lines drawn in the MDS plan.[6] The Commission openly linked the Kennedy Round to UGPs. Mansholt reminded the Germans that they were preventing agricultural talks from taking place according to the MDS outline and urged them to accept the lowering of grain prices so as not to disproportionately and artificially increase EEC production, causing a hostile

---

[3]   CM2 1964/86, PV de la 134ème session du Conseil de la CEE, June 1–3, 1964. PRO BT 241/842 The Secretary of State's meeting with Lahr, Bonn, May 25, 1964; Telcon Dillon-Ball, May 25, 1964, reporting the conversation between U.S. secretary of Treasury Dillon and Lahr, Ball papers, box 4, LBJL.

[4]   PRO BT 303/167 Note, "German Agriculture-Talks in Bonn, October, 30–31, 1963" reporting conversation between British officials and German officials of the Ministry of Agriculture.

[5]   MAEF, DE/CE, 1961–66 GATT 932, Premier Ministre, Secrétariat Général, Note CE/6450 "Conseil des Ministres des 29 et 30 juillet 1964," July 24, 1964.

[6]   AECB, PV 269 April 15, 1964 and PV 275, June 2, 1964; AECB BAC38/194 309 Mansholt cabinet papers, Note d'information de la Commission, June 19, 1964; HAEC— JMAS/95 Memorandum of conversation between Hallstein and Tuthill in Brussels, June 23, 1964.

American reaction. "Le problème de la fixation des prix des céréales est donc incontestablement un problème international," Mansholt argued to the recalcitrant Germans.[7] The Commission also counted on the pressure Washington could put on Erhard and urged the Americans to push the Germans to set UGPs.[8]

The hope that Washington would move Bonn turned out to be vain. The Americans rejected the nexus between UGPs and the Kennedy Round on the grounds that what mattered were quantitative assurances. They deemed the Commission prices too high to maintain an EEC market for U.S. grain exports.[9] When Erhard and Schröder visited Washington in June 1964, Herter took the view that a decision on UGPs was not an essential precondition for the GATT. The EEC had to abandon its rigid application of the MDS plan, guarantee access to its market, and set the lowest possible prices. Washington made it known that an immediate decision on UGPs was not indispensable, and it did not require of Erhard any definitive action in the short term. This was, of course, an attitude very welcome to the German chancellor. The American stance reduced the pressure for early decisions and apparently eased Erhard's position within the EEC.[10]

The U.S. attitude affected the EEC's internal discussions. Favoring forward movement in the GATT negotiations, Dutch minister Frans Andriessen dropped the link between UGPs and the Kennedy Round.[11] Most importantly, made bold by the American stance, the German member of the 111 Committee, Reinhardt, took the line that UGPs were not necessary. Asked by the French representative, Jean Wahl, if he had "une 'solution miracle'" to bargain over in Geneva, Reinhardt spelled out his miracle solution: for the next three or four years the agricultural policies of the Six would remain national, and each member state would negotiate on a national basis in Geneva.[12] Bonn in this way once again displayed its

---

[7]   CM2 1964/70, PV de la 129ème session du Conseil de la CEE, April 13–15, 1964; AECB PV 268, April 8, 1964, CM2 1964/86, PV de la 134ème session du Conseil de la CEE, June 1–3, 1964; AECB BAC38/194 309 Mansholt cabinet papers, Note de Hijzen à Messieurs Rey, Marjolin, Mansholt, June 24, 1964.

[8]   HAEC MK40 Conversation with Spierenburg (Dutch PERMDEL), April 10, 1964.

[9]   Telegram no. 4400 from McGhee to State Department, May 1, 1964, NSF—Subject files, Trade: Kennedy Round, box 48, LBJL. "Erhard Background Paper, Kennedy Round," draft written by Auchincloss, June 3, 1964, Herter Papers, box 8, JFKL. HAEC—MK 40, Note "Le prix du blé et le Kennedy Round," June 5, 1964, reporting a conversation between Kohnstamm, Tuthill, and McGhee.

[10]   FRUS, 1964–68, vol. XIII, Western Europe Region 26. Telegram from Rusk to Certain Posts, June 15, 1963, reporting a conversation between Herter, Blumenthal, Roth, Erhard, Schröder; PRO BT 241/842 Telegram no. 3498 from UK Embassy in Washington to Foreign Office, June 30, 1964.

[11]   NA 59 1964–66, box 450, Telegram from Hwe of the American Embassy in The Hague, July 22, 1964. CM2 1964/102, PV de la 139ème session du Conseil de la CEE, July 7, 1964; CM2 1964/389 PV de la 62ème réunion du Comité 111, July 23, 1964.

[12]   MAEF, DE/CE, 1961–66 GATT 932, Entretien de M. Wahl avec Dr Reinhardt et le Dr Sachs, Bonn June 23, 1964.

antagonism towards the CAP. In light of these German declarations, some of the extreme French tactics, illustrated below, make more sense. The German threat to the CAP was not just a figment of de Gaulle's imagination.

All of these various stances became evident at the Council of Ministers meeting at the end of July 1964. Here Jean Rey resolutely restated that it was impossible to make progress in the GATT until an agreement on prices put the EEC in the position to negotiate under the MDS plan. In response, Andriessen asked the Commission to take a flexible approach. Progress could be made without UGPs by applying the MDS plan and reading the December 1963 mandate in a non-rigid way. Predictably, Rolph Lahr supported Andriessen. Belgium, Italy, and Luxembourg reaffirmed the need to set UGPs and the value of the MDS plan in general. However, they too asked the Commission to be flexible. Giscard d'Estaing adopted a rather quiet attitude, leaving the task of defending French interests to the Commission. To the rescue of Rey came Mansholt, who pinpointed the difficulties of negotiating on the ground of access guarantees without setting UGPs. Third countries' requests for import quotas would depend on the EEC level of prices. Mansholt acknowledged that, since EEC and U.S. positions on the rules were still far apart, the discussion in Geneva had not yet arrived at a point where a decision on UGPs was urgent. Nevertheless, he maintained, the EEC would find itself in a difficult position if this decision was not taken by the end of the year.[13] Lahr left the meeting still asserting that the Six had agreed that UGPs were not critical to discussions in Geneva, and that there was no need for the Commission to limit itself to the MDS approach. The grain issue "had been unmasked as a Commission maneuver against the Germans," noted Lahr, who remained optimistic that the agricultural rules could be established without fixing grain prices, and that the November 16 deadline could be met.[14]

The Germans remained adamant in their resistance. The meeting of the ministers of agriculture in Brussels on October 20, 1964 again discussed the issue, again unsuccessfully.[15] At this point, de Gaulle concluded that the time had come to make the Germans understand that the French government required the CAP as the price for its participation in the EEC. On October 21, Alain Peyrefitte, the government spokesman, declared that France would not negotiate with the Americans so long as the EEC's policies—including its agricultural policy—remained unspecified and that France would cease to participate in the EEC unless the CAP was agreed

---

[13]   CM2 1964/11 PV de la 141ème session du Conseil de la CEE, July 28–30, 1964; NA 59, 1964–66 Ecin 3 box 795, telegram TAGG 2263 from Evens to Herter, August 11, 1964, reporting a conversation between Evans and the Belgian Ambassador Rothschild.

[14]   Telegram no. 414 from McGhee to State Department, August 1, 1964, NSF—Subject files, Trade: Kennedy Round, box 48, LBJL, reporting conversation with Lahr.

[15]   CM2 1964/134 PV de la 146ème session du Conseil de la CEE, October 19–21, 1964. The Germans stance on UGPs has been carefully researched by Knudsen, *Farmers on Welfare*, 207–65.

to.[16] Thus, because of German ambivalence and foot-dragging, the French position hardened. In order to appreciate de Gaulle's firmness, it is worth noting that Paris also considered the CAP a means to tie Germany to the EEC. Without an EEC solution to the problems in agriculture, each member state would look for its own interests, and concessions would be made to the Americans in the Kennedy Round. The Germans would look to relations with the United States, to a European free trade area, and to the British. Thus, the issue for France was Germany's attitude towards this common policy, the EEC, and third countries.[17]

German reaction to de Gaulle's threat combined disdainful irritation over the constant replenishment of French pressure with calmness regarding the substance of the matter. Erhard judged the ultimatum a mere bluff. For its agricultural surplus France had no good alternative to the EEC market, and its industrial sector was doing extremely well within the Community. Indeed, France was the main beneficiary of European integration. Therefore, hinted Erhard, there was no chance the German government would modify its position, except by resisting even more firmly pressure from either the French or the Commission.[18] At the same time, however, the Germans were afraid that the French president would block the Kennedy Round. Even if the French government did not withdraw from the EEC, it could well undermine the trade negotiations. This was a fact Erhard could not afford to ignore. French determination to set UGPs thus awakened the Germans from their illusion that the decision could be postponed until after the September 1965 election.[19]

The Commission's Brinkmanship

In the meantime, talks over agriculture carried on in Geneva. In September 1964, meetings between the Commission and Blumenthal intensified in an effort to work out mutually acceptable rules. Flexibility was demonstrated on both sides. Blumenthal was ready to abandon U.S. insistence that access guarantees be preliminary to agreeing on the rules.[20] On the Commission side, the internal EEC discussion led the

---

[16]   MAEF, DE/CE, 1961–66 GATT 932, Note 185/CE, "Politique agricole commune," November 5, 1964. On the French threat see Ludlow, *The European Communities and the Crisis of the 1960s*, 40–71.

[17]   HAEC—MAEF 21–209, Secrétariat General, Entretiens et Message, Entretien entre de Gaulle et Adenauer, November 9, 1964.

[18]   FRUS, 1964–68, vol. XIII, Western Europe Region, document 41. Telegram from the Embassy in Germany to the Department of State 3, October 23, 1964; and AAPD document 307 Gespräch des Bundeskanzler Erhard mit dem amerikanischen Botschafter McGhee, November 3, 1964.

[19]   Memorandum of conversation between German Ambassador in Washington Knappstein and Ball, October 28, 1964, Herter papers, box 15, JFKL.

[20]   Telegrams 2354/235 from Blumenthal to Herter, October 10, 1964, NSF Subject Files: Trade—Kennedy Round, box 48, LBJL.

institution to be less dogmatic in its application of the MDS approach. Moreover, the Commission had started to recognize that its plan was too complicated to be applied to all products. Equally important, Rey wanted the November 16 deadline for producing exceptions lists to be respected in order to force the Six to face up to the complicated process of agreeing on these exceptions. The Commission therefore suggested that the MDS plan be applied only to key countries—the EEC, the United States, and the United Kingdom, leaving out such relevant exporters as Canada and Australia—and key commodities, such as grains. The Commission presented proposals that went beyond the 1963 mandate by introducing the notion of primary countries and commodities. It did so without consulting national governments. Moreover, it bilaterally negotiated with Blumenthal, without the presence of member states and only loosely informing them of discussions. The Commission's strategy consisted of reaching an accord with the United States and, only then, fully informing the national governments. The aim was to confront them with a *fait accompli* that would be politically difficult to undo. The Commission thus attempted to exploit its negotiating role to enhance its preferences and promote its agenda.[21]

At the bilateral U.S.–Commission meeting of October 9, 1964 the Americans toughened their position. They asked again for access guarantees as a condition of agreeing on the rules. With the presidential election of November 1964 drawing closer, the American delegation aimed to show its resoluteness in winning concessions from the EEC. In response to the refusal of the Commission to accept these conditions, Blumenthal brusquely interrupted the talks.[22] The EEC member states learned about the suspension and the content of the discussions from the American delegation, not from the Commission.[23] At the Council of Ministers meeting on October 13, 1964, the Dutch and the Germans supported the Commission. They wanted the agricultural negotiations to move ahead, and the Commission's strategy corresponded to their interests. By contrast, the policy position and the strategy of the Commission enraged the other four members of the EEC. In the end, the Commission was urged to pursue the discussion in the framework of the mandate of December 1963 and to keep member states fully informed.[24]

Despite these instructions, the Commission continued discussions with Blumenthal without promptly informing the member states, behavior that infuriated Paris. The Commission's proposals questioned the full applicability of the MDS plan, which, from the French point of view, provided the double advantage of

---

[21]   AECB PV 288, October 7, 1964.

[22]   FRUS 1964–68, vol. VIII, International Monetary and Trade Policy 252. Telegram from the Mission to the European Office of the United Nations to the Department of State, October 10, 1964.

[23]   AECB PV 289, October 12, 1964.

[24]   CM2 1964/128, PV de la 144ème session du Conseil de la CEE, October 12–13, 1964. HAEC BAC 511 "Intervention du Ministre Mattarella au Conseil du 13.10.1964," October 16, 1964. MAEF, DE/CE, 1961–66 GATT 932, Telegram 1078/90 Boegner au Quai d'Orsay, October 14, 1964.

forcing both importers and exporters to discuss their domestic policies and putting pressure on the Germans to establish UGPs. French annoyance was so strong because Paris had not expected the Commission to try to reach a compromise with the United States at all costs. Until this point, Paris and the Commission had seen eye to eye, with the result that the French trusted the Brussels institution. However, on this occasion, their positions parted ways. The French wanted to delay the discussions in Geneva, since the Germans were stalling on setting UGPs, while the Commission was trying to reach a vague agreement with Blumenthal that would allow Washington to put exceptions on the table.[25]

As a result the French made a striking move. The French permanent representative, Jean-Marc Boegner, personally handed the president of the Commission, Walter Hallstein, a no-confidence note threatening to publicly disown the institution. The French government informed the other member states and the Americans of the note.[26] In the note the French government made it clear that, if any commitment to the Americans were made outside the terms of the 1963 mandate, Paris would openly reject the agreement and disown the Commission.[27] Faced with this threat, the Commission suspended its talks with the Americans.[28] Thus at the end of October 1964, with the date for producing exceptions lists approaching, no agreement on the rules for agriculture had been set, de Gaulle was threatening to leave the EEC, and Washington was refusing to provide its list.

The episode reveals the limits of the Commission's potential for action. If, on the one hand, it could attempt to influence the outcome of the negotiations by bargaining in Geneva and thanks to privileged information, it was equally the case that member states could put a stop to its actions when they disapproved of the course it set. Privileged information and negotiating authority did not automatically mean that the Commission was able to influence the outcome of the bargaining.

Moving the Round Ahead

With the failure to agree on rules for agriculture, the most urgent matter Washington had to resolve was whether to offer its exceptions list. The State Department and

---

[25]   MAEF, DE/CE, 1961–66 GATT 932, Telegram 1078/90 Boegner au Quai d'Orsay, October 14, 1964; ibid., Note de Wahl, "La situation actuelle de la négociation Kennedy," October 20, 1964; ibid. Telegram 2155/57, Wormser à DELFRA Bruxelles, October 19, 1964.

[26]   MAEF, DE/CE, 1961–66 GATT 932, "Note remise à la Commission," October 27, 1964; and ibid., Telegram 1182/84 Boegner au Quai d'Orsay, October 28, 1964. HAEC— MAEF OW 36 R132, Telegram 2304/07 Wormser à Boegner, October 27, 1964.

[27]   AECB PV 291, October 28, 1964 and MAEF, DE/CE, 1961–66 GATT 932, Telegram 1176/81 Boegner au Quai d'Orsay, October 28, 1964.

[28]   AECB PV 291, October 28, 1964 and PV 292, November 3, 1964; Memorandum of telephone conversation between Herter and Blumenthal, October 29, 1964, Bator Papers, box 12, LBJL.

National Security Affairs assistants Francis Bator and McGeorge Bundy were convinced of the need to go ahead with the industrial negotiations. Further efforts to get the agricultural negotiations underway would be futile until the EEC agreed upon UGPs. Moreover, putting the exceptions list on the table could bring an intangible benefit, that is, a quantum of impetus in the Kennedy Round. However, for Bundy and Ball, there were other issues at stake, including transatlantic relations, European unity, and the German bargaining position. Erhard's dithering put the German government, on whom Washington counted to make progress in Geneva, in a weak bargaining position in Brussels. France was in a legally sound position and Washington expected de Gaulle to make the most of his advantage by embarrassing the Germans, the EEC, the Kennedy Round, and the United States. In these circumstances, the German foot-dragging represented a threat to the EEC, the Atlantic partnership, and the round.[29] From the Americans' point of view, Germany had to regain diplomatic strength in Brussels, and it was also for the sake of the Germans that the United States had to present its list of exceptions. The other element essential to escaping the impasse was getting the Germans to finally agree to UGPs.[30]

One last consideration also encouraged the State Department, Bator, and Bundy to support the offering of the U.S. exceptions list. The United States could not risk wasting the possibility of reducing protection in the industrial sector for an agreement on agriculture, for it was in the former sector that the greatest gains to the United States from the Kennedy Round would be found. Concentrating its efforts on the more difficult objectives in agriculture "at the worst time and with clumsy tactics," the United States might sabotage more important trade benefits elsewhere.[31]

President Johnson adopted the line of his assistants and the State Department, overruling the opposition of the USDA. He agreed that the best prospect for obtaining concessions and keeping the Atlantic Alliance together lay in adhering to the established schedule.[32] The U.S. decision to present its exceptions list set off a chain of events that allowed progress in both Geneva and in Brussels.

---

[29] Memorandum of Conversation between Herter, Ball, Bundy, Bator, October 27, 1964, Bator Papers box 12, LBJL. Memorandum to Mr Bundy, October 26, 1964, Bator Papers, box 1, LBJL and Note of McGeorge Bundy "Kennedy Round Strategy," October 27, 1964, NSF Subject Files: Trade—Kennedy Round, box 48, LBJL.

[30] NARA 59 1964–66, box 450 from Fessenden to State Department, February 4, 1965 and PRO BT 241/948 Telegram no. 1028 from Roberts (UK Embassy in Bonn) to Foreign Office, October 23, 1964.

[31] Memorandum to Mr Bundy, October 26, 1964, Bator Papers, box 1, LBJL and Note of McGeorge Bundy, "Kennedy Round Strategy," October 27, 1964. NSF Subject Files: Trade—Kennedy Round, box 48, LBJL; Letter of Former Secretary of State Dean Acheson to Bundy, October 24, 1964, Bator papers, box 1, LBJL. Draft letter from Bundy to Dean Acheson, October 29, 1964, Bator Papers, box 12, LBJL.

[32] NARA 364 Records of the USTR, box 1, Memorandum for the President from Herter, November 9, 1964.

When the Six gathered for the Council of Ministers meeting of November 10–15, 1964 scheduled to approve the EEC's exceptions list, first they had to settle whether to do so and then present the list in Geneva. Couve de Murville asserted that approval of UGPs was a condition for both negotiations in Geneva and further progress within the EEC, and that, to conclude the Kennedy Round, Paris required the full elaboration of the CAP. Lahr, once more, rejected the link between the CAP and the Kennedy Round. However, he also stated that the German government attached great importance to the December 15 date for setting UGPs, and asked the other delegations to attach equivalent importance to presenting the exceptions list on that date. Couve de Murville expressed his satisfaction with Lahr's declaration and agreed to the presentation of the EEC list in Geneva.[33]

The French were aware that refusal to approve the list could cause a stalemate in Geneva, and their decisions showed their interest in attending the round and in liberalizing international trade in the industrial sector. Had the French been concerned simply with elaborating the CAP, all they needed to do was insist on setting UGPs before allowing the EEC to present its exceptions list. After all, the synchronization plan had been introduced by Bonn, and it was Bonn that was not treating it with respect. Moreover, the French government hoped that its goodwill would be rewarded by a German decision on UGPs. Lastly, France was aware that, in such a difficult period for the EEC, it was wise not to dangerously exacerbate conflict.[34] With the French decision offered by Couve de Murville, the negotiations in Geneva over the industrial sector could begin.

While France decided to put the exceptions list on the table, Erhard concluded that UGPs had to be resolved because they were delaying the Kennedy Round and impeding further development of the EEC. Equally important, Germany had put itself in a dangerously weak diplomatic position, undermining its credibility and precluding any new initiative or action in Brussels. Bonn had to alter its image as a stumbling block and thus be in a position to urge progress in other fields. Here the French would have to make concessions.[35]

---

[33]   CM2 1964/143, PV de la 149ème session du Conseil de la CEE, November 10–15, 1964; MAEF, DE/CE, 1961–66 GATT 932 Note, "Négociation tarifaire au GATT," November 20, 1964.

[34]   MAEF, DE/CE, 1961–66 GATT 932 Note 184/CE, "Négociation tarifaire au GATT," November 5, 1964 and MAEF, DE/CE, 1961–66 GATT 932, Telegram 1274/91 Boegner au Quai d'Orsay, November 16, 1964.

[35]   AAPD 1964 document 338 Gespräch des Bundeskanzler Erhard mit Staatssekretär Ball, amerikanisches Außenministerium, November 16, 1964; ibid., document 347 Bundesminister Schröder an Bundeskanzler Erhard, November 19, 1964; AECB PV 293, November 9, 1964, reporting conversation between Hallstein and Erhard on November 4–5, 1964; PRO PREM 13/306 Record of conversation between Hallstein and British Foreign Secretary, December 4, 1964. For a description of Erhard's decision see Knudsen, *Farmers on Welfare*, 207–65.

At the Council of Ministers meeting of December 15, 1964, the Six agreed to establish a common market for grains from 1967 onwards. The decision provided for unification of prices at the levels suggested by the Commission: U.S.$106.25 per metric ton soft wheat, roughly midway between French and German prices; U.S.$125 for hard wheat; U.S.$91.25 for barley; and U.S.$90.65 for maize. Compensatory payments to German, Italian, and Luxembourgeois farmers for income loss resulting from the reduction of prices would be allotted.[36] The level of the UGPs, 60 percent higher than world prices, showed that the EEC would enter the agricultural talks in Geneva with a clear manifestation of a protectionist stance. After the numerous difficulties encountered in setting these prices, it was unlikely that the EEC could reduce them in Geneva.

The decision was seen in Brussels as a milestone in the elaboration of the CAP, leading to agricultural integration among the Six, and strengthening the EEC. Furthermore, the Council's decision seemed to bring to an end to a period of tension.[37] The Commission considered the decision on UGPs its victory. It had presented the original plan in December 1963, and had stuck to it, a springboard for further important progress.[38]

The internal development of the EEC dictated the rate and timing of progress at the Kennedy Round; at the same time, the need to make progress at the GATT talks led EEC members to move forward with the elaboration of the CAP in Brussels, since the GATT was used as a lever to promote the CAP.

The State Department, Bator, and Bundy were satisfied with the agreement on grains, which they judged to be a clear gain in terms of Atlantic policy. However, the setting of prices at such high levels provoked a debate within the Johnson administration on their consequences for U.S. trade and on the ability of the U.S. government to obtain concessions in agriculture. The USDA considered the decision on UGPs as a serious threat to U.S. agricultural exports, and was not swayed by the political advantage of the decision. By contrast, Bundy and Bator held that the problem was the determination of EEC governments to protect their farmers' income, largely through price supports, and the technological revolution in European agriculture. Thus even if the UGPs were set at the lower French level, EEC production would increase and U.S. sales shrink. In their eyes, the USDA tended to ignore the fact that the "US lacks the bargaining power to make the EEC import grain beyond its needs." The U.S. threat not to negotiate in the industrial sector without tangible results in agriculture "would not work vis-à-vis the French," for "they are protectionist across the board, and they have been in

---

[36]   Ibid.

[37]   Memorandum for the President from Bundy and Bator "European Agricultural deal," December 16, 1965, Bator Papers, box 1, LBJL. Ludlow. *The European Community and the Crises of the 1960s*, 62.

[38]   AECB, PV 298, December 16, 1964; NARA 59–250–57, 1964–66 Ecin 3 box 795, Airgram A-512 from Fessenden of U.S. mission to EC to State Department "EEC Commission's bright Prospects for 1965," January 25, 1965.

the driver's seat at Brussels. More generally, we do not have the cards to force Europe to keep its farmers poor on our behalf." The USDA wanted "Herter to dig in his heels and make unbargainable demands at Brussels." However, by so doing, Washington could push itself "into a corner and lose the chance for a really profitable deal on industry without making a nickel for agriculture."[39] Moreover, the EEC had no significant interest in exporting to the U.S. market and making concessions in this sector in order to decrease U.S. protectionism. In addition, nothing in the GATT obliged a contracting party to make concessions beyond those it regarded as beneficial. Equally important, Washington's bargaining power was reduced by its refusal to challenge the CAP, considered an important tenet of European unity. With the struggle to agree on rules and the high level of UGPs, the Johnson administration saw that a Kennedy Round without a meaningful result in agriculture was a serious possibility.

Despite the stalemate, Washington still considered it worthwhile to insist on including agriculture in the Geneva talks. To the aid of the Americans in this effort came the GATT director, Wyndham White, who, recognizing that the EEC and the United States had aims that were impossible to reconcile in a shared set of rules, believed that the best way to move ahead consisted in setting a date for putting agricultural offers on the table in the form governments judged appropriate. Herter and Blumenthal adopted Wyndham White's proposal. It could overcome the impasse in agricultural negotiations by testing the EEC's willingness to make offers in this sector. Therefore, Herter decided to stop quibbling about rules, and sought to get the EEC to agree to present agricultural offers in April 1965.[40]

Herter met Mansholt and Rey in the early part of 1965 in order to obtain their agreement on Wyndham White's proposals. Mansholt was deeply disappointed. He had envisaged the Kennedy Round as a part of a "grand design," as he put it, for global management of markets. With this framework in mind, he did not want to give up the MDS plan, which he judged a valuable approach to controlling markets. Yet Mansholt was aware that some progress had to be made. In any case, he opposed putting offers on the table in April 1965. The EEC could not do so until its agricultural and financial regulations had been settled. As a consequence, he suggested September 16, 1965, by which date, or so he hoped, the new part of the CAP would have been approved. In truth, Mansholt had doubts about the EEC's willingness to accept even the September 16 date. A commitment to that deadline implied the fixing of meat and dairy product prices and the approval of financial regulations, thorny issues among the Six. The date had a strong political

---

[39]   Memorandum for the President from Bundy and Bator, December 16, 1965, Bator Papers, box 1, LBJL.

[40]   Letter from Blumenthal to Herter, December 15, 1964, Herter Papers, box 1, JFKL; Memorandum for the President from Herter "Agriculture in the Kennedy Round," January 19, 1965. NSF Subject Files: Trade—Kennedy Round, box 48, LBJL; PRO FO 371/183399 Telegram no. 165 from UK Embassy in Washington to Foreign Office, January 26, 1965, reporting conversation between Roth and Chadwick of the UK Embassy in Washington.

relevance, as it affected the pace of setting up the CAP and the working agenda of the EEC. Mansholt cautioned Herter that it was uncertain whether the EEC could hold to any date. The two countries most eager to attend the round, the Netherlands and Germany, were also those most hesitant about completing the CAP regulations, the Germans because of September elections, and the Dutch because of increases in food price that would probably result. Mansholt supported the September date to obtain leverage on the German and Dutch. Thus, once again, the Commission was hoping to exploit the GATT talks to complete the CAP.[41] Moreover, Mansholt retained his plan to use the Kennedy Round to organize world agriculture. He suggested that a decision on which elements of protection and the domestic support system affected international trade had to be made on a joint basis, and not simply left to each participant.[42]

The final agreement between the Commission and Herter consisted of presenting offers on grains on April 1, 1965; then, before September of the same year, an inventory of border protections and domestic support measures affecting trade in commodities other than grains would be carried out, in order to reach agreement to the greatest extent possible on the protective elements to be included in the negotiations; and, finally, on September 16, 1965, offers on commodities were to be unconditionally presented.[43]

Aware that a rejection of the Herter–Mansholt timetable could have serious repercussions for the GATT talks, at the Council of Ministers meeting in early March 1965 the Six approved it with no discussion. They specified that, in elaborating its offers, the Council would take into account the results of negotiations on cereals, the confrontation over agricultural policies between GATT members, and the progress in elaboration of the CAP.[44] In Geneva on March 18, 1965, the Herter–Mansholt timetable for agricultural negotiations was adopted.[45] After daunting discussions, a schedule for negotiations had been approved.

The situation, however, remained complicated, as is suggested by a last-minute difficulty created by the Germans in Geneva. While they accepted the September

---

[41]   NARA 59, 1964–66, box 450 Telegram no. 379 from Herter to various U.S. Embassy "Mansholt and the Kennedy Round," February 9, 1965; Letter from Roth to Murphy (U.S. Under Secretary USDA), February 23, 1964, Roth Papers, box 1 LBJL.

[42]   PRO FO 371/183399 Telegram no. 9 from O'Neill to Foreign Office, February 2, 1965, reporting conversation between the Commission, Herter and Blumenthal given by the Americans to O'Neill; AECB BAC 62/1980-54, PV 304, February 3, 1965.

[43]   Note on visit Mansholt, February 8–9, "Kennedy Round and agriculture" from Roth to McGeorge Bundy, February 9, 1965, NSF Subject Files: Trade—Kennedy Round, box 48, LBJL.

[44]   CM2 1965/15 PV de la 160ème session du Conseil de la CEE, March 2, 1965; NARA 59 1964–66, box 460, Telegram no. 946 from Tuthill to State Department, March 4, 1965.

[45]   NARA 59 1964–66, box 460, Telegrams 2871 and 2872 from Blumenthal to Herter, March 11, 1965. Letter from Richard Powell to Herter, March 17, 1964, Roth Papers, box 1 LBJL.

16 date so as not to appear once again the barriers to progress, Bonn and, to a lesser extent, The Hague withheld unconditional consent. The Herter–Mansholt agreement postulated more than Germany could possibly deliver by September 16, 1965. Erhard was anxious to avoid repeating the wrangling over UGPs, an episode in which a fixed international deadline had been used to pressure him into unpopular domestic decisions. Moreover, Germany's intra-EEC bargaining position could weaken if the French obtained another favorable batch of CAP provisions while giving nothing in exchange. The French were simply exploiting the Kennedy Round to obtain progress on the CAP, Erhard believed. He instructed German officials in Brussels that no final decision could be taken on agriculture before the German elections. When he met de Gaulle in mid-March, Erhard informed the French president that the new CAP provisions would only be approved after Germany had gone to polls.[46]

Following the suggestion by the German minister of agriculture, Werner Schwarz, who opposed the new CAP lot, the German delegate to the GATT, Stedfeld, confidentially floated to Blumenthal the suggestion that the EEC spokesman in Geneva make a qualifying statement, specifying that in September 1965 the EEC could only make imprecise offers.[47] In the face of U.S. irritation over this communication, Lahr reassured the Americans that he and the foreign minister Gerard Schröder would urge the German government to "take reasonably prompt action" on meat and rice, while, for dairy products and sugar, the delay in fixing prices would not be overlong.[48] Once again progress in agriculture in Geneva gave rise to German ambivalence towards the CAP, putting Bonn in an equivocal position. The German government appeared to include ministers who were in a state of permanent disagreement, rendering its decision-making incoherent. If one judged by the way the German government was getting ready for the negotiations over the CAP, another EEC storm was brewing. Against the categorical refusal of the Americans to consider any more qualifications, and the irritation of the Commission, France, and Italy, the impasse was overcome through an ambiguous declaration by Hijzen, issued only after the EEC and the United

---

[46]   NARA 364 Records of USTR, box 6, Staff meeting, document 28/Staff 7, February 8, 1965. PRO BT 241/844 Telegram no. 96 from British Ambassador Roberts in Bonn to Foreign Office, May 5, 1965. For de Gaulle-Erhard meeting see HAEC MAEF, OW 36 Note, March 17, 1965.

[47]   NARA 364 Records of USTR, box 6, Staff meeting, document 72/Staff 27, April 14, 1965; NARA 59 1964–66 box 450, Telegram no. 3513 from Cronk of U.S. Embassy in Bonn to State Department, March 15, 1965 and ibid., box 460 telegram 1022 from American Embassy in Brussels to State Department, March 16, 1966.

[48]   NARA 59 1964–66, box 460, Telegram no. 2881 from Blumenthal to Herter, March 15, 1965; PRO FO 371/183385 Telegram no. 59 from Cohen to Foreign Office, March 19, 1965; NARA 59 1964–66, box 450, Telegram no. 3513 from Cronk of U.S. Embassy in Bonn to State Department, March 15, 1965. NARA 59 1964–66, box 460, Telegram no. 2943 from Blumenthal to Herter, March 25, 1965.

States had already settled on a schedule. In considering the content of its offers for September 1965—asserted the Commission's representative—the EEC would take into consideration the state of CAP elaboration.[49]

With the March 1965 agreement, it seemed that the Kennedy Round was well on its way to realization. Yet, as already suggested by the German–Dutch attitude toward the Herter–Mansholt plan, tensions continued within the EEC that exploded into a full crisis at the end of June 1965.

The Outbreak of the Empty Chair Crisis

At the end of May 1965 it seemed that the Kennedy Round had gained a certain momentum. Negotiations over exceptions lists continued, discussions over the international grain agreement had just been kicked off, and an unconditional date for offers in agriculture had been settled. Yet the situation was still complicated and replete with obstacles to satisfactory bargaining at the round. The Six still had to agree on another crucial portion of the CAP, and the members states were frustrated with the way the EEC was developing.[50]

Believing that it had made a great sacrifice by accepting UGPs, Germany entered 1965 convinced that it was owed something in return, above all, steps toward its project for a political union in the EEC.[51] However, the Germans' hopes on that score receded rapidly. In March 1965, Couve de Murville made it known that progress on a union would be possible only after the approval of the financial regulations. France continued to require the preliminary settling of the CAP as a condition for forward steps in other areas. It had no intention of compensating Germany for the UGPs, since the completion of the CAP was required by the Treaty of Rome. The French stance increased German suspicions that de Gaulle desired to impose his own agenda. Erhard and Schröder thus became convinced that the approval of financial regulations had to be exploited as a means to compel France to make progress in other areas. The agricultural part of the Kennedy Round made concessions from France more urgent than ever. The September 16 date presupposed progress on the CAP that Bonn was reluctant to commit to, and pushed the Germans to urgently seek a French quid pro quo.[52]

---

[49]   HAEC BAC 512—Conseil des Ministres, Note "Négociations commerciales multilatérales du GATT," March 19, 1965; PRO FO 371/183385 telegram 58 from Cohen to Foreign Office, March 19, 1965.

[50]   N. Piers Ludlow, "Challenging French Leadership in Europe: Germany, Italy, the Netherlands and the Outbreak of the Empty Chair Crisis of 1965–1966," *Contemporary European History* 8 (1999), 231–48.

[51]   CM2 1965/6 PV de la 158ème réunion du Conseil de la CEE, February 2, 1965.

[52]   HAEC—MAEF, OW 36, Note, January 19, 1965 reporting conversation between Schröder and Couve de Murville; CM2 1965/6 PV de la 158ème réunion du Conseil de la CEE, February 2, 1965.

While the Germans stalled, French insistence on seeing this policy accomplished escalated for two reasons. First, Germany had been warned repeatedly that high UGPs would artificially increase EEC production, in particular by French farmers, owing to the higher prices on offer. In the absence of EEC financial regulations, the cost of this surplus would be borne by the French government. Paris considered approval of the financial regulations economically necessary, and an instrument with which to make Germany pay for its choice of high UGPs. Second, France had to make sure that the agricultural part of the Kennedy Round did not undermine the UGPs through concessions made to third countries.[53]

As N.P. Ludlow notes, the tension within the EEC at the beginning of 1965 arose from sources other than Franco-German relations. Italian and Dutch discontent about the EEC agenda also created strain.[54] Since 1958 Italian agricultural exports had not increased in a meaningful way, as French exports had done. Until 1965, the CAP had not addressed products of primary concern to Italy, such as fruit and vegetables, olive oil, rice, and wine. What was worse, Italy had experienced a huge surge of imports of meat from outside the EEC. Because of the CAP financial rules, the poorest EEC member had become the largest net contributor to the EEC agricultural fund. Moreover, Italy resented French actions within the EEC, believing that France should pay the other member states back for having obtained UGPs in December 1964, which, lowering prices for hard wheat, imposed sacrifices on Italy. Rome was also displeased with the priorities that the EEC had pursued. The economic integration of the EEC had increased competition in the Italian markets, and Rome had requested common regional and social policies in order to lessen economic inequalities among the EEC regions. Yet little attention was paid to these issues. As a result of its discontent, in March 1965 Italy shifted from the conciliatory role it had often played since 1958 to a more confrontational stance.[55] As for the Dutch, in February 1965 they made clear the importance they attached to giving the European Parliament a central role in setting the EEC's budget procedures. With the adoption of financial regulations, national parliaments would not control portions of the financial sources of the EEC, and the Dutch wanted the European Parliament to exert control over the budget. If this requirement went unmet, the Netherlands would not approve the financial regulations.[56]

---

[53] Ludlow, *The European Community and the Crises of the 1960s*, 63–71.

[54] Ludlow, "Challenging French Leadership in Europe."

[55] On Italian discontent see Italian declarations at the EEC Council of Ministers of February 2, 1965 CM2 1965/6 PV de la 158ème réunion du Conseil de la CEE, February 2, 1965. On Italy and CAP see Galli and Torcasio, *La partecpazione italiana alla political agricola comunitaria*, 85–6 and Giuliana Laschi, *L'agricoltura italiana e l'integrazione europea* (Bern, 1999). On Italy and EEC social policy see Antonio Varsori, *Il Comitato Economico e Sociale nella costruzione europea* (Venice, 2000).

[56] Anjo G. Harryvan, "A Successful Defence of the Communitarian Model? The Netherlands and the Empty Chair Crisis," in Jean Marie Palayret, Helen Wallace and

Until the early part of 1965, the Five had made concessions to the French, fearing that otherwise they would abandon the EEC. However, by 1965 the economic advantages that France enjoyed in the Community were such that the other states doubted that France would ever leave it. They were now united in their desire to be recompensed for the sacrifices they made to keep Paris in the fold. In this strained environment, the Commission presented its audacious March 1965 proposals for progress in many fields, throwing fuel on the smouldering fire. The need to finance the CAP provided the Commission with an opportunity to make political progress. It put forward its proposals on the financing of the CAP, seeking French agreement to strengthen the supranational qualities of the Community and giving more power to the Commission and the European Parliament, in exchange for highly favorable financial arrangements. The Commission would be provided with independent funding based on the transfer of customs duties and duties levied by the national governments on imports of foodstuffs into the EEC. The European Parliament would have the power to scrutinize the Commission's receipts and expenditure. The Commission's suggestions were based on a miscalculation: that de Gaulle would be willing to pay a political price to get final approval of the CAP. The proposals were discussed among the Six through the end of June 1965 and took up the entirety of the ministers' attention. France, as it turned out, had no intention of obtaining the financial regulations of the CAP at the cost of increasing the power of the Commission and the Parliament. France rejected what it considered blackmail, that is, making huge concessions to obtain the financial regulations. In contrast, the Dutch, the Germans, and the Italians, though they did not fully support the Commission's proposals, insisted on their indivisibility as a tactic to get French concessions. Under the leadership of the German foreign minister, Schröder, the three countries repudiated the French goal of approval of the financial regulations without parallel progress on institutional reform. With this line drawn in the sand, the French did what they had threatened many times. After several warnings on the consequences of a failure to agree on the CAP, on the night of June 30 French foreign minister, Couve de Murville, chairman of the Council of Ministers, announced the impossibility of reaching an agreement. Instead of sitting down to further negotiations, as had become customary, he declared the Council of Ministers session over. In the followings days France withdrew from the work of the Council and other policymaking committees of the Community, including the 111 Committee. The crisis of the Empty Chair had broken out.[57]

Pascaline Winand (eds), *Visions, Votes and Vetoes: The Empty chair Crisis and the Luxembourg Compromise Forty Years On* (Brussels, 2006), 129–52.

[57]   On the crisis, in addition to Ludlow's works mentioned, see Wilfried Loth (ed.), *Crisis and Compromises*, and Jean-Marie Palayret, Helen Wallace, and Pascaline Winand (eds) *Visions, Votes and Vetoes: The Empty Chair Crisis and the Luxembourg Compromise Forty Years On* (Peter Lang, 2006).

The U.S. Reaction: Keeping the Round Alive While Supporting European Integration

The EEC crisis had immediate repercussions in Geneva, making uncertain the destiny of the EEC and, consequently, of the GATT talks. To describe the impact of the Brussels breakdown on the EEC's participation in the Kennedy Round, it is necessary first to illustrate the U.S. reaction, as this set the stage for the EEC's response. Although the United States had a considerable interest in the outcome of the crisis, it decided to take no initiative to resolve it. Washington maintained a discrete silence in order to avoid accusations from the French of interference with the EEC's internal affairs. Washington feared the consequences the crisis could have for the Kennedy Round, European integration, and the Atlantic Alliance. Failure of the round would set back U.S. postwar policies of liberalization. Moreover, Washington had never seen GATT negotiations as an exercise in mere tariff reduction; rather, the U.S. government counted on them to strengthen its alliance with Europe. Equally important, the breakdown of the European Community would impede the U.S. postwar policy of European integration and Franco-German reconciliation. Washington thus hoped that the Five would hold firm, offering no concessions to the French that would weaken the EEC.[58]

Because of the suspension of talks in Brussels, the Six could not respect the September 16 deadline for putting offers in the agricultural sector on the table. At this point, Washington had to determine whether to proceed with the negotiations. President Johnson, following the request of Herter, the State Department, Bator, and Bundy, decided to present the American agricultural offers. Bundy held that, if the Geneva negotiations were formally halted, they would be difficult to revive and would probably collapse. Thus, an indefinite postponement of the agricultural talks had to be avoided, allowing useful discussions to begin with other countries. The crisis in the EEC and the stalemate on agriculture could be exploited by Japan, the United Kingdom, and other agricultural importing countries more interested in the industrial part of the Kennedy Round as an excuse to delay progress in agriculture. Proceeding with the agricultural talks would maximize pressure on the EEC to present satisfactory offers at a later date and Washington could make it absolutely clear that the round had to include agriculture.[59]

Moreover, in the view of the State Department, persevering with the Kennedy Round could be of crucial importance for the Community and the Commission. Once the crisis had passed, negotiations in Geneva could well emerge as a venue in

[58] Memorandum from Klein to Bundy, "De Gaulle and the Common Market," July 7, 1965, NSF Country File United Kingdom, box 215, LBJL; Memorandum 'Impact of EEC Crisis on the Kennedy Round', July 12, 1965, Bator Papers, box 12, LBJL.

[59] FRUS 1964–68, vol. VIII, International Monetary and Trade Policy, document 287. Letter from Herter to Bundy, July 20, 1965; ibid., document 289. Memorandum from Herter to President Johnson, August 9, 1965. Memorandum, Bundy to President, August 17, 1965, WHCF, Confidential Files, box 91, LBJL.

which the Six could maintain their integrity as a Community.[60] Given the hostility de Gaulle displayed towards the Commission in the crisis, it was important not to undercut the institution's role. Since Geneva was an important framework where it was negotiating on behalf of the Community, continuation of the round could play a significant role in the Commission's survival as a political force. It was for this reason that Washington refused to consider the proposal from Wyndham White to continue the round by replacing the Commission with the six member states, which would negotiate on an individual basis. The State Department considered this option as incompatible with the key political objective of fostering unity in Western Europe. The Kennedy Round had to be negotiated by the Community, represented by the Commission. Persistence with the round, the Americans believed, would help the Six to regain unity and the Commission to maintain its role in international trade policy. One last consideration held sway in Washington. Continuing the negotiations in Geneva would be the most effective way to ensure that the solution to the EEC crisis would include a connection to the Kennedy Round. In short, American national interests dictated going ahead with the trade negotiations, despite the complications introduced by de Gaulle's action.[61]

With this decision, Washington attempted to support both trade liberalization and European integration. The U.S. stance in this phase was dictated by an interest in supporting and sheltering European regional integration. The Johnson administration conducted the round in such a way as to help the EEC members to maintain their unity, and the Commission to keep its role in the EEC's trade policymaking.

It was on this ground that, on August 19, Herter announced that the United States would present offers in the agricultural sector, while withholding those of interest to the EEC.[62] Having decided to make its offers, Washington had to use all its political weight to force the British to attend, and, once this had been achieved, to convince the other countries to follow suit. On September 16, the United States and the other main participants in the round put their agricultural offers on the table, hoping in this way to prevent a dangerous halt to discussions in Geneva.[63]

---

[60] Memorandum from Leddy and Solomon to Ball and Mann, "The EEC Crisis, Agriculture and the KR," July 30, 1965, Bator papers, box 12 LBJL.

[61] NARA 59-250-57, 1964–66, box 460 Telegram no. 3063 from Rusk to U.S. mission in Geneva, September 15, 1965.

[62] Statement of Christian A. Herter, August 19, 1965, NSF Subject file, box 48, LBJL.

[63] NARA 59 1964–66 FT 13-2 box 979, Telegram no. 3343 from U.S. mission in Geneva to State Department, July 7, 1965. FO 371/183399 Telegram no. 178 from Cohen in Geneva to Foreign Office, July 23, 1965; NARA Recs. of USTR, box 6 Telegram no. 3040 from Rusk to U.S. mission in Geneva and U.S. Embassy in Copenhagen, September 1, 1965; ibid., telegram 3046 from Rusk to U.S. mission in Geneva and U.S. Embassy in Copenhagen, September 3, 1965.

Divided in Brussels, but not in Geneva

After the French withdrawal in Brussels, the other members had to decide whether to continue the Community's activities or wait for the French to come back into the fold. In particular, the Five had to determine whether and how to carry on the Kennedy Round negotiations. They wanted to demonstrate their willingness to go ahead in spite of the French empty chair, and one of the ways to do so was to allow the Commission to negotiate in Geneva. Yet they did not want to antagonize the French by taking confrontational steps. Negotiating in the GATT over issues that involved France could be seen as a provocation, and hamper a resolution to the crisis. It would not ease reconciliation for the Five to proceed as a unit as if the French were also represented. At the end of July, the Five and the Commission concluded that, while they could discuss the industrial sector and grains, they could not present offers in the agricultural sector on September 16 without a new Council of Ministers mandate.[64]

Ultimately, the Five decided to negotiate under the existing mandate, but refrain from laying agricultural offers on the table. In this way, the Commission could attend the Geneva meetings under the mandate previously received, without annoying the French with a new mandate given in their absence. The solution chosen was in line with the Five's desire to keep the Community functioning while refraining from substantive decisions. Moreover, Rey and the Five held that the internal crisis of the EEC should not be allowed to interfere with the Community's external relations or to stall the round.[65]

As for the French, they never obstructed the GATT talks and never opposed the right of the Commission to continue negotiating in Geneva. They were perfectly aware that meaningful negotiations would resume only once the internal crisis of the EEC was solved. Given the fact that the Commission was acting under the existing mandate, they judged it wise not to spark an unnecessary battle with the Five. Furthermore, the French were just as interested as the other EEC states in the Kennedy Round, and therefore did not want to undermine it. They stayed well abreast of progress made in Geneva.[66] Also revealing of Paris' attitude towards the EEC and the Commission was its proposal at the end of October 1965 on the issue of American subsidies. Washington had decided to subsidize chicken exports, and the French delegation to the GATT asked the delegations of the Five in Geneva to set

---

[64] AECB PV 326 "Communication de la commission au Conseil," July 22, 1965; CM2 65/86 173ème session du Conseil, July 26–27, 1965.

[65] AECB, PV 326, 22 July 1965; PRO FO 371/183387 Telegram no. 2104 from Washington to Foreign Office, December 12, 1965. NARA 59, 1964–66, box 460 Telegram no. 250 from Tuthill to State Department, September 30, 1965 and CM (IA 16726/182451824), 204ème réunion du comité de l'article 111, October 18, 1965.

[66] MAEF, DE/CE, 1961–66, GATT 932 Telegram no. 12624/27 from Brunet (Service de Coopération Economique du Quai d'Orsay) to French embassy in London, October 25, 1965 and ibid., Note sur le Kennedy Round, October 1965.

up a coordinating meeting which the representatives of Commission could attend as technical assistants. Thus Paris, even while bypassing the formal EEC framework, sought the cooperation of the Five, and even wanted the Commission present at the meeting. This request revealed that Paris had no intention of sabotaging the EEC or of excluding the Commission. However, the Commission refused the French proposal, as any consultations needed to take place within the framework of the 111 Committee.[67] Even during the crisis of the Empty Chair, the importance of the regional dimension of the EEC was evident. Its members maintained their unity in Geneva despite the French boycott of the meetings in Brussels.

In continuing the talks in Geneva, the Commission took care not to go beyond the remit of the mandate. Moreover, it kept in close contact with the French delegations to the GATT and to the 111 Committee, informing them of steps taken and progress made. For example, in November 1965, the Commission authorized its delegation in Geneva to agree to the creation of the GATT working groups on chemicals, pulp and paper, and aluminum, and to attend the working group on textiles. This decision was taken at the strong insistence of Rey, and despite the opposition of Commissioner Marjolin, who feared the move would annoy Paris. The Commission specified to its delegation that it had to remain strictly within the bounds of its mandate and that no concessions on tariff reductions could be made. In addition, Rey informed the French delegation in Geneva about the stances assumed in these working groups.[68]

No major decision was taken in Geneva during the crisis. Although technical work continued under the existing mandate, it was understood that any significant step forward required a new authorization from the EEC Council of Ministers. The Commission became progressively less able to actively and meaningfully attend the discussions, and the necessity for the Council of Ministers to give new instructions was strongly felt. In October 1965, the Council of Ministers requested that the Commission submit a report on the Kennedy Round by January 31, 1966 so that an appraisal of the situation could be made.[69] Then, at the end of November, the Council discussed with the Commission the state of the talks. Rey and the Five agreed that the Commission needed new instructions if it was to play any further part in the Geneva discussions. In spite of the efforts by Washington, the Commission, and the Five to treat the Kennedy Round as business-as-usual, it had, in fact, ground to a halt because of the EEC's paralysis. The Five were therefore at a crossroads. Bearing in mind that American authority to negotiate lapsed on June 30, 1967, they concluded that they could wait for the French until January 1966. However, if Paris persisted in its boycott, they would be obliged to consider

---

[67]   AECB PV 335, October 27, 1965.

[68]   AECB, PV 326, July 22, 1965; CM2 1965/314 PV de la 73ème reunion du Comité 111, October 27, 1965; AECB, COM (65) PV 337, December 17, 1965; Interview of the author with Paul Luyten, July 7, 2003.

[69]   AECB BAC 512, Note d'information-Négociations commerciales au GATT, June 29, 1965 and CM IA 16726/182451824 204ème réunion du Comité 111, October 14, 1965.

whether to go ahead in the Kennedy Round as a Community composed of five members. The Five believed that they had to stop the French from letting the crisis drag on until progress in Geneva became impossible.[70]

Ending the Crisis

Hopes of settling the crisis improved when, in November 1965, the Five and France agreed to meet in Luxembourg in January 1966 without the Commission. While the six states got ready for the meeting, Washington urged Wyndham White to publish a report to illustrate the state of play in Geneva. In so doing Washington had a double aim. First, the U.S. negotiators were concerned by the slow pace of the Kennedy Round and wanted to assist the bargaining with a bold stroke. Second, the Americans wanted to ensure that the GATT negotiations were considered in Luxembourg.[71] On January 3, Wyndham White circulated his report, which, for tactical reasons, exaggerated the need to act quickly and tried to inject renewed impetus into the round.[72]

The Luxembourg meetings that brought France back to Brussels have already been analyzed by many scholars. What matters here is the relation with the Kennedy Round. The Six discussed qualified majority voting (QMV) within the Council of Ministers and the power of the Commission. De Gaulle requested that QMV, which was scheduled to apply to Council of Ministers decisions after January 1966, be abandoned and that the Commission stop acting as an independent political authority. As for the first issue, none of the Six wanted to apply QMV to important matters, such as the CAP and the Kennedy Round, and run the risk of being outvoted on a critical policy. Before June 1965, a tacit agreement had been reached that important issues would be decided when unanimity had been achieved.[73] Therefore, France was not the only government to refuse the application of QMV to the most crucial issues. As Schröder put it to Dean Rusk and U.S secretary of Defense Robert McNamara, "no Common Market member should be outvoted by a majority on any question of vital importance" and, in any

---

[70]   CM2 1965/66 PV de la 175ème session du Conseil de la CEE, November 29–30, 1965; CM2 1965/314 PV de la 76ème réunion du Comité 111, December 17, 1965; NARA 59 1964–66, box 460 Telegram no. 106 from American Embassy in Rome to State Department, December 4, 1965. PRO FO 371/182398 Telegram from British Embassy in Rome to FO, November 26, 1965 reporting conversation between Marjoribanks, Colombo, Ferrari-Aggradi and Ortona.

[71]   NARA 364 Records of USTR, box 5, Telegram no. 3172 from Kaiser of the American Embassy in London to State Department, January 8, 1966.

[72]   PRO FO 371/189597, "The GATT Trade Negotiations" report by the Director General, January 3, 1966.

[73]   MEAF, DE/CE 1961–66, Folder 402, Note 107/CE, May 21, 1965.

case, a further mandate for the Kennedy Round had to be based on unanimity.[74] Even before de Gaulle's request, it was unlikely that a member's strongly held position would be overruled by the majority. This proves that, despite the fact that de Gaulle appeared to be the only one screaming against the majority vote, the other Five also actually had an identical, even if silent, position. However, what mattered to the Five was how to assert this position without modifying the Treaty of Rome, formally abolishing QMV, or recognizing a veto power.

As for the Commission's powers, the French wanted it to abandon aspirations to political authority, relegating it to its allotted role under the Treaty of Rome. As shown in the previous chapter, the Dutch and the Germans had often tried to reduce the negotiating role of this institution. The French, by contrast, had supported it. The only quarrel between the French and the Commission had taken place in October 1964. Here the squabble was not dictated by a French wish to downgrade the Commission, but motivated by a desire to terminate discussions with the Americans. For Paris, the Commission had acted appropriately until December 1964, and the French government wanted to return to that more acceptable institutional performance.[75]

When the Six gathered in Luxembourg on January 17 and 18, 1966, Couve de Murville submitted his "Decalogue" concerning the working style of the Commission, and insisted that QMV be reformed. The Five replied with firmness: no breach to the Treaty of Rome would be allowed and no right of veto could be recognized. Couve de Murville also presented a timetable in order to bring the crises to an end: agreement on the Decalogue and QMV by the end of January, and adoption of CAP financial regulations, described by the French minister as a "precondition to overcoming the crisis," by March 31, 1966. However, financial settlement of the CAP without parallel mention of the Kennedy Round was unacceptable to the Germans and the Dutch. Given the impossibility of reaching an agreement, the Council of Ministers meeting was adjourned until the end of the month.[76]

In the meantime, Washington heightened its pressure on the Five to insert the Kennedy Round in the final settlement with France.[77] Their strong support for trade liberalization made the Germans particularly receptive to this pressure. In Bonn's view, any final agreement on the agricultural financial settlement could

---

[74]   Memorandum of conversation between Rusk, Ball, McNamara, Bator and German Ministers Schröder and Von Hassel, Washington, December 20, 1965, Francis M. Bator's papers, box 21, LBJL.

[75]   NARA 59, 1964–66, box 460 Telegram no. 104 from American Embassy in Paris to State Department, October 26, 1965.

[76]   CM2 1966/1, Verbal du Conseil de la CEE, Luxembourg, January 17–18/28–29, 1966. For the Decalogue see John Lambert, "The Constitutional Crisis of 1965–1966," *Journal of Common Market Studies*, 4 (1966), 221–3. HAEC, Max Kohnstam Conversation with Monnet, Davignon, Spierenburg and Robinson, January 20, 1966.

[77]   NARA 59 1964–66 Ecin 3 box 792. Telegram no. 4382 from Bohlen to State Department, January 26, 1966.

be reached only if, in return, France would cooperate in the Kennedy Round. The German government considered it unacceptable that the French would again dictate the agenda, and adopted a tough stance to force them to abandon their blocking tactics.[78] Lahr asked the U.S. government—unofficially—how the would respond if the Five were to renew the Commission mandate in the Kennedy Round.[79] Rusk gave Bonn a response that bolstered the Germans' intention to remain firm: "US is negotiating in Kennedy Round with Commission acting on behalf of Community. Whether Commission's instructions come from Six member States or from Five acting for Community is internal matter for determination by EEC members involved."[80]

On 19 January 1966, the Commission presented the Council of Ministers a detailed report on the round, setting out in detail the problems that had to be resolved to enable the EEC to negotiate in Geneva. The Commission hoped, in this way, to make sure the trade conference remained the center of attention in Luxembourg.[81]

Meeting on January 28–29, 1966, the Council of Ministers easily reached an agreement concerning the Commission. The French "Decalogue" was turned into a "Heptalogue" that did not downgrade the Commission's role but restricted it to the limits defined in the Treaty of Rome. The QMV issue proved more difficult to settle, giving rise to an agreement to disagree. The Council's decision merely outlined the disagreement and noted that it did not prevent the resumption of the EEC's work. Then, when the issue of voting seemed settled, Schröder insisted on unanimous decisions on all questions that had to be settled by 1965 and, in particular, on the CAP. Couve de Murville, pointing out that the problem had not been raised by the French, refused to give special treatment to these issues. He mused out loud that such an approach would imply unanimity on any agricultural mandate for the Kennedy Round, which was also supposed to be approved in 1965. For the French minister, both questions had to be governed by the same agreement reached on the basis of QMV. Schröder nonetheless remained steadfast on the need for a unanimous vote on the CAP. For a brief period at the very end of the meeting, it looked as if the CAP and the Kennedy Round might develop into stumbling blocks. Ultimately, however,

---

[78]   NARA 59 1964–66 Ecin 3 box 792. Telegram from American Ambassador to Bonn McGhee to State Department "KR and EEC crisis," January 28, 1966; Ludlow, *The European Community and the Crises of the 1960s*, 94–100.

[79]   Note of Permanent Secretary Fritz Neef for Foreign Minister Schröder, Minister of Trade and Industry Schmücker and Permanent Secretary Lahr, January 28, 1966, PAAA, B1, vol. 214; taken from Henning Türk, "'To face de Gaulle as a Community'—The Role of the Federal Republic of Germany in the Empty Chair Crisis," in Palayret, Wallace, Winand (eds) *Visions, Votes and Vetoes*, 113–28.

[80]   FRUS 1964–68, vol. XIII, Western European Region document 125. Telegram from the Department of State to the Embassy in Germany, January 27, 1966.

[81]   CM2 1966/17507, Rapport de la Commission au Conseil sur les négociations commerciales au GATT, January 19, 1966.

the Six agreed that both the CAP and the Commission negotiating mandate for the agricultural sector in Geneva would be decided on the basis of unanimity. As regards the decisions the Six had to take in the Kennedy Round in the other sectors, these important matters would be covered by the agreement reached by QMV. Following the suggestion of Couve de Murville, the Six then considered the agenda of the Community. While recognizing the importance of the GATT negotiations, the French minister stated that priority had to be given to the financial settlement of the CAP. Representatives of the Five, and in particular Schröder, made clear that no progress would be made in the CAP without parallel progress in the Kennedy Round. They agreed nonetheless that the Council of Ministers would deal with the financial settlement of the CAP as a priority.[82]

The Luxembourg meetings brought France back into the fold, but did not eliminate tensions. An agreement on the CAP and the GATT negotiations still had to be reached, and in the nervous aftermath of the Empty Chair it would not prove an easy task.[83] The risk of acrimony mounted when, in March 1966, France withdrew from NATO. At this point, it seemed that the EEC could become entangled in a new crisis over security issues. The Six agreed that every effort had to be made to keep the conflicts surrounding the two institutions separate, in order to prevent disagreements over NATO from paralyzing the EEC. NATO could live without France, while the EEC could not.[84]

The Six still had various decisions to take in order to get to Geneva with an updated position. They had to specify their proposals for the commodity agreement on cereals, work out offers for the rest of the agricultural sector, and take positions in the industrial sector. However, the Six had a huge amount of agricultural business to settle in Brussels before they would be in a position to negotiate in the GATT.[85]

The Six proceeded with the approval of the CAP regulations and the Kennedy Round mandate in a parallel way. Using a formula suggested by Couve

---

[82]   CM2 1966/1, Verbal du Conseil de la CEE, Luxembourg, January 28–29, 1966. NARA 364 Records of USTR, box 5, Telegram no. 658 from Tuthill to State Department, January 30, 1966. On Schröder's request see also Maurice Couve de Murville, *Une politique étrangère 1958–1969* (Paris, 1971).

[83]   For the tension in the aftermath of the Luxembourg meetings see Ludlow, *The European Community and the Crises of the 1960s*, 100–24.

[84]   NARA 59 1964–66 Ecin 3 box 792. Memorandum of Conversation between Rey and Ball, Tuthill, Schaetzel and Hinton on U.S.–EEC relations, May 25, 1966. FRUS 1964–68, vol. XIII, document 140 Circular Telegram from the Department of State to Certain Posts in Europe, March 10, 1966; for the German debate on de Gaulle's move see Ronald J. Granieri, *The Ambivalent Alliance. Konrad Adenauer, the CDU/CSU, and the West 1948–1966* (New York, 2002), 215–17.

[85]   CM2 1966/17509, PV de la 222ème réunion du Comité 111, February 23–24, 1966, March 1, 1966; CM2 1966/17509, Aide-Memoire du Conseil des Ministres, March 11, 1966.

de Murville and then elaborated by the German minister of economics, Kurt Schmücker, decisions on the CAP and the Kennedy Round were to be taken, but finally approved only when comparable progress was achieved on both fronts. Thus, Germany could agree on the financial regulations, but this agreement would not be taken out of the "box"—formally approved—until the following Council of Ministers meeting had made progress on the Kennedy Round.[86]

Despite the firmness with which Paris called for the approval of the CAP, the French actually followed this working method in a flexible way. In April 1966, they agreed to the Commission negotiating in Geneva over chemicals, even if not all the CAP elements had been approved.[87] This agreement proved French willingness to move ahead in the GATT talks, and it confirmed two aspects of Paris' policy. Once again, the round remained a lever to obtain concessions. German and Dutch keenness for the round gave the French government a valuable bargaining chip it could use to move forward with the CAP. However, Paris was also keen to reduce tariffs. Thus, it was always careful not to push too hard, requesting concessions but not endangering the round itself.

Moreover, the EEC elaborated its decisions on the basis of the proposals presented by the Commission. It is worth pointing out that, despite the Empty Chair crisis—often described as having weakened the Commission—the latter was still able to act vigorously. As the two following chapters—dedicated to the content of the industrial and agricultural negotiations—show clearly, the Commission's role in the EEC's trade policymaking was undiminished, and in the last phase of the round in 1967, the Commission was even able to increase its autonomy. The French, who had attacked it during the crisis, never questioned its negotiating role, as they were aware of the advantages of negotiating with a single voice.

The turning point in the EEC's preparations for the round came in mid-May when the Six agreed on the financial regulations for the 1966–70 period.[88] As a result of this progress, the Council of Ministers on June 14, 1966 approved the EEC common stance on cereals, tropical products, and the industrial sector, and authorized the Commission to start negotiations in Geneva immediately. Again, even though decisions on the Kennedy Round had to be kept "in the box" until the entire CAP issue was settled, France allowed the talks in Geneva to begin.[89] At the end of July, the EEC reached a package decision on the Kennedy Round mandate and the CAP. The Six achieved a final agreement on agricultural finance regulations, and on a phased program up to July 1, 1968 for implementing common prices on a wide range of agricultural products. They also agreed on July 1, 1968 as the date for achieving full internal free trade and for completing the move

---

[86]   CM2 1966/17509, Note d'information du COREPER, 1 April 1966, and ibid. Conseils CEE/CECA, April 4–5, 1965, Note à l'attention de M. le Président, April 1, 1966. Ludlow, *The European Community and the Crises of the 1960s*, chapter 4.

[87]   CM2 1966/16 PV de la 182ème session du Conseil de la CEE, April 4–5, 1966.

[88]   CM2 1966/22 PV de la 185ème session du Conseil de la CEE, May 9–12, 1966.

[89]   CM2 1966/34 PV de la 188ème session du Conseil de la CEE, June 14, 1966.

towards the CET. This agreement opened the way for the final debate on the offers in the agricultural sector. In a four-day marathon that ended in the early hours of July 27, the Council of Ministers approved offers for agricultural products other than cereals.[90] At this point, the French deputy permanent representative Maurice Ulrich could claim, "The crisis is over."[91]

In the aftermath of the crisis, the EEC was able to adopt a common negotiating position for the final part of the Kennedy Round, showing again the importance EEC members attached to attending the GATT talks as a trading unit.

[90]   CM2 1966/48 PV de la 191ème session du Conseil de la CEE, July 22–23 and 26–27, 1966.

[91]   NARA 59 1964–66 Ecin 3 box 791. Memorandum of Conversation between Ulrich and Russell Fessenden of the American Embassy in Brussels, July 29, 1966.

Chapter 5

The EEC and Negotiations in the Industrial Sector: Enhancing Freer Trade

EEC Trade Patterns

As noted in the previous chapters, at the GATT ministerial meeting of May 1964 the EEC, the United States and the other participants in the Kennedy Round agreed to exchange lists of exceptions for the industrial sector in November of that year. Once these lists had been put on the table, negotiations over this sector slowly got under way. Before describing the bargain struck among the EEC's members in Brussels to establish their exceptions list and then focusing on the negotiations in Geneva held until December 1966, it is useful to illustrate the trade patterns of the EEC to understand how they were evolving. It was by considering these trade flows that member states set their tariff policy.

Table 5.1 shows the EEC's exports to major areas of the world. While during these years intra-EEC trade grew in importance for all of the Six, the EFTA remained a significant destination. The U.S. market remained of particular importance to Germany. It is also worth noting that, whereas in 1959 the EEC exported more to the rest of the world than to itself, by 1962 this pattern had reversed.

Table 5.2 shows the composition of exports of the Six in 1964. The most important sectors were machinery and transport equipment (the major type of export for Italy, Germany, and the Netherlands) and manufactured goods (the major type of export for France and Belgium–Luxembourg).

Machinery and transport equipment held a significant place in negotiations during the round, representing 36 percent of OECD countries' exports.[1] It is worth examining additional data on this sector. Table 5.3 illustrates the destination of exports machinery and transport equipment by the EEC's members. EFTA and the U.S. markets were of particular significance for Germany; these two markets combined took more German exports than did the EEC. This aspect of its trade profile should be borne in mind as one considers Germany's stance in the bargaining over the industrial sector.

Table 5.4 shows the dynamism of this sector, illustrating the growth of the EEC member states' exports from 1958 to 1972 by destination. To provide a complete idea of the EEC's patterns of export by sector, Tables 5.5 and 5.6 illustrate the growth in exports of chemicals and machinery, the two other areas of world trade that were most dynamic.

---

[1]   *Source: OECD SITC Rev. 2—Historical Series 1961–1990* (Paris, 2000).

Table 5.1   EEC exports to major areas, 1959, 1962 and 1964 (U.S.$m f.o.b.)

Exporter	EEC	EFTA	United States	Rest of the World
1959				
France	1,527	760	470	2,953
BLEU	1,522	524	444	789
Netherlands	1,597	847	209	926
Germany	2,731	2,649	913	3,643
Italy	792	642	345	1,097
EEC	8,169	5,422	2,381	9,408
1962				
France	2,712	1,175	426	3,049
BLEU	2,458	620	414	833
Netherlands	2,256	1,057	200	1,071
Germany	4,512	3,687	965	4,100
Italy	1,625	957	441	1,643
EEC	13,563	7,496	2,446	10,696
1964				
France	4,115	1,571	594	3,768
BLEU	3,947	791	532	1,112
Netherlands	3,561	1,210	244	1,378
Germany	6,306	4,830	1,436	5,320
Italy	2,891	1,199	618	2,480
EEC	20,820	9,601	3,424	14,058

Source: Statistical Office of the European Communities, Basic Statistics of the Community 1960, 1963, 1965.

Table 5.2   Composition of total exports of the Six in 1964 (%)

SITC		France	Italy	Germany	BLEU	Netherlands
0	Food and live animals	12.7	22.7	1.8	5.2	22.7
1	Beverages and tobacco	3.3	1.2	0.3	0.6	1.2
2	Crude materials, inedible, except fuels	7.1	7.9	2.7	6.2	7.9
3	Mineral fuels, lubricants, and related materials	3.5	9.2	4.9	4.0	9.2
4	Animal and vegetable oils, fats and waxes	0.3	0.8	0.3	0.2	0.8
5	Chemicals and related products, n.e.s.	9.7	9.2	11.6	5.6	9.2
6	Manufactured goods classified chiefly by material	28.4	19.4	22.0	50.0	19.4
7	Machinery and transport equipment	25.4	23.6	46.2	19	23.6
8	Miscellaneous manufactured articles	9.1	5.2	9.0	7.2	5.2
9	Commodities and transactions, n.e.c	0.6	0.9	1.3	2.2	0.9
Total		100	100	100	100	100

Note: n.e.s. stands for "not elsewhere specified"; n.e.c. stands for "not elsewhere classified."
Source: *OECD SITC Rev. 2—Historical Series 1961–1990* (Paris, 2000).

Table 5.3   Exports of the Six in machinery and transport equipment (SITC Classification 7, in percentages) in 1964 by destination

	EEC	United Kingdom	EFTA + Finland	United States
BLEU	69.2	3.6	10.3	3.4
Germany	31.5	4.0	28.0	9.3
France	33.3	3.3	15.7	3.7
Italy	36.9	4.2	15.2	4.6
Netherlands	52.0	6.1	18.2	4.8

Source: SITC Classification. *OECD SITC Rev. 2—Historical Series 1961–1990* (Paris, 2000).

Table 5.4   Index of growth of EEC member states' exports in SITC 7, machinery and transport equipment

	1958	1964	1967	1972	1958	1964	1967	1972
	EEC				*United States*			
BLEU	100	469	593	1,641	100	448	707	2,530
FRG	100	263	345	823	100	223	352	870
France	100	580	858	2,752	100	117	207	457
Italy	100	670	985	2,413	100	189	528	1,181
Netherlands	100	516	470	1,211	100	352	575	1,068
	EFTA				*Rest of the World*			
BLEU	100	252	379	1,030	100	161	221	494
FRG	100	187	202	470	100	144	200	415
France	100	394	498	1,523	100	204	291	588
Italy	100	432	655	842	100	300	476	777
Netherlands	100	280	324	741	100	237	334	649

Source: *OECD SITC Rev. 2—Historical Series 1961–1990* (Paris, 2000).

Table 5.5   Index of growth of EEC member states' exports in SITC 5, chemicals

	1958	1964	1967	1972	1958	1964	1967	1972
	EEC				*United States*			
BLEU	100	344	600	2,156	100	189	190	376
FRG	100	244	1,397	1,011	100	165	256	629
France	100	531	2,211	2,303	100	351	399	819
Italy	100	644	4,689	2,021	100	224	385	766
Netherlands	100	353	1,076	2,235	100	126	164	520
	EFTA				*Rest of the World*			
BLEU	100	140	176	510	100	133	168	490
FRG	100	219	274	531	100	293	422	641
France	100	306	374	655	100	250	350	499
Italy	100	294	417	952	100	456	601	868
Netherlands	100	286	429	883	100	280	403	825

Source: *OECD SITC Rev. 2—Historical Series 1961–1990* (Paris, 2000).

Table 5.6   Index of growth of EEC member states' exports in SITC 6, manufactured goods classified chiefly by material

	1958	1964	1967	1972	1958	1964	1967	1972
		EEC				United States		
BLEU	100	329	396	873	100	190	244	361
FRG	100	291	388	828	100	140	294	495
France	100	391	450	1,054	100	276	424	965
Italy	100	527	756	2,141	100	243	351	697
Netherlands	100	330	422	980	100	117	154	477
		EFTA				Rest of the World		
BLEU	100	212	222	399	100	114	140	220
FRG	100	181	207	378	100	94	153	266
France	100	297	299	492	100	135	154	236
Italy	100	292	330	579	100	193	271	483
Netherlands	100	199	199	387	100	130	176	302

Source: OECD SITC Rev. 2—Historical Series 1961–1990 (Paris, 2000).

To gain a clear picture of the EEC members' stances in the Kennedy Round, it is worth considering the EEC's trade patterns with the United States, its main negotiating partner. Table 5.7 illustrates the U.S. trade balance with the EEC in 1964. Although the volume of U.S. exports to the EEC was greater in the industrial sector than in the agricultural, Washington gained a good share of its surplus in the latter sector. Trade in manufactured goods was a two-way street; that is, the United States exported to the EEC and vice versa. By contrast, in the agricultural sector U.S. imports from the EEC were much lower than exports to it. These trade patterns go some way toward explaining what led to a reduction in protectionism in the industrial sector, but no such progress in agriculture. The United States and the EEC had a reciprocal interest in increasing exports to each other in the industrial sector, while the same could not be said for agriculture.

Establishing an exceptions list was a complicated process for all participants in the Kennedy Round. Business sectors vigorously lobbied their national governments, which had to balance these requests with what they considered the broader interests of the country. For the EEC this process was particularly thorny. Each member had its own domestic sectors to protect or liberalize. These sectors did not necessarily correspond to those that other members identified for greater or lesser tariffs. Compromises were necessary. Most importantly for the EEC, choosing which sectors to put on the list had twofold implications: it entailed reaffirming a willingness to establish a common commercial policy as well as defining how liberal it would be.

The task of preparing the draft list of exceptions fell to the Commission. In performing this task, the Commission considered its own preferences in addition to those of the member states. In particular, it sought to use the round to sway member states to implement a common commercial policy that also covered NTBs

Table 5.7   Composition of U.S. trade balance with the EEC in 1964 (in thousands of U.S.$)

SITC	Imports from the EEC	Exports to the EEC	Balance
Total trade	2,837,977	4,590,854	1,752,877
0 Food and live animals	122,663	769,676	647,013
1 Beverages and tobacco	83,905	129,145	45,240
2 Crude materials, inedible, except fuels	110,783	830,959	720,176
3 Mineral fuels, lubricants, and related materials	11,215	311,382	300,167
4 Animal and vegetable oils, fats and waxes	11,598	169,797	158,199
5 Chemicals and related products, n.e.s.	178,204	512,293	334,089
6 Manufactured goods by material	822,332	564,035	−258,297
7 Machinery and transport equipment	850,724	1,063,669	212,945
8 Miscellaneous manufactured articles	521,896	228,709	−293,187
9 Commodities and transactions n.e.c.	124,657	11,179	−113,478

Source: OECD SITC Rev. 2—Historical Series 1961–1990 (Paris, 2000). The Commission's Exceptions List.

and was grounded on a common industrial policy. The Geneva talks were a lever to move member states in the direction of commonality. The Commission's role as "guardian of the Treaty" shaped its preferences as it fostered the full implementation of the promises made in Rome. This was rather remarkable considering that none of the member states shared these priorities.

Since 1963 the Commission had been consulting trade associations in order to improve its knowledge of the effects of a tariff reduction.[2] In early 1964, it started working on the exceptions list, consulting with representatives of business sectors and the national officials of member states. In gathering this information, the Commission attempted to elaborate a draft list that could gain broad support from the six governments. However, it also tried to transform the requests of the member states into a common position representing what the Commission judged to be an accurate reflection of the EEC's commercial interests. An indication of this desire is given by its consultations with various business sectors. The director general for the Internal Market, the French Pierre Millet, consulted them through their representatives in Brussels rather than on a national basis. Moreover, only after they had been heard did the Commission approach national officials.[3]

[2]   AECB PV 213, January 20, 1963; NARA 59 State Department Central file subject numeric, box 3489, FT 4 US/TEA, telegram ECBUS A-645 from U.S. mission to EEC to State Department, April 9, 1963.

[3]   AECB—PV 274, May 27, 1964; CM2 1964/86 PV de la 134ème réunion du Conseil de la CEE, June 1–3, 1964. See also David Coombes, Politics and Bureaucracy in the European Community: A Portrait of the European Commission (London, 1970), 180.

The Commission considered that, in 1963, total EEC industrial imports amounted to U.S.$14.7 billion. These products were covered by about 2200 tariff lines; after the elimination of 150 zero-duty tariffs, representing around U.S.$4.9 billion, exceptions would concern roughly 2050 tariffs lines. Various business sectors asked for 850 exceptions, of which 600 were total—completely excluding the product from the linear cut—and 250 partial—a reduction of less than the target of 50 percent. These requests amounted to around U.S.$3.8 billions of imports, 40 percent of industrial imports, and 57 percent of dutiable imports of the EEC. They concerned textiles; ferrous and nonferrous metals; paper, wood, and ceramics; chemicals; and the machinery and transport equipment sector. In their consultations with the Commission, national administrations identified 300 total and 300 partial exceptions, representing U.S.$2.6 billion in imports, and making up 18 percent of industrial imports and 27 percent of dutiable imports. The types of products these requests addressed were similar to those singled out by business sectors.[4]

The Commission deemed these requests too numerous and not justified by the commercial and competitive strength of the EEC on world markets. The Community could afford a more liberal attitude.[5] Thus in October 1964, the Commission presented to the member states a considerably shorter list. Not including paper, for which the Commission had been unable to formulate a proposal, this enumeration identified 55 total exceptions and 195 partial ones. The exceptions represented 11.9 percent of the EEC's total tariffs and 13 percent of positive tariffs, that is to say, excluding zero duties (Table 5.8).

Table 5.9 illustrates how the proposed protected tariffs affected different sectors. Exceptions represented 4.9 percent of the EEC's total industrial imports and 11.5 percent of dutiable imports (excluding paper and ECSC products).[6]

The Commission tried to limit the list to what it considered a reasonable number while satisfying member states' most urgent interests. This outlook corresponded to its aim of implementing a liberal common commercial policy while affirming the regional dimension of the EEC in world trade. The Commission was perfectly aware that, once in the hands of the member states, the desired exceptions would grow in number. Its objective was to convince members to adopt a list that would constitute no more than 20 percent of the EEC's dutiable imports.[7]

---

[4] AECB BAC 118/83 851 Discussion du fevrier 28, 1964 entre Millet et Reimer, Oorschot et Hoogland (Dutch members of 111 Committee); AECB BDT 144/92 Marjolin cabinet papers box 777, Note à l'attention de Marjolin, June 1, 1964.

[5] AECB PV 274, May 27, 1964 and PV 275, June 2, 1964.

[6] CM2 1964/128, PV de la 144ème session du Conseil de la CEE, October 12–13, 1964. For a description of the Commission's list see also AECB BDT 144/92 Marjolin cabinet papers, box 777, Note, "Déroulement des débats au Conseil sur le problème des exceptions," November 11, 1964.

[7] AECB BAC 122/1991–24 Rapport du Comité 111 en ce qui concerne la proposition de la Commission relative à la liste d'exception de la Communauté, November 4, 1964; AECB

Table 5.8   Tariff lines excluded from the linear cut, for each sector (Commission proposals), as a percentage of total number of tariffs

Sector	Total exceptions		Partial exceptions		Total	
	Total number of tariffs	Positive tariffs	Total number of tariffs	Positive tariffs	Total number of tariffs	Positive tariffs
Chemicals	11	12	82	86	92	98
Textiles	22	24	10	109	122	133
Mechanical	32	32	91	91	122	124
Minerals and metals	55	69	12	151	175	221
Other	18	2	76	84	94	103
Total (excluding ECSC products and paper)	26	28	92	101	119	13
Total + conditional exceptions on textile					132	145

Source: AECB 122/1991–16, Négociations commerciales au GATT, Liste des exceptions (présentée par la Commission au Conseil), October 13, 1964.

Table 5.9   Exceptions as a percentage of the EEC's total imports and dutiable imports by sector and in total in 1963

Sector	Total imports	Dutiable imports
Chemicals	7	105
Textiles	23	8
Mechanical sector	94	96
Minerals and metals	38	227
Other	27	91
Total (excluding ECSC products and paper)	49	115
Total including conditional exceptions on textiles	61	144

Source: AECB 122/1991–16, Négociations commerciales au GATT, Liste des exceptions (présentée par la Commission au Conseil), G/415/64, October 13, 1964.

PV 293, November 13, 1964; HAEC—MAEF OW 36 R.132, Marjolin's Note reporting the Commission attitude towards the settng up of the exception list, November 13, 1964.

Negotiating the EEC Exceptions List

As the Commission expected, member states wanted modifications to its proposal. Italy, France, and, to a lesser extent, Belgium called for additional exceptions, while Germany and the Netherlands wanted the list trimmed. Only Luxembourg approved of the Commission's enumeration as it stood. The additions suggested by France and Italy were so numerous that, if accepted, the list would double in length. They justified their requests on the grounds that foreign competitors enjoyed natural, financial, and technical resources that put the Italians and French at a severe disadvantage. Moreover, the EEC had not yet reached a level of integration that would suppress the concept of national economies, and national governments still had to bear the consequences of the GATT negotiations. Equally important, France and Italy noted that they would have to withstand the cumulative reductions of joining the CET and those stemming from the round itself. Consequently, additional reductions in tariffs at the multilateral level had to be moderated.[8]

Germany and the Netherlands were deeply concerned by the French and Italian attitude. They underlined that the economic strength of the EEC and the ongoing expansion of its exports proved that protectionism was not needed. The EEC had to demonstrate a preference for freer trade in order to encourage other countries to do the same. A long list of exceptions would undermine the liberalizing aim of the Kennedy Round and work against the overall interests of the EEC, which, given its competitive capacity, had to make an effort to reduce tariffs and foster the expansion of world trade.[9]

After preparatory discussions in the 111 Committee and COREPER, final bargaining over the EEC's list of exceptions took place between November 11 and 15, 1964 in a Council of Ministers night-and-day endeavor.[10] The meeting was attended by the ministers of foreign affairs, commerce, and finance. The difficult, drawn-out nature of the proceedings should come as no surprise. Since 1958 the most important decisions within the EEC had resulted from marathon sessions, and in this instance major trade interests were at stake.

The discussion touched upon a vast number of industrial products. Attention in this chapter focuses on sectors that were most important in terms of trade volume and relations or that reveal a critical aspect of the EEC's trade policymaking.

---

[8] MAEF, DE/CE, 1961–66 GATT 932, Note de la Direction des Relations Economiques Extérieurs (DREE)—Ministre des Finances, November 4, 1964; ibid., Note 184/CE, "Négociation tarifaire au GATT," November 5, 1964.

[9] CM2 1964/128, PV de la 144ème session du Conseil de la CEE, October 12–13, 1964; AECB BAC 122/1991-24 Rapport du Comité 111 en ce qui concerne la proposition de la Commission relative à la liste d'exception de la Communauté, November 4, 1964.

[10] CM2 1964/143 PV de la 149ème session du Conseil de la CEE, November 10–15, 1964.

Directed by these criteria, the following discussion considers machinery and transport equipment, chemicals, aluminum, paper, and textiles.

Machinery and Transport Equipment

Because of the volume and dynamic growth of trade in machinery and transport equipment across the Atlantic and in Western Europe, this sector was crucial for the Kennedy Round. The members of the EEC had significant interests at stake and opposing aims to pursue. This made a common position particularly tough to achieve. Indeed, machinery and transport equipment produced the toughest confrontation between France and Germany. France demanded limited reductions in tariffs in order to protect its market from the United States and EFTA competition and retain its preferential access to Germany. French business sectors had requested exclusion of the mechanical electric and electronic sectors, machine tools, aircraft, and tractors. Moreover, French automobile builders wanted restrictive conditions, acquiescing to cuts in tariffs on cars only if equivalent reductions were made not just by the United States and the United Kingdom, but also by EFTA and the Commonwealth countries of Canada, Australia, New Zealand, and South Africa. On top of all this, French car-makers insisted on exceptions for cars weighing less than 2.5 tons, trucks, buses, and their detached accessories, keeping the EEC market closed to British and EFTA competition.[11] Couve de Murville and Giscard d'Estaing judged these requests untenable, considering that for transport equipment the CET was more than double U.S. tariffs and that Bonn was firmly advocating reductions. However, the two ministers accepted the automobile manufacturers' requests as a starting point from which to bargain. Italy shared French worries and asked for numerous exceptions to protect its industry and maintain preferential access to the German market. The Italian automobile industry, supported by the Italian government, wanted the whole sector to be excluded from tariff cuts on the ground that it was already reducing its duties to join the CET and that American multinationals controlled greater financial and industrial resources.[12]

As a net exporter competitive on a global scale, Bonn had a major interest in reducing tariffs. Machinery and transport equipment represented one-third of Germany's total exports, and in this sector it enjoyed a trade surplus with the United States. Half of Germany's production was exported, and it had a crucial interest in shrinking the CET as a bargaining chip to obtain reciprocal reduction

---

[11]   MAEF DE/CE GATT 930, Direction des Affaires Economiques et Financière—Service de Coopération Economique, Rapport adopté par la Chambre de Commerce et d'Industrie de Paris, May 9, 1963; MAEF, DE/CE GATT 932, Lettre de Erik d'Ornhjelm (Vice Président délégué de la Chambre syndacale des constructeurs d'automobiles) à Couve de Murville, July 7, 1964.

[12]   HAEC—MAEF OW 36 R.132, Note reporting the Commission attitude towards the setup of the exceptions list as described by Marjolin, November 13, 1964; AECB BDT 144/92 Marjolin cabinet papers, box 777, Liste d'exceptions Kennedy, November 13, 1964.

of EFTA and U.S. tariffs. Bonn did not share Italian and French qualms about competitiveness, arguing that numerous exceptions in a sector where the EEC's industries were robust could not be justified. As a net exporter, the EEC had every interest in adopting a liberal attitude so as not to provoke other countries, whose industries were less competitive, into creating their own exceptions.[13]

The broad issue was how liberal the EEC had to be in this critical sector. The diverging interests of members were so complicated that the debate among ministers was repeatedly shifted to the 111 Committee. Here the Commission played a mediating role, advancing package proposals in order to downplay differences of opinion. It held the middle ground and made a series of suggestions that proved successful, demonstrating that it possessed the technical expertise to set the terms of discussion, effectively define problems, and present solutions. Commissioners Jean Rey and Robert Marjolin made appeals to Rome and Paris to moderate their requests and persuaded the Dutch and the Germans to show an understanding of French and Italian anxieties. Also easing the deal was the urgent need to approve the list of exceptions. Eventually, the French representative in the COREPER, Jean-Marc Boegner, realizing that Paris had to eliminate some of its demands if it wanted to obtain the approval of others, withdrew 30 percent of its demands. Italy, after presenting additional requests for exceptions, completely abandoned them, showing a rather hesitant diplomatic position.[14]

The final compromise was a balanced and complicated set of concessions. Cars would be subject to a 50 percent reduction—as Germany desired—on the condition that reciprocity of concessions be attained—as France insisted. Buses and trucks and their parts, at the insistence of Italy and the Netherlands and despite German opposition, were included, but limited to trucks heavier than 4 tons. The list also included motors and detached pieces for heavy trucks; tractors; heavy buses and their parts, including motors; bicycles; and light aircraft and diesel motors, as France asked. Further exceptions covered sewing machines, certain machine tools, air conditioners, computers, nuclear reactors, radios, helicopters, airplanes (less than 2000 kilograms), public works machinery, and optical equipment. Primarily because of French insistence, an additional 2.8 percent of dutiable imports were protected from tariff cuts. Germany accepted this compromise with the clear understanding that the number of exceptions would be reduced in negotiating with other countries in Geneva.[15]

---

[13]   CM2 1964/143 PV de la 149ème session du Conseil de la CEE, November 10–15, 1964.

[14]   MAEF, DE/CE, 1961–66 GATT 932, Note, "Négociation tarifaire au GATT," November 20, 1964.

[15]   Ibid.

The Chemical Sector

The chemical sector is worth attention because of its importance to world trade. Moreover, it became the major stumbling block to the conclusion of the negotiations in May 1967, because of the U.S. customs valuation system of the ASP, which affected certain categories of products entering the U.S. market, in particular, benzenoid chemicals. Among the Six, Germany, France, and Italy had the most at stake. Germany had a strong and competitive industry and was willing to remove tariffs across Europe and the Atlantic. The German chemical industry attached considerable importance to abolition of the ASP, and it pressed the German government to exempt organic chemicals from reductions in tariffs if it was not eliminated.[16] France, too, was convinced of the need to eliminate the ASP. However, it had less at stake than the Germans, as the French chemical industry had only a small share in the American organic chemicals market. The French government was prepared to make moderate cuts, provided Washington removed the ASP, a stance was shared by the entire French chemical industry.[17] Italy, meanwhile, held that it was already bearing the pressure of increased competition within the EEC. It was wary of bargaining away tariff advantages for its newly developed enterprises. Italy opposed substantial tariff reductions and had no intention of making any meaningful concessions, hoping to defend the status quo by exploiting American unwillingness to abolish the ASP.[18]

The Commission, Italy, Germany, and the Benelux countries wanted to present the list of exceptions while simultaneously announcing that the EEC would reject any reduction in tariffs on organic benzenoid chemicals if Washington did not remove the ASP. In contrast, France wanted the EEC to refuse all negotiations unless the ASP was eliminated in advance. If the United States rejected this proposal, the EEC should withdraw the entire chemical sector from the round. Germany was reluctant to adopt such a tough attitude at the outset for fear that Washington would reciprocate, deadlocking the talks and dropping the chemical sector from the round. Several meetings between the 111 Committee and the Commission took place to work out a compromise. Here the Commission did not try to mediate. It stuck to its position, and eventually the German president of the Council of Ministers suggested accepting the French line. Thus, the Six adopted

---

[16]   PRO BT 241/844 Telegram no. 96 from Roberts, British Ambassador in Bonn, to Foreign Office, May 3, 1965, reporting conversation between Keiser, Stedfeld and Horn of the German Ministry of Economic, and Roberts, Hughes and Denman, and PRO FO 371/183386 Letter from Hughes to O'Neill, May 18, 1965.

[17]   MAEF, DE/CE GATT 931, Note, "Préparation de la Conférence KENNEDY—Opinions des producteurs français," February 5, 1964.

[18]   CM2 1964/143 PV de la 149ème session du Conseil de la CEE, November 10–15, 1964. The Italian stance is also described in NARA 364, Recs of USTR, box 5, Report of discussions between American officials and senior representatives of the Commission, June 28, 1966.

a firm stance in hopes of putting an end to the ASP. This bargaining chip might also be useful in responding to the pressure that the United States would apply in other sectors.[19]

Aluminum and Paper

Aluminum and paper played a key part in the round. They were central to trade relations between the EEC and the Nordic countries of Sweden, Norway, Denmark, and Finland, which exported the bulk of these two products, an important share of their total exports, to the EEC. To put pressure on the Six, the Nordics adopted a confrontational attitude. If the EEC was interested in enhancing its exports in other sectors—machinery and transport equipment in particular—tariffs had be reduced on aluminum and paper.[20]

The elaboration of a common position for primary aluminum required a tough clash between France, on the one hand, and the Commission, Germany, and Benelux, on the other. The problem, again, was how to reconcile diverging trading interests in a common commercial policy. In 1960, the CET had been fixed at 10 percent: France and Italy had decreased their respective duties of 20 and 25 percent, while Germany and the Benelux countries increased them, respectively, from 0 and 7 percent rates. The latter were granted a 5 percent tariff contingent, so that they could import a fixed quantity at this lower tariff. In the Dillon Round, the CET was fixed at 9 percent, with the retention of the tariff contingents. Within the EEC, France, with its leading firm Pechiney, was the largest producer of aluminum and was trying to establish a regional protected aluminum market in the EEC. The French had no intention of reducing barriers to imports from outside the EEC. By contrast, Bonn, pursuing a goal larger than that of protecting its state-owned firm, Vereinigte Aluminiumwerke AG, considered the requirements of its transforming industry, which sought primary aluminum from traditional suppliers at advantageous prices. In 1964, Germany imported 165,000 tons of primary aluminum, of which 15,000 tons came from the EEC and the rest from other countries, mainly Norway, the United States, and Canada. Given this position within the industry, Bonn favored a reduction of the CET. The Benelux countries also preferred a reduction, possibly to zero. They had no relevant national production and, in 1964, imported about 40 percent of their consumption from countries outside the EEC. The Italian aluminum industry held

[19]   CM2 1964/389 PV de la 65ème réunion du Comité 111, October 13, 1964; MAEF, DE/CE, 1961–66 GATT 932, Telegram no. 1217/30, Boegner au Quai d'Orsay, November 10, 1964; AECB BAC 122/1991–24 Aide-Mémoire du COREPER, November 10, 1964; AECB BAC 122/1991–24, Mise en œuvre des décisions prises par le Conseil lors de sa session des November 11/16, 1964.

[20]   AECB BAC 118/83 851 Discussion du fevrier 28, 1964 entre Millet et Reimer, Oorschot et Hoogland (Dutch members of 111 Committee); ibid. Note de Millet pour M. Verloren van Themaat, April 2, 1964.

the same position as Pechiney. It aimed to increase its production, was making new investments, and believed that a reduction of the CET would endanger this goal. The Italian government, however, could not ignore the fact that in 1964 it imported 88 percent of its aluminum from outside the EEC.[21]

The Commission proposed to reduce the CET to 7 percent with the elimination of the 5 percent tariff contingents. This latter element corresponded to the Commission's aim of implementing a full common commercial policy. Only the Netherlands approved this proposal. Germany, Belgium, and Luxembourg refused to abandon contingents, whereas France, weakly supported by Italy, would not reduce the duty. These stances were observed with concern by Rey. They would cause problems with the Nordics, endangering the possibility of reducing discrimination in other sectors. The Commission made no new suggestions, refrained from playing the role of mediator, and stuck with its proposal. Needing to elaborate a final compromise, the German president of the Council suggested that, unless it agreed on another solution in the course of the GATT talks, the duty of 9 percent would be maintained and the EEC would offer in Geneva the binding of the 5 percent tariff contingent. This solution added to the EEC's list of exceptions and differed greatly from the Commission's proposal.[22]

Not much easier were discussions over paper. All of the Six maintained that their own national paper industry was incapable of facing the Nordic competition. Their national enterprises were less developed and did not enjoy the same abundance of raw materials—indeed, for raw material the EEC depended on the Nordic countries, the dominant suppliers to Europe and providing the EEC with two-thirds of its pulp. The EEC claimed that the Nordic firms maintained artificially high pulp prices to ensure that foreign manufactured products could not compete with their exports.[23]

In framing its proposals, the Commission bore in mind the reaction of the Nordics and the difficulties that a substantial reduction of protectionism could cause to the EEC's industries. Equally important, it considered how to develop common commercial and industrial policies for this sector. Pulp paper and newsprint represented two-thirds of the EEC's imports from the Nordic countries in the paper sector. The EEC had an ad valorem duty of 6 percent on pulp paper, plus a free quota (bound in the GATT) of 2.1 million tons out of a total of 3 million tons imported in 1964. The growing EEC need for pulp explained the free quota, while the 6 percent duty was an instrument to encourage EEC industry to further invest in this sector. The Commission proposed to halve the duty and renounce tariff contingents. As for newsprint, the EEC had a 7 percent duty accompanied by an unbound free quota for France and Germany of 0.6 million tons (out of a total

[21]   AECB Marjolin cabinet papers, box 791, "L'aluminium au regard de la négociation Kennedy," November 11, 1964.

[22]   CM2 1964/143, PV de la 149ème session du Conseil de la CEE, November 10–15, 1964.

[23]   Ibid.

EEC consumption of 1.8 million tons). The Commission recommended reducing the duty by 50 percent and giving up contingents. Moreover, it suggested setting up a para-fiscal tax on the EEC consumption of paper and using the collected funds to subsidize the paper industry in order to compensate it for the tariff reduction. These concessions were conditional on a preliminary agreement with the Nordic countries addressing their producing and marketing policy. This solution would allow the EEC to cut tariffs while fostering its paper industry, in harmony with a regular expansion of its imports. The Commission tried to combine tariff cuts with measures of industrial policy that would favor the progressive adaptation by domestic enterprises to the tariff reductions.[24]

The Six agreed that the interests of the Nordics had to be considered, but disagreed on how to do so. Their position was complicated by their domestic industries' strong opposition to lowering barriers.[25] Bonn and The Hague held that some concessions had to be made to get tariff reductions in other sectors. They opposed the Commission's solution based on a para-fiscal tax, on the grounds that only national parliaments could impose taxes. The Italian Minister of Commerce Bernardo Matterella, Olivier Wormser of the French delegation, and Albert Borschette, the Luxembourger member of COREPER, believed that the Commission should inform the Nordics of the EEC's willingness to begin discussions on reductions in tariff and nontariff barriers. In the meantime, exempting the entire sector from cuts to tariffs was the best policy. Italy and France considered financial aid to be a preliminary to any concessions.[26]

The Commission strongly opposed the proposal to fully exempt the paper sector, as doing so would extend the EEC list. Rather than suggest a compromise, it stuck to its prior stance and avoided the role of broker. Once more, the final compromise was suggested by the German presidency of the Council of Ministers. Pulp paper and newsprint would be on the conditional and partial exceptions list; the rate of the partial cut was not specified. In presenting the list in Geneva, the EEC would underline that the rate of the exceptions depended on the results of discussions with the Nordic countries. Clearly, the concessions the EEC was prepared to make fell far short of what this group of countries expected, and troubles with them were just around the corner.[27]

---

[24] Ibid.

[25] MAEF, DE/CE GATT 931, Note, "Préparation de la Conférance KENNEDY— Opinions des producteurs français," February 5, 1964. Schulte, "Industrial Interest in West Germany's Decision against the Enlargement of the EEC," 35–61.

[26] CM2 1964/143, PV de la 149ème session du Conseil de la CEE, November 10–15, 1964.

[27] Ibid.

Cotton Textiles

The only sector on which the Six easily reached a compromise was cotton textiles. It is worth considering this product, as it well illustrates that the common commercial policy was still under construction and that liberalization in the GATT concerned, above all, trade among the industrialized countries. The EEC cotton textile industry was united in asking protection from competition from the LDCs. Particularly strong were the requests from the French, Italian, and German industries, which feared the competition of low-wage countries such as India, Pakistan, Hong Kong, and Sri Lanka. Moreover, within the EEC, Italy was a major textile producer and aimed to keep the EEC's current preferences. The textile industries of the other five members were already facing pressure from the Italians, and were not ready to be exposed to increased competition.[28] The member states wanted to avoid putting the entire sector on the exceptions list. Thus, they accepted the Commission's suggestion of a conditional list, claiming to being willing to reduce tariffs by 50 percent or to increase quota imports, provided that the Long Trade Agreement (LTA), which regulated textiles and which had been signed in 1962 for a duration of five years, was renewed.[29] The LTA was the first worldwide commodity-type agreement set up for specific manufactured products. Shorn of its embellishments, it was a market control scheme by which importers— mostly the advanced industrial countries—imposed quotas on exporters—mostly LDCs, plus Japan and Hong Kong. The agreement had little to do with *free* trade and much to do with regulation to the advantage of the inefficient importers.[30]

For at least two reasons, a common commercial policy was far from ready for cotton products. First, member states maintained national quantitative restrictions and different NTBs, among them safeguard clauses. For the Commission, negotiations on textiles had to serve the purpose of filling out the EEC common commercial policy by adopting a common regulation on the safeguard clause. Moreover, the Commission suggested combining the common commercial policy with harmonizing measures of industrial policy in order to allow the EEC members to face competition from low-wage countries, accelerate the structural adaptation of the EEC industry to global competition, and allow a progressive reduction in barriers to trade. For the Commission, elaboration of these two common policies

---

[28] AECB BAC 118/83 851 Discussion du février 28, 1964 entre Millet et Reimer, Oorschot et Hoogland (Dutch members of 111 Committee); AECB BDT 144/92 Marjolin cabinet papers box 777, Note à l'attention de Marjolin, June 1, 1964. MAEF, DE/CE GATT 931, Note, "Préparation de la Conférance KENNEDY—Opinions des producteurs français," June 5, 1964. For German industry, see Schulte, "Industrial Interest in West Germany's Decision against the Enlargement of the EEC," 35–61. For the Italian industry, Ruggero Ranieri, "Italian industry and the EEC," 185–98.

[29] CM2 1964/143, PV de la 149ème session du Conseil de la CEE, November 10–15, 1964.

[30] Curzon, *Multilateral Commercial Diplomacy*, 254–8.

went hand in hand. However, member states were completely unreceptive to these suggestions. Second, the EEC was not a signatory to the LTA. Only member states were. Despite the Commission's request that it be the sole negotiator for textiles, as it was for agriculture, also regulated by NTBs, member states decided that they would negotiate on the quantitative restrictions on a national basis, while the Commission would do so for tariffs. Thus, the common commercial policy was not completely common as it was deployed in Geneva.[31]

The EEC Exceptions List and its Implications

The final EEC list covered 19–20 percent of Community's dutiable industrial imports and 9 percent of all industrial imports.[32] The average level of the CET, which in 1963 was 12 percent, would be reduced by 33.4 percent, setting a new average of 8 percent. A total of 1148 tariffs were submitted to general linear cuts and 409 were exempted, 117 totally and 292 partially. Thirty-one tariffs were reduced conditionally. Member states added exceptions for a further 4.6 percent of the EEC dutiable imports beyond those the Commission had suggested. Table 5.10 shows the additional exceptions approved by the Council of Ministers.[33]

Many partial and conditional exceptions were necessary to reach a compromise, and in many cases difficult decisions were postponed. The exceptions rule permitted the EEC—and the other GATT members—to shield the most sensitive sectors from linear cuts, allowing the pursuit of the neomercantilism that characterized the EEC's commercial policies. Protectionism and freer markets managed to coexist in the political economy of trade liberalization by the Six. Yet overall, the final list showed that the EEC was assuming a liberal posture in world trade.

In a tense period, often described as dominated by the quarrel over grains, the Six were able to approve their joint list of exceptions. Their willingness to reach a compromise was never in doubt, and all of them demonstrated an eagerness to achieve it. The ability to establish a common list despite differing

---

[31] AECB BDT 144/92 Marjolin cabinet papers box 781, Note de la Commission sur l'opportunité d'accélérer la mise en place d'un politique commerciale commune dans l'industries du textile, April 30, 1964; ibid., "Politique Commerciale commune dans le secteur des industries textiles." Note d'information diffusée sous l'autorité de Rey et Levi Sandri, July 13, 1964.

[32] For the EEC final list AECB 122/1991-24, Mise en oeuvre des décisions prises par le Conseil lors de sa session des November 11/15, 1964, November 16, 1964; AECB Marjolin's cabinet paper box 791, Liste d'exceptions de la CEE pour le produits industriels, December 4, 1964.

[33] AECB, BDT 144/92, Marjolin cabinet papers, box 144, Répercussion des abaissements prévus par le Kennedy Round et des hypothèse adoptées par le Conseil de Ministres du novembre 14, 1964 and MAEF, DE/CE, 1961–66 GATT 932, Note, "Négociation tarifaire au GATT," November 20, 1964.

Table 5.10   Exceptions proposed by the Commission and further exceptions approved by the Council of Ministers (millions of U.S.$)

Exceptions proposed by the Commission		Further exceptions approved by the Council of Ministers	
Textile conditional list	156	Textile	10
Textile nonconditional list	48		
Chemicals	91	Chemicals	3
Mechanical sector	259	Mechanical sector	195
Metals and minerals	235		
		Pottery	7
Various	38	Various	35
Paper	68	Paper	150

Source: MAEF, DE/CE, 1961–66 GATT 932, Note "Négociation tarifaire au GATT," November 20, 1964.

national circumstances and needs showed the paramount interest the Six had in attending the round as a regional trading unit. These combined interests pushed them to reach a common position and, more generally, to meld their disparate commercial approaches into a common commercial policy. The participation in the round moved the Six in the direction of unity, and drove them to make the necessary adjustments to national preoccupations. The GATT talks represented an external stimulus. Equally important, trade interests were able to keep the six countries together, despite difficulties in other areas, showing that the customs union and the common commercial policy were the most critical undertakings of the EEC.

The interest of the EEC member states in attending the Kennedy negotiations as a regional trading area pushed them to find a compromise between states that wanted more exceptions to tariff reductions and those that wanted fewer. The GATT negotiations led the Six to define a common commercial policy, as the need to defend their regional unity and negotiate as a whole led them to compromise on their different trade interests in order to agree on this policy. Equally important, in the industrial section of the round, the Six were prepared to reduce tariffs. An interest in enhancing their exports worldwide led them to adopt a liberal stance so as to obtain, on a reciprocal basis, a reduction in other countries' trade barriers. They thus delineated the EEC's common commercial policy along freer trade lines, contributing to the liberalization of international trade.

The Commission demonstrated satisfaction with the results of the discussions. The list had been kept under the envisaged 20 percent limit and, according to Rey and Marjolin, reflected overarching EEC purposes rather than merely a collection of fragmented national interests. Moreover, the Council of Ministers set the EEC negotiating procedure in Geneva on terms that could strengthen the Commission's role as negotiator. Along the lines of the practice adopted at the Dillon Round, the 111 Committee would meet in Geneva so that the Commission could consult it. One observer for each member state could attend the negotiations with third countries without speaking rights. Most importantly, the Commission was given the right to set up informal meetings with the other participants, meetings that only its delegation could attend. Furthermore, the Commission expressed satisfaction with the role that it had played in the formulation of the list of exceptions. In effect, the Commission was able to provide essential technical expertise and play a key role as broker in disputes among the Six. With its technical fund of knowledge, it could make suggestions born out of its own preferences and, in this way, influence final decisions by the member states.[34]

Yet the approval of the exceptions list reveals the limits of the Commission's ability to determine the outcome in Brussels. Thanks to its technical expertise, it could propose compromises that advanced its own preferences, play the role of broker, and influence the final outcome. This was the case for mechanical and transport equipment sector. Here the Commission held a middle ground against the requests of the member states. Rey, Marjolin, Hijzen, and Millet made great efforts to mediate and elaborate acceptable compromises. However, the mediating roie of the Commission should be considered in light of the fact that Member states had a priority interest in reaching an agreement. As a matter of fact, they aimed to attend the GATT talks as a trading unit and this provided them with a strong incentive to compromise. This aspect eased the brokering role of the Commission. Moreover, the Commission was not always a neutral mediator, as the cases of aluminum and paper illustrate. Here, rather than occupy the middle ground, it maintained a rigid stance and stuck to its own preferences. In these cases member states reached an agreement through the mediating role of the presidency of the Council of Ministers. As it turned out, neither the Commission's right of initiative nor its capacity to mediate was crucial in producing a final agreement. National governments did not supply proposals and provide brokering while the supranational actor was doing so. However, when the Commission was not active or when its suggestions did not suit them, the member states themselves advanced proposals and mediation. Members were aware of one another's preferences and were able to reach an agreement that sidelined the Commission. The latter was able to implement its wishes—and therefore influence the final outcome in Brussels—only when its proposals appealed to the interests of the member states. When the Commission acted without making that appeal, member states modified or ignored its suggestions. Thus they kept in their hands the reins of the decision-making process and, hence, of commercial policy.

---

[34] AECB PV 294, November 18, 1964.

The Presentation of Exceptions Lists in November 1964

On 16 November 1964, exceptions lists for nonagricultural products were exchanged between the United States, the EEC, the United Kingdom, Japan, and Finland. Austria, Denmark, Sweden, Norway, and Switzerland declared that, conditional on reciprocity from other countries, they would not claim exceptions. All these countries would attend the round on the basis of the 50 percent reduction rule and were denominated the "linear" countries. Others would attend proposing specific offers rather than exceptions lists. These were either less developed countries or those with a special economic structure—exporters mainly of farm products or those whose economy lagged, without being considered LDCs.

The United States presented a list concentrated on a limited number of products, and with a few partial exceptions. Herter held that the United States had to play the leading role in increasing the scope of negotiations by appearing in Geneva with a shortlist to pressure other GATT members to do the same. Eighteen percent of U.S. industrial dutiable imports were exempted from the 50 percent tariff cut, but 8 percent were made up of oil products, not traded in the GATT.[35]

As for the EFTA, the small members did not present exceptions lists. Their course of action can be explained by tactics rather than by a real willingness to make 50 percent cuts across the board. Their goal was to put pressure on the EEC by emphasizing their liberal stance. London presented a short exceptions list, concentrated on a few items. It accounted for 4.7 percent of total British industrial imports in 1962 on an MFN basis, excluding, therefore, Commonwealth and EFTA preferences. The main items on the list were cotton textiles and associated man-made fibers, plastics materials, jute goods, lead, and zinc. In drawing up its list, the British government had encountered remarkably little resistance from British business sectors. After the French veto of British entrance into the EEC, the Kennedy Round constituted far and away Britain's best hope of reducing barriers to European trade.[36]

As soon as the lists had been exchanged, the bazaar began. The U.S. delegation pointed out that the EEC list was longer than its own; the Commission disagreed, claiming that the U.S. and EEC positions were perfectly comparable; Britain asserted that it was in "credit" with both of these trading partners; the latter two claimed that, on the contrary, a balance existed in this respect; Japan maintained that its list was in equilibrium with the others, but no other country was ready to

---

[35] "Products proposed to be excepted," Annex A-3, NSF National Security Council History, box 52, LBJL; NARA 364-130-51-23 Recs of USTR, box 1, Memorandum for the President from Herter, November 9, 1964. On the U.S. list see also, Preeg, *Traders and Diplomats*, 84–5 and Zeiler, *America Trade and Power*, 183–6.

[36] PRO BT 241/842 Note of the Board of Trade "Kennedy Round: List of Exceptions," May 29, 1964; PRO BT 241/843, Note of the Tariff Division of the Board of Trade written by Neale, November 5, 1964; ibid., "Kennedy Round—Lists of Exceptions," November 13, 1964.

recognize this assertion; the small EFTA countries claimed that, having offered no exceptions lists, they necessarily had a credit with everyone.[37]

Washington labeled the EEC list "disappointing at best," finding it restrictive both quantitatively and qualitatively, with elements of uncertainty, owing to largely unspecified partial offers.[38] According to U.S. data, in terms of dutiable nonagricultural imports, the U.S. offers to the EEC substantially outweighed the EEC linear offer to the United States. Washington asserted that the EEC exceptions hit 29.1 percent of dutiable nonagricultural imports from third countries and 26.1 percent from the United States. These figures disagreed with the 18.8 percent figure given by the EEC. Moreover, Washington claimed that tariff cuts on its dutiable nonagricultural imports from the EEC averaged roughly 45–46 percent, whereas the EEC's offers were between 30 and 40 percent, depending on whether conditional offers on chemicals were included. Most crucially, the EEC list hit the most dynamic sectors of U.S. exports, as Table 5.11 shows.[39]

Table 5.11   Categories of U.S. imports affected by EEC exceptions list

Brussels Tariff Nomenclature chapter	Description	Volume of U.S. trade affected (U.S.$m, 1961)	U.S. trade affected (%)
38	Miscellaneous chemical products	24	35
39	Artificial resins and plastic	38	55
47	Papermaking material	36	60
48	Paper, pulp, paperboard	35	95
51	Continuous man-made fibers	18	65
73	Iron and steel articles	24	15
84	Machinery and mechanical appliances	150	25
85	Electrical machinery and equipment	46	30
87	Vehicles	43	50
90	Miscellaneous instruments and apparatus	41	40

Source: NARA 364, Recs of USTR box 4, Memorandum of the Chairman, Country Committee I (EEC), November 2, 1964.

[37] AECB BDT 144/92, Marjolin cabinet papers, box 777, Note d'information "Négociations commerciales multilatérales du GATT—justification des listes d'exceptions," February 16, 1965.
[38] NARA 364, Recs of USTR, box 4, Memorandum of the Chairman, Country Committee I (EEC), December 2, 1964.
[39] NARA 364, Recs of USTR, box 4, Memorandum of the Chairman, Country Committee I (EEC), November 23, 1964 and ibid., Memorandum of the Chairman, Country Committee I (EEC), December 2, 1964.

Despite the complaints issued from all sides, in comparison to the previous GATT talks the Kennedy Round was launched with far more liberal initial offers, in terms of both the sectors of trade covered and the rates of tariff reductions. The initial offers were already greater than the final cuts achieved in previous rounds. The four major trading entities, the United States, the EEC, the United Kingdom, and Japan, made offers representing a substantial linear cut covering from 80 to 95 percent of their industrial tariffs. The United States recognized that considerable scope for reduction in world trade barriers existed and that the total EEC offers held out the possibility of significant improvement in U.S. trading opportunities.[40] A reciprocal interest in boosting export was evident and led governments to reduce duties and make concessions. Valuable results were attainable, despite the many barriers to progress.

The Negotiations in Geneva

Once lists were on the table, the bargaining started at a slow pace. Governments evaluated the lists of their partners and studied the obstacles to a reduction of tariffs in various sectors. The pace of the negotiations further slowed during the crisis of the Empty Chair. Equally important as a drag on progress, the agricultural part of the round remained locked until September 1966. Governments were biding their time, waiting for developments in this crucial sector. It was only at the beginning of 1967 that the bargaining got going in earnest.

As previously noted, the primary interests of the industrial countries lay squarely in machinery and transport equipment. The United States proposed no exceptions in this sector. Its industry was strong enough to bear a 50 percent reduction in duties, and it wanted a cut in other countries' protection. Washington was worried by the EEC exceptions, which heavily hit U.S. exports in this growing sector. The American delegation counted on the fact that the Six had to shrink their list of exceptions if they wanted to obtain reductions from the EFTA countries.[41] The British and the other EFTA countries had not presented exceptions, hoping that their liberal stance would push the EEC to significantly reduce duties. The machinery and transport equipment sector was the biggest group of British exports to the EEC. British discontent with the EEC's reserved tariffs was limited to certain items, notably radio sets and parts, machine tools, pumps, diesel engines, tractors,

---

[40] NARA 364, Recs of USTR box 1, U.S. delegation to the Sixth Round of GATT Trade Negotiations "EEC—Part 1, Delegation Evaluation of Offers," November 1, 1966.

[41] AECB—BAC 122/1991-3, Rapport no. 32 de la Commission, March 29, 1965; NARA 364, Recs of USTR box 1, Briefing for Governor Herter "USA–EEC talking points," June 3, 1966. For the automobile sector see Sigfrido M. Pérez Ramírez, "The role of multinational corporations in the foreign trade policy of the European Economic Community: the automobile sector between 1959 and 1967", *Actes du Gerpisa*, no. 38—"Variety of capitalism and Diversity of Productive Models."

and heavy lorries, for which the United Kingdom was the primary supplier to the EEC. With the EEC agreement to include cars in the 50 percent reduction and the Americans' lack of concern for the rest of the automobile sector, it became the subject of what amounted to an intra-European negotiation. None of the EFTA countries proposed any exceptions in the automobile sector, hoping that their markets would be attractive enough to push the Six to make concessions in such items as pulp paper and paper, aluminum, and wood products. Moreover, Sweden had a 24 percent duty on cars and believed that offering to halve it might push the EEC to match this cut with respect to trucks, tractors, and buses.[42]

Within the EEC, the Germans paid close attention to the Americans' and the EFTA's requests and attended the Geneva sessions with the clear intention of shortening the EEC's list.[43] The pressure of third countries combined with the German stance made machinery and transport a likely candidate for better offers by the EEC in the final agreement. However, because no particular obstacle impeded reductions in tariffs, apart from the willingness of participants, this sector was set aside while negotiations took place on the other industrial products and agriculture. Only in the final phase would it become central in the discussions.

As already observed, chemicals represented one of the talks' most turbulent topics. Herter and Blumenthal were irritated by the EEC's focus on the ASP and claimed that, for bargaining purposes, the EEC was exaggerating its importance. After all, the system applied to only 10 percent of U.S. chemical imports.[44] However, the EEC's stance was fully supported by the British, and the combined European pressure was too great to be ignored. Washington could not insist that its trading partners assume a liberal posture while it retained a protectionist and legally inconsistent device.[45]

The Europeans' stance put the U.S. delegation in Geneva in a difficult position. The American chemical industry did not feel such an urgency to reduce European tariffs that it would willingly relinquish the broad protection afforded by the ASP. On the contrary, it opposed the abolition of this NTB and preferred to enhance its exports through corporations in Europe. Moreover, the ASP had been established by Congress and eliminating it would necessitate congressional action. The U.S. government had subjected virtually the entire chemical sector to the 50 percent reduction, apparently a drastic step, since most of these tariffs had remained

---

[42]   PRO BT 241/844 Telegrams nos 17 and 28 from Cohen (UK Delegation to GATT) to Foreign Office, February 15, 1965.

[43]   PRO BT 241/844 Telegram no. 96 from Roberts, British Ambassador in Bonn, to Foreign Office, May 3, 1965, reporting conversation between Keiser, Stedfeld, Horn of the German Ministry of Economy, and Roberts, Hughes and Denman.

[44]   PRP FO 371/18339, Telegram no. 165 from Lord Harlech of the British Embassy in Washington to Foreign Office, January 25, 1965, reporting conversation between Roth and Commercial Minister at the Embassy Chadwick.

[45]   Memorandum for the President from Bator, December 7, 1965, Bator Papers, box 13, LBJL.

unchanged since the 1930s. In truth, it would have been difficult to do otherwise. The U.S. chemical industry was highly competitive. Thus, Washington had to cut across the board to appear credible in its effort to liberalize trade.[46] Despite this logic, internal difficulties meant that only in April 1966 did Blumenthal announce that his government would present a working hypothesis to remove the ASP.[47]

At this point, Rey pressed member states to put their exceptions on the table. The firm attitude that the EEC had displayed up to that time had pushed the Americans to present proposals to eliminate the ASP. Now it had to assist the discussions by listing its exceptions. The Commission's position was strongly supported by Germany. Critically, contrary to the position that the French had always taken, Couve de Murville concurred.[48] Accepting the proposals presented by the Commission, the Council of Ministers specified the rates of the partial exceptions. The Community would offer tariff reductions of between 22 and 30 percent and would indicate that it was doing so on the assumption that the ASP would be eliminated. Its offers on chemicals thus remained conditional, but at least the EEC had agreed to present them.[49]

At the beginning of May 1966, Blumenthal put forward the U.S. working hypothesis, which had two aspects. First, the ASP was to be replaced by a system of tariff protection, translating ASP duties into ad valorem equivalents. The converted rates would then be subjected to the 50 percent tariff cuts. Second, the United States would make a formal offer only in the framework of a package deal, separate from the tariff negotiations on the rest of the chemical sector. In exchange for the abolition of the ASP, GATT partners would make additional offers. This last point was crucial. It was the only way to present Congress and the American chemical industry with a settlement in which valuable concessions had been obtained. The U.S. tactic was clear: the ASP could not be the linchpin of the negotiations; if it were, the entire Kennedy Round would stand or fall on the basis of what Congress chose to do.[50]

The reaction of the U.S. partners to Blumenthal's plan was one of great frustration. They rebuffed the American request for additional offers and wanted the United States to cut its higher rates by more than 50 percent in order to eliminate disparities. To cap it all off, in Blumenthal's working hypothesis the outcome

---

[46]   PRO BT 241/844, Telegram no. 137 from Baker (UK delegation to GATT) to Foreign Office, June 25, 1965; Trade Talk Review, vol. XI, no. 2, February 26, 1964, Herter Papers, box 13, JFKL; Memorandum for the President from Roth, October 5, 1965, Roth Papers, box 1, LBJL.

[47]   AECB—BAC 122/1991-4 Rapport no. 62 de la Commission, June 3, 1966.

[48]   CM2 1966/4 PV de la 177ème réunion du Conseil de la CEE, February 28 to March 1, 1966.

[49]   AECB BAC 62/1980-55 PV de la 227ème réunion du Comité 111, March 29, 1966; AECB PV 355, April 4, 1966; CM2 1966/16 PV de la 182ème session du Conseil de la CEE, April 4–5, 1966.

[50]   Memorandum for Bator from Roth, April 25, 1966, Roth Papers, box 2, LBJL.

would be subject to the whims of Congress, with the American legislative body having final say on the negotiations.[51]

Within the EEC there was a large range of views. Despite its dissatisfaction, the Commission believed that it was dangerous to dismiss the only proposal on the table. Bonn was willing to accept the American suggestion as a starting point in order to avoid a stalemate. France adopted a similar position. By contrast, Italy was firmly opposed to Blumenthal's idea. As previously stated, Rome was using the ASP as a pretext for blocking or limiting negotiations over chemicals. The Netherlands, too, took a tough position. Thus, the Commission was unable to convince the Council of Ministers to accept the working hypothesis even as a point of departure for discussions. It was only under strong pressure by the Germans, in the absence of opposition by the French, that the Council of Ministers, rather than dismiss it out of hand, agreed to charge the 111 Committee with analyzing the implications of the American proposal.[52] However, the EEC remained paralyzed by internal divisions and, by the end of 1966, had not yet decided whether to accept the plan as a basis for negotiation. The year ended in deadlock.

While the chemical sector was a transatlantic negotiation, aluminum and paper composed a predominantly intra-European one. The decision by the EEC to exempt aluminum from cuts to tariffs was predictably criticized in Geneva. The EEC's aluminum industry was made up of strong and efficient enterprises, well equipped to face a reduction in protective tariffs. Companies had gone beyond their national boundaries and joined in investments in other countries with their principal foreign competitors.[53] The insistence of Canada, United States, and, above all, Norway led the Commission to reopen the issue in Brussels with the full support of Germany and the Benelux countries. The Commission insisted on its 1964 proposal, consisting of reducing the duty from 9 to 7 percent and eliminating the tariff quota. The entire negotiations until May 1967 consisted of convincing the French to reduce the duty. However, the pressure from the Commission and the other five members was not enough to move France, for Paris had never been unwilling to defend a stance it took in isolation. Given this resolve, the Council of Ministers could only reaffirm the level of the duty at 9 percent and charge the 111

---

[51]   PRO FO 371/189598, Telegram no. 63 from Melville to Foreign Office, May 4, 1966; AECB—BAC 122/1991-5, Communication de M.M. Rey, Marjolin et Colonna di Paliano, "Etat d'avancement des travaux dans le secteur de la chimie," June 8, 1966.

[52]   CM2/17509, Rapport de Borschette à la Présidence du Conseil de la CEE, June 12, 1966; CM2 1966/34 PV de la 188ème réunion du Conseil de la CEE, June 13–14, 1966; NARA 364, Recs of USTR box 5, Report of discussions between American officials and senior representatives of the Commission, June 28, 1966; PRO FO 371/189598 Telegram no. 118 from Melville to Foreign Office, July 12, 1966.

[53]   AECB PV 345, January 19, 1966, Annex "Rapport de la Commission au Conseil."

Committee and the Commission with defining the volume of the 5 percent tariff contingents to be presented in Geneva.[54]

Negotiations on the contingents were no less thorny. France wanted to allow only a small contingent, so as not to nullify the retaining of the duty. Germany, Benelux, and the Commission wanted a larger allocation in order to import from third countries at lower prices and improve the quality of offers to Norway.[55] It was only at the Council of Ministers of mid-June 1966 that the Six finally reached an agreement. Under the proposals presented by COREPER president Borschette, the Council maintained the 9 percent duty and offered the consolidation of a 5 percent tariff contingent on imports totaling 100,000 tons. This was a compromise between the French, who had demanded a level of 50,000–60,000 tons, and the others, who had asked for 120,000.[56] Germany was disappointed by this settlement. However, because of the French intransigence and the necessity of offering a proposal in Geneva, Bonn reluctantly accepted it. Germany, Benelux, and the Commission, however, had no intention of giving up. Thus the EEC approached the Geneva talks with France firmly determined to defend the agreement reached in Brussels and with the Commission, the Benelux countries, and Germany resolutely determined to modify it.[57]

Predictably, in Geneva the offer was labeled disappointing, as it did not provide improved access to the EEC's market. Hijzen defended the offer, pointing out that the EEC foresaw an increase in production, a slowdown in consumption, and, as a consequence, a decreased level of imports from the EEC. Thus, the consolidation of the contingents represented an important guarantee for exporters. Ultimately, no other meeting took place because the various positions were so far apart that an agreement appeared impossible for the time being.[58]

As for the paper sector, bilateral negotiations between the EEC and the Nordics started in early 1965. By early 1966, Hijzen and the Swedish ambassador,

---

[54]   AECB PV 355, April 4, 1966 and CM2 1966/16 PV de la 182ème session du Conseil de la CEE, April 4–5, 1966.

[55]   ANF 724711 1964–67, box 3, Telex COMICECA/642 Boegner au SGCI, May 25, 1966, AECB BAC 62/1980-59, PV de la 86éme réunion du Comité 111, June 6–8, 1966. AECB—BAC 122/1991-5, Communication de M.M. Rey, Marjolin et Colonna de Paliano, "Etat d'avancement des travaux dans le secteur Aluminium," June 8, 1966.

[56]   CM2/17511, Note de la Présidence, June 10, 1966; CM2/17509 Rapport de Borschette à la Presidence du Conseil de la CEE, June 12, 1966; CM2 1966/34 PV de la 188ème réunion du Conseil de la CEE, June 13–14, 1966.

[57]   CM2 1966/34 PV de la 188ème réunion du Conseil de la CEE, June 13–14, 1966; PRO FO 371/189598, Telegram no. 833 from Foreign Office to Bonn on the Anglo-German Economic Committee meeting of July 20–22, 1966.

[58]   AECB BAC 62/1980-59, Compte rendu "Réunion du Group sur l'aluminium— juillet 1966," July 26, 1966; AECB—BAC 122/1991-5, Rapport no. 74 de la Commission, July 18, 1966; PRO FO 371/189599, Note, "Aluminium" by the Tariff Division of the Board of Trade, October 1966.

Nils Montan, representing the Nordic countries, were getting nowhere. The Commission insisted on an agreement determining the price and marketing policy of the Nordics. Montan claimed that these policies concerned the Nordic firms and, therefore, were not within governmental competence.[59]

This stasis was looked upon with concern by the Commission, which started to pressure the member states to take important steps to unlock the talks. It suggested completing the elaboration of exceptions and presenting them in Geneva despite the lack of agreement on price policy. The Commission offered its November 1964 proposals. In response, the Dutch and the Germans suggested alternatives, consisting of maintaining the tariff rates while consolidating large zero-duty contingents together with annual increases in the consolidated contingent, corresponding to a percentage linked to the increase in EEC consumption. In this way, they hoped to favor the Nordic countries while maintaining protection. The Dutch–German proposals were opposed by France, Italy, and Belgium, which backed the Commission's version.[60]

Against Dutch and German opposition, the Commission suggested a compromise. Grounded on new proposals offered by the Commission, in June 1966 they agreed to offer a 50 percent reduction on pulp paper; the resulting 3 percent duty would then be suspended at a pace to be determined. On the internal front, subsidies could be granted by the member states, but would depend upon national legislations. On newsprint, the 7 percent rate would be maintained and a zero-tariff contingent would be offered and bound for 420,000 metric tons—lower than the existing unbound quota—as the Germans and Dutch had requested. For other basic paper, paper products and cartons, the reduction would be between two and four percentage points, as the Commission had requested. As a result, the CET for these products, which currently ran at 16–21 percent, would be reduced to 13–17 percent. The paper sector would be subjected to an average reduction of 14.7 percent, with 85 percent of dutiable imports and 52 percent of all imports exempted, most of them partially. Moreover, the offers remained conditional on concluding a bilateral agreement on the Nordic countries' price and marketing policy.[61] In this case as well, Germany accepted these proposals to start off the

---

[59]   AECB BAC 62/1980-59, "Deuxième rencontre entre la CEE et les pays scandinaves concernant les produits de l'industries papetière (24.11.1965)," December 7, 1965.

[60]   AECB BAC 62/1980-55, "Note de la réunion du Comité 111, March 21, 1966." AECB BAC 62/1980-59 "Proposition des délégations allemande et néerlandaise relatives au secteur des pâtes et du papier-journal," June 13, 1966; CM2/17509, Note d'Information de la réunion du Comité 111, March 30, 1966; CM2 1966/16 PV de la 182ème session du Conseil de la CEE, April 4–5, 1966.

[61]   AECB BAC 62/1980-59 PV de la 85ème réunion du Comité 111, May 23, 1966; AECB—BAC 122/1991-5, Communication de M.M. Rey, Marjolin et Colonna di Paliano, "Etat d'avancement des travaux dans le secteur pates et papier-autres," June 8, 1966; AECB BAC 62/1980-59 PV de la 86ème réunion du Comité 111, June 6–7, 1966; CM2 1966/34 PV de la 188ème réunion du Conseil de la CEE, June 13–14, 1966.

talks with the Nordics, with the clear understanding that they would be improved in the course of the negotiations, despite a request to increase protection coming from the German paper industry.[62]

As predicted, the reaction of the Nordics was negative. They considered the EEC offers insufficient to permit them a share in the increased level of consumption and asked a 50 percent reduction, with abolition of contingents. Moreover, in a turbulent meeting in November 1966 with Hijzen, the Nordic delegation refused to subject the tariff reduction to an agreement on marketing conditions. They interpreted the request as an excuse not to make concessions. These bilateral negotiations were interrupted and shifted to the multilateral level at the end of 1966.[63]

No easier were the discussions over textiles. During the 1960s, worldwide exports of cotton textiles were losing ground to other textiles, particularly man-made fibers. While exports of other textiles grew by more than 60 percent from 1960 to 1966, cotton textiles increased only marginally. However, cotton textiles were becoming important in the economies of the LDCs. From 1960 to 1966, the volume of exports of cotton yarns and woven fabrics of the industrial countries declined by 21 and 13 percent respectively, while exports from the LDCs increased by 22 and 10 percent. Thus, cotton products were crucial in the relations between LDCs and the industrialized countries.[64] When the Kennedy Round was launched, the former had been told that the round would represent an opportunity for LDCs to increase their exports. This assurance was intended to mollify critics who considered the GATT a rich men's club. To prove their goodwill, the developed countries agreed that LDCs would not be required to grant reciprocity in the exchanges of concessions with them. However, when such promises needed to be transformed into facts, trouble emerged. The industrialized countries did not appear to intend to concede a great deal. The case of cotton textiles fully illustrates their reluctance.

As noted, this sector was regulated by the LTA, and by 1964 the LDCs' disappointment with the agreement was evident. They criticized the rich countries' loose interpretations of market disruption, which triggered barriers to imports, and complained that importing countries were the sole judges of whether their markets had been disrupted. The LTA represented legalization of discriminatory actions in order to frustrate, rather than promote, the LDCs' exports. Thus, they demanded

---

[62] PRO FO 371/189599, Note, "Pulp and Paper" by the Tariff Division of the Board of Trade, October 1966.

[63] AECB BAC 122/1991-19, "Entretiens entre la délégation de la CEE et les délégations unique des pays nordiques, 8.11.1966," November 9, 1966; AECB—BAC 122/1991-7, Rapport no. 88 de la Commission, November 22, 1966.

[64] For a good account of the negotiations in the textile sector, see Norbert Kohlhase and Henri Schwamm (eds), *La négociation CEE Suisse dans le Kennedy round* (Lausanne, 1974), 139–57.

an end to the LTA and warned that results in this area would be crucial to their assessment of the negotiations and the GATT in general.[65]

While the LDCs tried to kill the LTA, the United States, the United Kingdom, and the EEC asked to renew it for five more years. Indeed, renewal represented an outstanding priority. If the LTA were not renewed, textile imports could be restricted only through violations of GATT rules.[66] Wyndham White looked with concern on the deep opposition this extension faced; it might bring no meaningful result and could dangerously increase the LDCs' dissatisfaction with the GATT. For this reason, he took an active role in elaborating a negotiating ground and ensuring that the LDCs would receive concessions. He tried to secure a package deal involving tariff reductions, an increase in quotas, and more liberal implementation of the LTA by importers in exchange for a renewal of the agreement by exporters.[67]

Among exporters, only Japan and Hong Kong accepted Wyndham White's plan. These two traditional exporters were subject to competition from new ones—Pakistan, India, South Korea, and the United Arab Republic—and were willing to renew the LTA so as to ensure for themselves part of the U.S. and European markets. However, the plan was rejected by the new exporters, which refused to renew the LTA in its current form, fearing that it would become permanent. In the face of these conflicting interests, the United States searched for bilateral agreements with the exporting countries.[68]

The negotiations between the EEC and the exporting countries adopted a slower pace. The exporting countries had preferred to await the end of the crisis of the Empty Chair before negotiating with the EEC. After January 1966, the EEC preferred to see what progress the United States made in bilateral negotiations to determine whether the LTA could be renewed. It was only at the end of October 1966 that the Commission met, on a bilateral basis, with the exporting countries. For the EEC these bilateral discussions were difficult. They included the general question of residual restrictions and other national import controls, over which the Commission lacked authority. Thus, a bilateral agreement first had to be made between the member states and exporters, and then the Commission could negotiate on the tariff side. As 1966 drew to a close, the renewal of the LTA looked far from certain: the EEC had just started its negotiations on cotton textiles, and, to the annoyance of other countries, it continued to hold up negotiations into early 1967.[69]

---

[65]   NARA Congressional Record—House, August 29, 1966, 20991–1001.

[66]   Evans, *The Kennedy Round in American Trade Policy*, 231.

[67]   PRO BT 241/845, Note by Hughes of discussion with Mr Wyndham White in Geneva on September 23, 1965.

[68]   PRO BT 303/152 "United States–United Kingdom discussions in Washington, November 8–10, 1965: Kennedy Round, brief for Sir Richard Powell," note by the British delegation to GATT, October 28, 1965.

[69]   NARA 364, Recs of USTR, box 5, Telegram no. 2343 from Rusk to various posts, May 27, 1966, reporting conversation between Hijzen and Herter; AECB—BAC 122/1991-6 Rapport no. 86 de la Commission, November 7, 1966.

Pressures on the EEC

In mid-1966, to move the bargaining in the industrial sector ahead, Wyndham White called on the participants to reach an assessment of other countries' offers by November 1966. They would have to specify the improvements they expected from other governments and the offers they would withdraw if additional concessions were not received. For the general secretary, "a brutal confrontation" among the participants was necessary to make progress.[70]

In this phase the EEC came under severe pressure. It cannot be explained simply by offers that were considered insufficient. The problem was also its trade policymaking. Other countries calculated that drawing more concessions from the Six would be difficult because of the EEC's political cross-currents and its complex decision-making machinery. Once a compromise had been reached in Brussels, after extended negotiations that balanced the different interests of the member states, it was difficult to change this equilibrium in a new bargain in the GATT. The Commission arrived in Geneva with a "take it or leave it" position, an inflexible mandate rather than a bargaining position. The Brussels institution demonstrated no flexibility in the exchange of concessions; it had little leeway, and talks were tortured and frustrating. The Commission's power to negotiate had been a major problem from the beginning, and it became particularly so in the last phase, during which concessions had to be given. Repeatedly, the United States and the EFTA countries had asked the EEC member states to give more flexible directives to the Commission, but to no avail. As noted in the previous chapter, until July 1966 the EEC's internal bargain on the trade negotiations was linked to approval of the CAP. With this approval still pending, the Commission's delegation had no freedom to negotiate; member states—France above all—wanted the CAP approved before the conclusion of the round. Moreover, some member states—and, again, France above all—tended to sit in an arm chair until third countries offered them concessions in order to successfully conclude the round. Thus, the EEC could afford to keep their negotiators in Geneva on a very tight leash, leaving almost no room for autonomy and discretion. While in this phase the Commission played an active role in setting a common stance in Brussels, in Geneva it acted as a mere *porte-parole*, since member states gave it no flexibility in bargaining with other countries.

Against this background, other countries concluded that changes in the EEC list of exceptions would only be achieved under the threat of specific withdrawals. The assessment in November called for by Wyndham White would crystallize the differences of opinion among participants and, accordingly, precipitate a crisis that could force the EEC to improve its offers. The purpose of the plan settled on by those across the negotiating table was to compel the EEC Council of Ministers to

---

[70]   NARA 364, Recs of USTR, box 5, memorandum of conversation among Wyndham White, Blumenthal and Roth, Washington, June 14, 1966.

make friendlier proposals and give the Commission leeway it had hitherto lacked.[71] It is worth noting that this same strategy was recommended by the Germans and the Commission. As the British put it, "friendly Commission and German sources" had repeatedly made it clear that the only way to extract improved offers was to confront the EEC with withdrawals of sectors of special interest to its national enterprises. The way to get concessions was to bare some teeth.[72]

On November 30, 1966, the United States, the United Kingdom, Japan, the Nordic countries, Switzerland, Austria, and Canada presented the lists of improvements of offers that they wanted from their trading partners, the offers they would totally or partially withdraw if improvements were not conceded, and the concessions they themselves were willing to make. The EEC decided not to offer any lists. Such formulations would have required another Council of Ministers marathon and painful negotiations. Neither the Commission nor the Six ever considered holding such talks. They preferred to receive the appraisals and get ready to negotiate the final phase.

When the lists were exchanged, it became clear that the EEC was the main target of the other delegations. Washington presented a withdrawal list hitting 5.4 percent of U.S. imports from the EEC.[73] The British list hit the mechanical sector.[74] The Nordics applied shock treatment. To maximize pressure, they pooled their lists, withdrawing 32.4 percent of their imports from the EEC. The mechanical sector was most affected, with automobiles making up one-third of the list. These withdrawals hit Germany in particular. The strategy was to push Bonn, with major interests in the Nordic market, to convince the EEC to make concessions.[75]

The EEC was now under fire to rectify the imbalance in negotiating positions to forestall extensive withdrawals. The United States and the EFTA countries clearly transmitted the message that the EEC represented the major stumbling block to successful negotiations. At this point, it was up to the EEC to respond.

---

[71]   NARA 364, Recs of USTR, box 1, Background Paper, "Negotiations with the EEC," July 1, 1966. Ibid., box 5, Letter from Blumenthal to Herter, October 23, 1966.

[72]   PRO BT 303/396 letter from Denman (Geneva) to Douglas Carter (Board of Trade), June 17, 1966.

[73]   NARA 364, Recs of USTR, box 1, U.S. delegation to the Sixth Round of GATT Trade Negotiations "EEC—Part 1, Delegation Evaluation of Offers," November 1, 1966; ibid., "Assessment of offers as of November 30, 1966," November 30, 1966.

[74]   AECB BAC 122/1991-18 Compte Rendu de la réunion du October 13, 1966, "Négociations bilatérales avec la Suède," October 27, 1966. AECB—BAC 122/1991-7, Rapport no. 91 de la Commission, December 9, 1966.

[75]   Administrative History of STR, Narrative History, vol. 1, box 1, LBJL.

Chapter 6

Negotiations in Agriculture: In the Shadow of the Common Agricultural Policy

Protectionism in Agriculture and the GATT: A Longer Perspective

In 1963, participants in the Kennedy Round agreed to try to "provide for acceptable conditions of access to world markets for agricultural products ... in furtherance of a significant development and expansion of world trade." However, the participating countries disagreed on the path to this goal because of their different conceptions of the purposes of the Kennedy Round. It was against this background that negotiations over agriculture started in May 1965, after almost three years spent haggling over the rules under which the talks would be conducted.

When agriculture was explicitly included as a point of negotiations in the Kennedy Round, governments were fully aware of the difficulty of reaching valuable results. Foreign trade in farm products was a complicated issue with a long tradition of protectionism among the developed countries. More recently, with the agricultural crisis of the 1870s and 1880s in Western Europe, barriers had been raised still higher. Grain prices fell dramatically as a result of the steady expansion of American and Australian production and a decrease in ocean freight rates. While some nations reacted by shrinking their agricultural sector, others reacted with trade protection. The Netherlands and Denmark specialized in livestock and dairy products, but France, Germany, Austria–Hungary and the countries of southern Europe reacted to competition from overseas by setting duties on grain, and then on the other agricultural products whose price depended on grain. During the interwar period, protection increased further when overproduction and falling demand caused prices and farmers' income to crash. Traditionally protectionist countries supplemented tariffs, which were ineffective because of the fall in prices, with quotas and licences, closing their markets to the flood of low-cost products. The Netherlands and Denmark, which had been relatively open to trade, reacted with export subsidies and pricing mechanisms to close the gap between domestic and export prices. As a result, virtually the entire agricultural sector was protected against outside competition. In this case the wave of protectionism also touched the United States. In the 1920s, the United States supported farm prices and incomes through increased tariffs. During the depression years of the 1930s the Roosevelt administration created a more direct form of intervention through price supports and subsidies to exports. The divorce between agriculture and marketplace pricing was thus complete.[1]

In 1947, under the pressure of big exporting countries like Australia and Canada, the GATT was applied to all trade, without distinguishing between agricultural and industrial trade. In truth, the United States and the Western European countries had no intention of weakening the protection and support they gave to their individual agricultural sectors. Instead, they pursued the goal of stabilizing and increasing the revenues of farmers and deemed the liberalization of trade incompatible with that aim. Moreover, domestic pressures created incentives to give special treatment to agriculture. The United States therefore asked and obtained—in Article XI of the GATT—the right to restrict imports of agricultural products when necessary to control domestic production. The Western European countries, which favored quantitative restrictions (QRs) for balance-of-payments reasons, got their wish in Article XII of the GATT, which authorized QRs. In 1955 the GATT contracting parties were forced to approve an open-ended waiver requested by Washington to enable it to comply with the Agricultural Adjustment Act enacted by Congress in 1954–55. That act imposed on the administration the duty to introduce QRs on a range of agricultural imports whenever such protection was needed to implement U.S. agricultural policies. On the other side of the Atlantic, practically all European countries were still facing balance-of-payments deficits, which allowed them to apply QRs on a wide range of farm products. Thus, the GATT did not prevent a widespread reinforcement of agricultural protectionism. Although its rules applied to agricultural and industrial trade alike, the first four rounds concentrated on cutting customs tariffs in the industrial sector, and agriculture escaped GATT discipline.[2]

In the mid-1950s, widespread concern grew over the agricultural sector. Canada, Australia, and New Zealand began to demand that agriculture be subject to GATT rules. The urgency of the issue increased when the Six presented the Treaty of Rome, which foresaw the organization of trade in agricultural products, in Geneva in 1958. With this major breakthrough at the European level, the big exporters and the United States insisted on bringing agriculture within the GATT rules so as to soften European discrimination. Discussions started in Geneva on agricultural protection, the inadequacy of GATT rules to promote the expansion of trade in agriculture, and appropriate corrective steps. In 1958 the Habeler report was published. It highlighted the high level of protection, the accumulation

---

[1]   For an account of protectionism of agriculture in Europe see Michael Tracy, *Government and Agriculture in Western Europe, 1880–1988* (New York, 1989) and Warley "Western Trade in Agricultural Products," 287–402. For American protectionism see Evans, *The Kennedy Round in American Trade Policy*, 61–77. For a broader view of the history of agriculture, see Giovanni Federico, *Feeding the World. An Economic History of Agriculture (1800–2000)* (Princeton, NJ, 2006).

[2]   For a description of agriculture treatment in GATT the best accounts remain T.E Josling, Stefan Tangermann, Thorald K. Warley, *Agriculture in the GATT* (London, 1996) and William P. Avery (ed.), *World Agriculture and the GATT* (Boulder, CO, 1993).

of surpluses by low-cost producers, and the inability of existing GATT rules to deal with these problems. A subsequent GATT working committee—Committee II—examined the policies of individual countries and reported in detail on the general autarky that had evolved in member countries.[3] In these circumstances, Washington clearly identified the trend toward greater agricultural protection in Western Europe, and the prospect that techniques of protection largely outside the procedures of the GATT might be applied by the EEC. Supported by the major exporting countries, it pressured the EEC to relax existing measures of protection.[4] The Americans' request to include agriculture in the Kennedy Round was therefore the continuation of attempts made since 1958 to diminish the discriminatory effects of the CAP and of conflicts in trade policy left over from the Dillon Round. The Kennedy Round was the first set of GATT talks in which agriculture came to the fore and a comprehensive attempt was made to deal with farm products.

As noted previously, the leading governments had decided to negotiate a new international agreement on grain, for which an arrangement already existed. In 1949, the International Wheat Agreement (IWA) had been signed by Australia, Canada, France, the United States, Uruguay, and certain wheat-importing countries. It had been renewed many times, most recently, in 1962, for five years. Addressing the two basic problems of international trade in cereals—the instability of prices and the surpluses produced by developed countries—the double aim of the IWA was to ensure supplies to importers and markets for exporters at stable prices, and to help with the disposal of surpluses. Importers promised to buy and exporters promised to sell certain fixed quantities of wheat to each other in each year of existence of the agreement's life. Maximum and minimum prices were also agreed upon. Guaranteed purchases and sales would operate only at the price limits.[5]

The agreement, however, was deficient. Argentina and the Soviet Union, two major producers, had not joined. Moreover, IWA had very limited engagements. It covered only prices and permitted a rather wide range, between U.S.$1.625 and 2.025 per bushel. In fact, prices on grain exchanges tended toward the higher limit, but they were not maintained by cooperation between importers and exporters. Rather, the United States and, to a lesser extent, Canada limited their sales, at considerable cost, to maintain stable wheat prices. In other words, the essential instrument to guarantee price stability was the concerted policy of Washington and Ottawa. In contrast, the market in feed cereals was not organized, and prices tended to drop.[6]

---

[3]   Curzon, *Multilateral Commercial Diplomacy*, 166–8.

[4]   NARA Department of State, 1960–63, CDF, box 872, GATT "Draft Progress Report of Committee II 'Effects of Protection on Trade'," October 18, 1960 and ibid., "Official report of the US delegation to GATT Committee II on Expansion of Trade, October 6–20," November 21, 1960.

[5]   On the origins of the IWA see Frank H. Golay, "The International Wheat Agreement of 1949," *The Quarterly Journal of Economics* 64, 3 (1950), 442–63.

[6]   ANF 724.713, box 4, Note pour le cabinet du Ministre 127/CE, "Project d'accord mondial sur les céréales," April 26, 1965.

At the ministerial meeting of the GATT in December 1961, the Cereals Group was set up to study trade in grain. It was tacitly understood that the major issue was continued access to the EEC's markets in light of its decision to subject cereal imports to a system of variable levies.[7] In 1963, the governments signatory to the GATT decided that the Cereals Agreement should be negotiated by this group. Divergences remained regarding its elements, in particular, access to supplies, the level and role of international prices, and the financing of food aid. At the 1964 session of the Cereals Group, Washington had been prepared to negotiate on the MDS, provided that UGPs were set at a low level and the EEC gave an access guarantee. The EEC had opposed the latter request as incompatible with the CAP and maintained that negotiations on price and MDS were sufficient to regulate trade in grain. The major disagreement between the EEC and the big exporters was clear: guarantees of access. It was on this question that discussions would concentrate.[8]

Trade Patterns in Grain and the Divergent Interests of the Six

The largest portion of the discussion in this chapter is dedicated to grain, which was of crucial importance in the Kennedy Round. It was the commodity with the largest volume of trade between the United States and the Western Europe and made up the bulk of U.S. exports to the EEC. Moreover, decisions about trade in meat and dairy products depended on the treatment of grain. Most importantly, grain was a test of how the EEC's variable levy mechanism would be accommodated in the world trading system. The negotiations in Geneva over grain would show what position the Six wanted to have in world trade in farm products.

To fully appreciate the development of, and results from, negotiations over grain, it is essential to observe the trade patterns. A look at the structure of trade will shed light on the difficulties the United States faced in its negotiations with the EEC, and in particular its lack of bargaining power. As noted in the previous chapter, although the volume of trade in the agricultural sector was smaller than that in the industrial sector, the United States exported substantially more in agriculture than it imported from the EEC, with the result that, in 1964, out of a total U.S.$1.752 million U.S. trade surplus, the agricultural surplus represented U.S.$700 million.[9]

Table 6.1 illustrates the composition of U.S. agricultural exports by major commodity. The bulk of these exports were in oilseeds, wheat and feed grain.

---

[7] Preeg, *Traders and Diplomats,* 152–3; NARA Department of State, 1960–63, CDF, box 872, Telegram no. CA-2508 Circular Telegram, April 18, 1962.

[8] MAEF DE/CE GATT 931, Note, "Session du group céréales du GATT", March 20, 1964; ibid., Réunion agricole du GATT, April 6, 1964.

[9] OECD SITC Rev. 2—Historical Series 1961–90 (Paris: OECD 2000).

Table 6.1   Composition of U.S. agricultural exports to the EEC, by commodity (thousands of U.S.$)

Commodity	1958	1960	1961	1962	1963	1964	1965	1966
Variable-levy commodities								
Wheat	79,000	46,332	173,039	50,606	63,365	67,085	70,283	107,259
Feed grains[a]	158,000	197,146	194,012	336,457	295,182	334,433	478,099	498,405
Rice	5,854	6,894	15,035	14,247	13,399	15,378	10,139	18,823
Beef and veal meat	31	38	49	64	163	1,064	1,511	647
Pork	400	418	561	341	2,061	8,624	377	1,334
Lard	2,100	2,326	3,401	2,134	2,543	2,489	1,062	1,104
Dairy products	1,800	2,997	2,084	3,603	22,551	54,398	30,473	1,213
Poultry and eggs	364	28,551	45,835	53,479	30,613	31,676	30,747	236
Non-variable-levy commodities								
Fruit and vegetables	71,631	57,665	69,952	93,070	102,225	88,695	106,402	91,851
Oilseeds[b]	71,052	120,245	134,294	174,028	169,860	235,840	245,208	301,624
Unmanufactured tobacco	96,452	97,003	97,384	106,609	104,983	106,877	107,738	122,690

Note: [a] Feed grains are SITC categories 043 (barley), 044 (maize), and 044 (rye and oats). [b] Includes soybeans.

Source: SITC Classification; *OECD SITC Rev. 2—Historical Series 1961–1990* (Paris, 2000) and OECD Exports, Series B, 1958 and 1960.

Table 6.2   U.S. exports by destination in 1965 (thousands of metric tons)

	Wheat and wheat flour	Feed grain
EEC	1,197	8,803
EFTA	584	2,439
Japan	1,864	3,971
Developing countries	14,435	1,473
Sino-Soviet bloc	71	416
Other	946	3,774
All countries	19,097	20,875

Source: OECD Commodity Trade: Exports, Series C, 1965.

Table 6.2 illustrates the major destinations of exported American cereals. The EEC was the second largest market after Japan for wheat and the largest market for feed grain.

These data indicate why cereals took on such importance and urgency for the Atlantic alliance. Wheat and other grains made up the bulk of trade in agricultural products. Indeed, it was for this basic commodity that the EEC established the CAP and the variable-levy system. With its prominent position in world trade in agriculture, and as the prime destination for U.S. exports, the EEC was the key to lowering barriers to agricultural trade.

As for the EEC's trade balances, its members were, with one exception, importers of grain. Only France was a significant exporter. Table 6.3 shows the grain suppliers to the EEC's members, excluding France. All of them imported more grain from outside the EEC than from France.

Table 6.3   Imports of cereals by EEC members, excluding France, in 1964, by country of origin (in tons)

SITC	Argentina	Australia	United States	Canada	France	Rest of the world
Italy						
041 Wheat	150	0	112,000	66,000	202,000	11,000
043 Barley	280,037	28,155	212,678	40,678	28,096	272,998
044 Maize	2,212,609	0	2,162,184	2,649	61,000	714,173
045 Other cereals	149,426	11,858	274	6,974	1,853	13,599
Federal Republic of Germany						
041 Wheat	137,000	105,000	394,000	676,000	170,000	161,000
043 Barley	88,561	63,302	285,169	687	383,905	382,247
044 Maize	139,000	0	1,079,000	2,000	364,000	410,000
045 Other cereals	177,181	125,319	166,392	56,773	16,828	136,462
The Netherlands						
041 Wheat	119,000	4,000	377,000	58,000	45,000	2,000
043 Barley	7,140	17,643	103,576	3,869	62,706	28,274
044 Maize	165,000	0	1,578,000	63,000	5,000	19,000
045 Other cereals	157,222	10,035	671,173	93,016	1,844	62,521
BLEU						
041 Wheat	37,000	1,000	58,000	267,000	134,000	1,000
043 Barley	102	1,781	12,368	—	153,778	56,333
044 Maize	163,000	0	464,000	1,000	6,000	72,000
045 Other cereals	86,235	995	43,275	17,822	27,952	25,175

Source: OECD SITC Rev. 2—Historical Series 1961–1990 (Paris, 2000).

Table 6.4   Rate of EEC members' self-sufficiency in cereals in 1964

	EEC	Germany	France	Italy	Netherlands	BLEU
Wheat	90	70	109	95	32	68
Rye	98	107	103	46	75	69
Barley	84	65	123	48	39	47
Oat	92	91	101	85	68	86
Maize	64	2	105	79	—	1
Average	85	77	110	87	35	51

Source: Istituto Statistico delle Comunità europee, Annuario di statistica agraria, 1970.

Table 6.4 illustrates the EEC's self-sufficiency rate (the ratio of total production to total domestic consumption) in grain. France was the only country self-sufficient in all grains, and thus a potential exporter, whereas the other five countries were not self-sufficient in any grain, with the exception of the Federal Republic's production of rye.

The elaboration of a common position for the EEC thus required a difficult compromise between the opposing interests of the one exporter, France, and the five importers. Agreeing on a stance from which to negotiate in Geneva meant holding a version of the Kennedy Round on a smaller scale in Brussels. The EEC as a whole wanted to regulate trade in cereals through a commodity arrangement and also hoped to gain its trading partners' acceptance of its farm policy. However, these common interests were opposed by country-specific differences that promoted disagreements among the Six.

In joining the EEC, France pursued the clear aim of getting preferential advantages for its agricultural products, wheat and feed grain in particular. French cereals were competitive at the EEC regional level but were uncompetitive on world markets, given cheaper American, Canadian, Australian, and Argentine alternatives. The level of world prices thus represented an obstacle to French exports, and Paris needed the EEC to purchase French surpluses, particularly of wheat. France counted on the CAP as a means to this end. Wheat was France's most serious problem in agricultural trade, posing questions of market access and the financing of exports and surpluses. As Table 6.5 shows, in 1964, about 61 percent of French exports in wheat went outside the EEC. Also for other cereals, the rest of the world took a considerable amount of its uncompetitive exports.

Uncompetitive on the world market, it required heavy subsidies at great financial cost. Moreover, the surplus required expensive stockpiling. French agricultural costs drained national finances, and an EEC solution appeared indispensable to the French government, which intended to shift the burden of surplus disposal to its EEC partners. Preferential access to the EEC's markets, combined with exclusion of competitive imports from third countries, would rid France of its surplus. France shared the U.S. interest in joining an international

Table 6.5   French exports of cereals by destination in 1964 (in tons)

SITC	FRG	Italy	Netherlands	BLEU	UK	Rest of the world
041 Wheat	273,000	227,000	41,000	134,000	474,000	1,818,000
043 Barley	487,058	114,163	35,720	157,775	51,150	1,737,853
044 Maize	366,000	61,000	5,000	7,000	44,000	340,000
045 Other cereals	17,544	1,562	1,004	27,946	306	25,234

Source: OECD SITC Rev. 2—Historical Series 1961–1990 (Paris, 2000).

arrangement. Provided that the CAP was not endangered, France was eager to stabilize the flow and prices of basic commodities, wheat in particular.[10] The long-standing French concern in a world agreement on grain was to bring discipline to exchanges by fixing minimum prices for commercial transactions. Paris wanted to set world wheat prices at as high a level as possible in order to shrink the gap between French and international prices and, consequently, reduce the need to subsidize exports. During the EEC's discussions on a common price for cereals, France had pushed for a low figure, as high prices raised the cost of exports and production. However, once high prices were established, France desired a boost in world prices to diminish the difference between the latter and the EEC price level.[11] Moreover, France held that the United Kingdom, Japan, and other developed importing countries, plus the whole Communist bloc, were "getting a free ride" from the existing market system, with low import prices that they made no effort to maintain. Hence, from the viewpoint of Paris, any agreement needed to include provisions whereby "freeriders" assumed the burden of maintaining the price level.[12]

French aims generated problems within the EEC, as they conflicted with those of Italy, Germany, and the Netherlands in particular. They were net importers of wheat and feed grain from outside the EEC, mainly from North America and Argentina. They hoped that the final arrangement would guarantee this flow and insisted that the EEC take into consideration the need to maintain a reasonable level of imports. The Germans repeated their request that quantitative assurances

[10] HAEC—MAEF 36 OW, Note, "Politique européenne de la France—Questions économique," May 17, 1963; ANF 724.713, box 4, Premier Ministre, Comité Interministériel pour les questions de Coopération Economique Européenne, Note, "Négociations commerciales multilatérales au GATT: secteur agricole," April 1, 1966.

[11] ANF 724.70/10, box 1, Premier Ministre, Comité Interministériel pour les questions de Coopération Economique Européenne, Note, "Vue d'ensemble sur les négociations commerciales au GATT," April 1, 1966.

[12] Telegram no. 5518 from Bohlen (U.S. Ambassador to France) to State Department, April 1, 1965, NSF, CF Germany, box 184, LBJL.

were to be given to third countries, while the Dutch insisted on an automatic safeguard clause in case EEC imports fell below a given level. The preparations of the Six for the Cereals Arrangement became entangled in these divergences.[13]

The EEC's Preliminary Discussions on a Commodity Agreement

In adopting its mandate for the Commission in December 1963, the Council of Ministers had approved the binding of the MDS as an instrument to bring discipline to world exchanges. Thus, a basic agreement existed among the Six. Yet it was fragile and could not hide the incompatible interests at stake. It was in the context of this clash of interests that on April 7, 1965 the Commission presented to the Council of Ministers its draft for the agreement on grain to be offered in Geneva. As already noted, the Commission considered the Kennedy Round an opportunity to regulate agriculture at the world level and deemed the commodity agreement a first step in this direction. The aim of the Commission was to promote worldwide cooperation to achieve a balance between production and long-term demand, the elimination of short-term fluctuations through an enlargement of existing demand and of international markets, and the stabilization of international prices at what the Commission deemed an equitable and higher level. Equally important, Mansholt was aware of the discriminatory effects of the CAP and considered the commodity agreement an opportunity to bring them under control. The elaboration of the CAP also had external ramifications that rose to the surface in the GATT talks, which would have the double function of establishing an international market compatible with the rules of the CAP, and of moderating its negative aspects. It was with these preferences in mind that the Commission drafted its proposals.[14]

These proposals centered on prices, cooperative management of surpluses, and the binding of the MDS. Regarding prices, the Commission considered the international price of reference a means to determine the support to be given to national producers, an instrument to stabilize world exchanges, and a North Star by which to orient long-term production and exchanges. Thus the Commission suggested setting a world price of reference below which sales on the world market would be prohibited. This price would be fixed so as to permit the most efficient producers to sell on the world exchanges without resort to export subsidies, implying a rise in international prices equivalent to the amount of such subsidies. The Commission insisted on stability in world markets as a means to stability

[13] MAEF DE/CE GATT 931, Note, "Session du group céréales du GATT", March 20, 1964; ibid., Réunion agricole du GATT, April 6, 1964; ibid., Compte-Rendu d'un entretien avec Rabot, April 9, 1964.

[14] AECB PV 313, April 7, 1965 "Schéma d'un arrangement général 'céréales' pour le Kennedy Round"; CM2 1965/314 PV de la 70éme réunion du Comité 111, April 7, 1965; ANF 724.713, box 4, Note pour le cabinet du Ministre 127/CE "Project d'accord mondial sur les céréales," April 26, 1965.

in the EEC market, and one way to achieve equilibrium was to fix and respect an international price of reference. The Commission considered its proposals on international prices essential to a coherent functioning of the CAP. For Mansholt, this common policy had to reduce the use of subsidies and increase prices paid to farmers. The international price of reference together with the variable levy was needed to stabilize domestic markets and world exchanges. If third countries respected the international price, the CAP levy would not be variable.[15]

To maintain the price level, the Commission plan foresaw limitation and discipline of global supply through consultations among exporters and importers, and engagements to finance stockpiling and the disposal of surplus among industrialized countries. In a parallel way, the Commission envisaged measures to enlarge nonsolvent demand in favor of LDCs through a food aid program. The third element of the Commission's proposal was the binding of the MDS for three years. This consolidation represented a pledge that all governments were to make, as the creation of acceptable conditions of access required commitments on domestic policies. The three basic elements of the Commission's proposal were fully compatible with the CAP principles. Thus, the establishment of rules at the multilateral level was the external dimension of the talks taking place in Brussels for the organization of the market in grain. The elaboration and operation of the CAP also had an external dimension, necessary for the stable functioning of the policy itself and for the world market.

The Commission showed a clear vision of how to organize agriculture and tried to promote its outlook through the GATT talks. It considered these negotiations crucial to implementing the kind of regulation of world trade it supported. Moreover, the Commission also saw in them an opportunity to affirm its role as negotiating agent for the EEC. Both the Commission and EEC member states attended the Cereals Group sessions with speaking rights. At a meeting of the group in 1963, the Commission showed up flanked by representatives of member states; its own participants were "very anxious not to state anything in any way that would upset the representatives of the six member countries sitting behind him. So it was not only difficult to make a decision but even to make a statement."[16] The aim of the Commission was therefore not only to prevent disruptions by member states, but also to get them out of the talks altogether.

The first matter on which the Six divided was prices. The Belgians, Italians, Dutch, and Germans opposed the Commission's proposal, which implied that an increase that would boost production and, consequently, surpluses. Importing countries would then be financially responsible for the disposal of surpluses created by exporters. Equally important, it would put companies that processed cereals in an unfavorable competitive position, as the raw commodities would

---

[15] AECB PV 313, April 7, 1965 "Schéma d'un arrangement général 'céréales' pour le Kennedy Round"; NARA 59 State Department 1964–66 box 450 Telegram ECBUS 826 from Fessenden to State Department, February 3, 1965.

[16] Eckes, *Revisiting U.S. Trade Policy*, 62.

become more expensive. The German minister of economics, Kurt Schmücker, also opposed an increase because it would reduce the EEC's budget revenues from levies. In contrast, Olivier Wormser of France wanted a rise in the international price of reference to reduce the gap between it and the EEC price, making French wheat more competitive on the world market. In addition, a much higher price would boost production and finance the sale of surpluses to LDCs. If revenues from customs protection decreased, it was wise to bear in mind, Wormser pointed out, that the aim of the agricultural policy was not to create revenues. However, Mansholt had no intention of giving up on international prices, so important to the Commission's vision of organizing agriculture on a global scale. Rather than elaborate a compromise, he remained firmly attached to the Commission's proposals.[17]

Divisions among the Six also existed over proposals to limit global supply. According to the Dutch, limits to production were necessary. The Germans pointed out that the Commission had not included any measure affecting access to the EEC market. Moreover, the Dutch and the Germans found the consultations procedure insufficient to ensure respect for the reference price and requested more rigorous measures, such as production limits and import quotas.[18] Germany, Benelux, and Italy, meanwhile, criticized the Commission's ideas on the food aid program. As net importers, they had no wish to finance disposal of surpluses. Germany, in particular, already concerned by the high costs of the CAP, did not want to absorb new expenses for surpluses it had not generated.[19]

The French deemed measures directly limiting production to be incompatible with the principles of the CAP, which were grounded on price mechanisms. They accepted the principle of discipline and shared responsibility to solve problems of imbalances in supply and demand. Until that time, the United States had borne the burden of keeping prices stable in world markets. In Geneva, the U.S. negotiators would surely ask importers for quantitative commitments on the level of their imports and stocks as a way to maintain discipline on world markets. These instruments would lead to restrictions on quantity that France rejected. Thus in the absence of such quantitative discipline, the French believed that it was dangerous to reject any financial responsibility to keep grain markets in balance. By offering to share the burden with the United States, the EEC would be in a stronger position to refuse any quantitative concessions.[20]

---

[17] CM2 1965/314 PV de la 70éme réunion du Comité 111, April 7, 1965; CM2 1965/30 PV de la 166ème réunion du Conseil de la CEE, April 8, 1965.

[18] BT 241/844 Telegram no. 96 from Bonn to Foreign Office, May 5, 1965 reporting conversation between the German Stedfeld and Hughes.

[19] ANF 724.711B—Agriculture, Premier Ministre, Comité Interministériel pour les questions de Coopération Economique Européenne, Note CE/5934, June 11, 1965.

[20] ANF 724.713, box 4, Note pour le cabinet du Ministre 127/CE "Project d'accord mondial sur les céréales," April 26, 1965; ibid., Note du Ministère de l'Agriculture, undated but written in May 1965.

According to the schedule approved in Geneva, talks over grain were to be started in May 1965. Lacking time to discuss the Commission's proposals, the Council of Ministers approved the plan of setting minimum and mandatory international prices of reference for commercial exchanges and establishing a food aid program whose cost would be borne by developed countries. Then it charged the 111 Committee and COREPER with further study of the issue.[21] Thus, the Commission received only vague instructions, but discussions in Geneva could start and the EEC could arrive with proposals, rough though they were.

The First Stage of Negotiations in Geneva

On May 17, 1965, the EEC, the United States, Australia, Canada, the United Kingdom, Japan, and Argentina presented their proposals for an agreement on grain. While in the industrial sector each major participant was both an exporter and an importer and therefore had an interest in reducing trade barriers, in grain there was significant polarization into exporting and importing countries. Japan and the EFTA countries were importers; the EEC was the largest importer, but France was an exporter of soft wheat and had a major interest in increasing its exports of feed grain to the EEC. Australia, the United States, Canada, New Zealand, and Argentina were exporters.

Undersecretary of State George Ball believed that a cereals arrangement was of great importance in establishing access to the markets of the importing countries and in multilateral sharing of the food aid burden. The EEC's unified grain prices could bring about an abrupt drop in U.S. exports as French producers shifted their sales from other countries into markets, such as Germany, that the United States had traditionally dominated. The arrangement on cereals was necessary to soften this effect and maintain and possibly enlarge the U.S. market. The Americans were aware that they would have to reduce their exports of wheat, as the EEC was almost self-sufficient and France had a great surplus. However, Ball held that Europe's total food requirements were likely to increase as improved living standards were reflected in a shift to protein consumption that would increase the EEC's demand for feed grain.[22]

The United States also wanted to set up a new food aid program. Such a program had been a major component of U.S. foreign assistance since the end of World War II. Originally, it had had the dual purpose of meeting both foreign policy objectives—by responding to needs for food abroad—and the domestic

[21]   HAEC BAC 512 Résumé des principaux problèmes de fond soulevé lors d'une premier examen préliminaire des propositions de la Commission en matière céréalière, undate but written in April 1965; CM2 1965/30 PV de la 168ème réunion du Conseil de la CEE, May 13–14, 1965.

[22]   "Components of a Strategy for the Kennedy Round," Preliminary Draft, written by Ball, December 10, 1963.

desideratum of exporting large U.S. stocks of agricultural products.[23] In the Kennedy Round the United States had above all the aim of managing wheat supplies. To the extent that other countries diverted excess production to food aid, room would be created for commercial imports, thus reducing pressure on export markets. This channeling of aid was central to the U.S. plan. Support from the EEC and other importers would alleviate the U.S. burden of aid and, above all, open an opportunity for U.S. sales to importers by keeping the EEC's surplus out of commercial markets. The Americans' emphasis on a cereals agreement increased after the EEC set common prices for grain at high levels. With the likely growth in EEC production, the agreement became an instrument to protect U.S. exports to the EEC.[24]

At the end of May 1965, the members of the GATT started extended negotiations on the Cereals Arrangement that would be completed only during the last hours of the round in May 1967. As the major net importer in the process of establishing a discriminatory and restrictive CAP, the EEC became the main target of exporters. Discussions concentrated on three major issues: access, international prices, and food aid. The three issues were interrelated, although debate centered on the most difficult one, access. Exporters were critical of the EEC's offers to bind the MDS. In view of the high level of EEC prices, they considered it of little value unless it was supplemented by a firm effort to provide access for a definitive volume of imports. Blumenthal requested specific engagements, such as the reduction of UGPs, direct measures to limit production, and quantitative guarantees.[25]

Pierre Malvé, representing the Commission in this first round of discussion, defended the EEC's position by referring to trade data. Since 1957, the EEC's average self-sufficiency rate had remained stable at 86 percent, and net imports of grain at 10 million tons. For 1969–72 the EEC aimed to maintain the same self-sufficiency rate and level of imports. In this sense, the consolidation of MDS was an indirect means to control production and continue this same level of imports. On top of this, Malvé expressed the irritation of the Commission over the progress of the negotiations. While the EEC was ready to make commitments, exporters focused on what importing countries had to do, but had not yet clarified the commitments they themselves were willing to make, in particular their domestic policies. Exporters and importers alike had to contribute. Blumenthal, however, rejected Malvé's approach. According to Blumenthal, the cereals agreement was to be placed in the context of the Kennedy Round; thus reciprocity was to be considered *global* reciprocity.[26]

---

[23]   Administrative History of the Department of State, vol. I, chapter III, International Economic relations, "Food aid abroad and PL 480," box 3, LBJL.

[24]   Letter from Kenneth Auchincloss to Herter, April 7, 1965, Herter papers box 1, JFKL.

[25]   AECB BAC 122/1991-3, Rapport 45 de la délégation de Commission pour les négociations du GATT, July 9, 1965.

[26]   Ibid.

As for the international prices of grain, the Commission presented its conception of prices and suggested a moderate rise. Japan and the United Kingdom firmly refused to go along with this offer, as they opposed paying higher prices for their imports. Exporters had mixed reactions and were divided in their preferred strategies. Higher prices would stabilize and perhaps increase revenues from exports, and for this reason were supported by Canada, Argentina, and Australia. However, rigid and unrealistically high prices might encourage additional production. On this ground, they were opposed by Washington, which bore the major burden of maintaining the agreed-upon level. For feed grain, the United States strongly resisted an arbitrary rise in prices that might weaken its strong competitive position in this growing market. Consequently, it considered the best option to be an agreed price range related to normal trading conditions.[27]

The EEC and the United States differed on how to arrange food aid. Washington wanted a flat annual commitment independent of commercial market conditions, while the Commission suggested that aid be tied to the disposal of surplus production. Japan and the United Kingdom were reluctant to contribute to any food aid program. Assistance was the concern of countries with a surplus to distribute, not importers, they claimed.[28]

Despite these differences, both the EEC and the United States had a strong interest in reaching a compromise. However, any meaningful negotiation was stopped dead when the EEC was caught up in the crisis of the Empty Chair. Thus, in November 1965, negotiations were suspended, with the EEC under heavy pressure from exporters to improve its offers.[29]

Completing the EEC Mandate: A Balance of Divergent Trade Interests

As shown in Chapter 4, the marathon talks that led to the approval of the EEC mandate for agriculture took place from February until the end of July 1966. They ran parallel to the approval of the CAP financial regulations, and progress in the two fields was synchronized. Exporters' firm opposition to negotiating only on the MDS and the EEC's desire to conclude the agreement encouraged the Commission and member states to adopt a more flexible approach. In elaborating

---

[27]   PRO FO 371/189781, Note, "Cereals in the GATT Kennedy Round" Draft, undated but written in April–May 1966.

[28]   PRO BT 241/844, "Note of a meeting held in the office of Ambassador Roth in Washington on 25th May," attended by Powell, Chadwick, Cullen for the British and Roth, Hedges (STR) and Greenwald (USSD); AECB BAC 122/1991-3, Rapport 45 de la Commission, July 9, 1965; ANF 724.713, box 4, Premier Ministre, Comité Interministériel pour les questions de Coopération Economique Européenne, Note, "Négociations commerciales multilatérales au GATT: secteur agricole," April 1, 1966.

[29]   AECB PV 345, January 19, 1966, Annex, "Rapport de la Commission au Conseil sur les négociations commerciales au GATT," NCG (66)3.

its additional proposals, the Commission considered that, if the EEC were able to create a provision guaranteeing access to its markets, the Americans could embark on negotiations with good prospects of success.[30] At the same time, the Commission had to keep in mind that Germany, worried about the financial impact of the CAP, remained hostile to common financing of surpluses and the food aid program. France would reject any quantitative guarantee to third countries, while the Italians, Germans, and Dutch opposed an increase in world prices.[31]

At the end of March, the Commission presented additional proposals. It suggested a rise in the price of wheat amounting to U.S.$4–5 a ton. Thus, if the average cost of Red Winter no. II United States (Free on Board Baltimore) for 1962–65 of U.S.$60.5 per ton were raised by such a figure, the international reference price would be U.S.$65. For feed grain, the Commission proposed only a partial and limited readjustment. The majority of feed grain entered the world market without export subsidies, with the exceptions of grain from the EEC and South Africa. The Commission suggested a limited readjustment ranging up to U.S.$3 for the different kinds of feed grain to avoid disrupting the existing relation between the prices of wheat and feed grain, following the increase in the international price for wheat.[32]

In order to be flexible and meet other countries' request for guarantees on access, the Commission suggested a mechanism to set a limit for surpluses that a country could produce, applying to importers and exporters alike. It proposed binding the self-sufficiency rate for three years. If it were exceeded, as an automatic corrective instrument, governments would set up mandatory consultations to discuss appropriate market reorganization measures and automatic mechanisms to limit supplies or to enlarge demand through the multilateral food aid program. This obligation would create a financial deterrent to excess production. Moreover, the penalty provisions would oblige the EEC member states to face up to the costs of their own domestic policies. With these proposals, Mansholt and Rabot hoped to reassure the Americans and, at the same time, rapidly gain the approval of the Six in order to start negotiating in Geneva.[33]

---

[30] PRO BT 241/845, Private office minute no. 62, Memorandum of conversation between Rey, van Kleffens (ECSC representative to the United Kingdom), Douglas Jay (President of Board of Trade), Hughes and Carter, January 25, 1966.

[31] CM2 1966/4 PV de la 177ème réunion du Conseil de la CEE, February 28 to March 1, 1966; CM2 1966/8 PV de la 179ème réunion du Conseil de la CEE, March 21, 1966.

[32] CM2 1966/8 PV de la 179ème réunion du Conseil de la CEE, March 21, 1966 and AECB BAC 122/1991-4, "Communication de la Commission au Conseil en vue de compléter la proposition de la CEE relativement à la négociation d'un arrangement général 'céréales' dans le cadre des négociations commerciales du GATT," March 25, 1966.

[33] Ibid.; NARA 364 Recs of the USTR, box 5, Telegram no. 1012 from Fessenden/ USEC) to State Department, reporting conversation between Blumenthal, Hedges, Rabot, Malvé and Schlosser in Brussels, May 17, 1966 and NARA 59 1964–66 ECIN 3, box

The Commission's hopes were short-lived. The French also presented a plan, one that had nothing in common with the Commission's. Consequently, progress slowed in Brussels. At the Council of Ministers meeting of March 21, 1966, Edgar Faure, the French minister of agriculture, presented the same Baumgartner–Pisani plan that the French government had unsuccessfully offered in Geneva in 1961. Faure claimed that, in the Commission proposals, food aid only had the residual role of eliminating surpluses that could not be absorbed otherwise. In contrast, the discussion over grain in Geneva had to allow the EEC to define its general conception of agricultural and food aid policy. Hence, the agreement had to be considered from two points of view: trade among countries that would purchase products at markets prices, and assistance to LDCs. This double orientation required a greater increase in the international price of grain than that suggested by the Commission, U.S.$10 a ton for wheat, in order to boost production to a level sufficient to cover the food requirements of the LDCs. From the French point of view, this plan had the advantage of reducing the difference between the world price and the EEC price, thereby making French exports more competitive worldwide.[34]

Italy, Germany, and the Benelux countries rejected the French plan. They wanted only a small increase in prices. Moreover, the French proposal put the burden of food aid on the shoulders of importers, who had to pay higher price for their imports. The Germans also opposed the plan because it decreased revenues from levies on imports. The strongest opposition came from the Netherlands. The minister for agriculture, Barend Biesheuvel, argued that the French suggestion raised a question of political choice. The Western world had to decide whether to follow an agricultural policy adapted to solvent purchasers or to carry out production and price policies adapted to the larger needs of the world population. The French proposal showed an orientation toward humanitarian needs, but was also extremely favorable to producing countries. For Biesheuvel, the Western countries had to improve living conditions in LDCs through a policy of aid in the field of technical assistance and investments and not through food aid. Thus Italy, Germany, and the Benelux countries approved of the Commission's suggestions as good basis for negotiations. Even if Germany was unenthusiastic about financial involvement, it welcomed the binding of the self-sufficiency rate as a device to meet the requests of third countries.[35]

792, Memorandum of conversation between Rabot and American officials of the State Department, "EEC grains proposals and related matters," May 23, 1966.

[34]   CM2 1966/8 PV de la 179ème réunion du Conseil de la CEE, March 21, 1966; ANF 724.713, box 4, Premier Ministre, Comité Interministériel pour les questions de Coopération Economique Européenne, Note, "Négociations commerciales multilatérales au GATT: secteur agricole," April 1, 1966.

[35]   CM2 1966/8 PV de la 179ème réunion du Conseil de la CEE, March 21, 1966; NARA 364 Recs of the USTR, box 5, Memorandum of conversation between Lahr, Blumenthal and Fessenden in Bonn, April 25, 1966.

From the end of March until the middle of June, the efforts of the Five and the Commission were concentrated on convincing the French to accept the Commission's ideas. As Lahr put it, the French were "alone in support of their extravagant plan for food aid."[36] Yet the French were aware that a compromise was needed if the EEC was to arrive in Geneva with a constructive position that would counter the American request for quantitative assurances. If, as a consequence of the Six's disagreements, the Commission showed up without plausible proposals, the Americans would insist on quantitative assurances or limits to the EEC's production, which were so dear to the Dutch and the Germans.[37] At the Council of Ministers meeting of mid-May 1966, the French made a step toward the Commission's proposals, backing away from advocacy of a massive jump in cereals prices. Renouncing a U.S.$10 increase in price, France gave up its plan. Under the Luxembourg presidency's suggestion, the Council of Ministers adopted an increase in the range of U.S.$2.50–3.50 a ton for wheat and no increase for feed grain. The level represented a compromise between the Commission's suggestion and the requests of Germany, Italy and the Benelux countries.[38]

However, if Faure had given up on price, he had no intention of doing so on the self-sufficiency rate. The Commission's proposal was especially objectionable, in the French view, because it represented a sort of access guarantee to third countries, which France had always rejected. Equally important, it froze the existing arrangements regarding the flow of imports. Yet nothing justified a system in which an economic unit refused to produce the quantities of cereals necessary to meet its own demand only to comply with other countries' requests. Moreover, Faure rejected the notion that the EEC had to accept the financial responsibility for surpluses. He pointed out a paradox: an economic unit such as the EEC, an importer whose production did not cover its consumption, would be financially responsible for surpluses on the world market.[39]

At the Council of Ministers meeting of May 26, 1966 discussions went badly. Faure restated the French opposition to the self-sufficiency rate. France could not accept that the self-sufficiency rate should set a limit to its production.[40] "Faure's filibuster," as the Dutch described it, irritated the Dutch minister, Biesheuvel, who described Faure's declaration as an "eloquent and long soliloquy, which included quotations from Kant, [but] failed to give any indication about what Faure would or would not accept." There followed sharp and open criticism of the French and a warning that the financial regulations in the CAP could be endangered if the

---

[36]   Ibid.

[37]   ANF 724.711B—Agriculture, Premier Ministre, Comité Interministériel pour les questions de Coopération Economique Européenne, Note CE/5934, June 11, 1965.

[38]   CM2 1966/22 PV de la 185ème réunion du Conseil de la CEE, May 10–12, 1966.

[39]   Ibid.

[40]   CM2 1966/32 PV de la 187ème réunion du Conseil de la CEE, May 25–27, 1966.

French blocked progress in the Kennedy Round.[41] Despite the Dutch warning, however, the Commission and the Germans were inclined to compromise. In order to meet the French part way, Commissioner Hans von der Groeben proposed setting the self-sufficiency rate at a higher level than the existing one, giving the EEC room to increase its production.[42]

Faure remained evasive. At the end of May, none of the other member states or the Commission had a clear idea of how Paris would play the grain issue. Clearly, Faure was withholding agreement so that Paris could use the grain proposal for bargaining purposes in the envisaged July package deal on the CAP.[43] Actually, Faure's performance was not solely dictated by the need to obtained concessions, but was designed to mask differences within the French government. While the Ministry of Agriculture was interested in increasing production, the Quai d'Orsay feared overproduction and was anxious to put a brake to the plans of the minister of agriculture.[44] Thus, the foreign minister was leaning toward accepting the Commission's proposal for the self-sufficiency rate as at least a basis of discussion. Even if no enthusiasm existed for this plan, the Quai d'Orsay was sure that Washington would never accept a self-sufficiency rate set on the grounds of the suggestions made by von der Groeben. Thus France ran no risk in accepting it. Moreover, thanks to this plan, the Commission could show up in Geneva with a strategy to resist U.S. requests. In the meantime, Rabot and Marjolin made considerable headway in bringing Faure and the French government around to accepting the self-sufficiency rate, with the provision that certain elements, such as the food aid program, which was dear to the French, would be strengthened. Equally important, the French realized that the CAP financial regulations might be imperiled if they did not move on the Kennedy Round.[45]

The Quai d'Orsay line eventually prevailed, thanks also to the flexibility of the new proposals by the Commission. At the 111 Committee meeting of June 9, the Six agreed, as suggested by the Commission, that the self-sufficiency rate would not limit production but rather bring into play the financial responsibility of the entire EEC if the rate was exceeded and a surplus created. Thus, in theory, a country could produce as much as it wished, provided it did not perturb the world market. The country that had exceeded the rate of self-sufficiency and overproduced could

---

[41]   NARA 59 1964–66 box 451 AGRI 3 EEC, Telegram ECBUS 1043 from Fessenden to State Department, May 28, 1966 reporting description of the Council of Ministers on the grounds of the Dutch account.

[42]   CM2 1966/32 PV de la 187ème réunion du Conseil de la CEE, May 25–27, 1966.

[43]   NARA 59 1964–66 box 451, AGRI 3 EEC, Telegram ECBUS 1043 from Fessenden to State Department, May 28, 1966 reporting description of the Council of Ministers on the ground of Dutch account.

[44]   NARA 59 1964–66 box 451, AGRI 3 EEC, Telegram ECBUS 1058 from Tuthill to State Department, June 1, 1966 reporting a conversation with Rabot.

[45]   Ibid.

chose whether to stock the surpluses or use them for food aid, but a minimum part had to be used for the latter.[46]

The Council of Ministers meeting of June 13–14 finally made the most important decision, defining the rate of self-sufficiency at a level higher than the existing one, as von der Groeben had suggested. As the Germans put it, "the Council played a number game."[47] Instead of the existing 85–86 percent rate, Mansholt suggested 88–89 percent. Faure countered with 95 percent and then, given the negative reaction of the other member states and Commission, proposed 90 percent. The Germans suggested 87–88 percent. As a compromise, the Luxembourg presidency proposed accepting the French suggestion of 90 percent. Mansholt recognized that 90 percent was too high and that he would have to come back to the Council for a modified mandate later. However, for the moment the pressure of time dictated making an offer of some kind to starting bargaining in Geneva. In the middle of June 1966, after extensive internal discussions, another important portion of the EEC mandate was added. The specific offer, however, was very loose. The self-sufficiency rate was offered at a level higher than the existing one; the duration of the binding would be on the order of three years, with no guarantee after that time. The commitment was, therefore, indirect and somewhat vague, and this explains why the French accepted it.[48]

After having agreed on the self-sufficiency rate, two crucial issues remained to be addressed: the principle of EEC financial responsibility for surplus. This last decision touched upon a critical question that was being discussed in Brussels, the high financial burden of the CAP. Bonn was not willing to assume more financial strain and was apprehensive about the financial cost of the Cereals Agreement. By contrast, France wanted the principle of EEC responsibility to be approved. As the only exporter within the EEC, it was the one country likely to have surplus. Given the recalcitrance that Germany had already demonstrated in the approval of the financial regulations of the CAP, its agreement to finance the surplus could not be taken for granted. Initially, German minister of agriculture Hermann Hoecherl tried to shift the financial burden, pointing out that, as his country was a big importer, it would not create a surplus. According to the German minister, the question was whether an importer could be considered responsible for surpluses. The German attempt to escape responsibility was promptly reigned in by Mansholt. The level of production within a member state was a result of the level of common price for cereals. The Germans had wanted high prices that would stimulate French production and now they had to bear the consequences. Eventually, the COREPER meeting of June 17 approved the principle of general

---

[46]   CM2 1966/17509, Note d'information du Conseil (S/400/66), June 9, 1966.

[47]   NARA 59 1964–66 ECIN 3, box 791, Telegram ECBUS 1086 from Fessenden to State Department, June 15, 1966.

[48]   CM2 1966/34 PV de la 188éme réunion du Conseil de la CEE, June 13–14, 1966. CM2 1963/305 PV de la 46ème réunion du Comité 111, June 17–18, 1966.

EEC financial responsibility.[49] Then, the Council of Ministers meeting at the end of July concluded the EEC's preparation for the cereals negotiations, by setting all the details of the EEC proposals.[50]

The talks were made difficult by the need to find compromises among the contradictory interests of the Six. However, as had already occurred in the industrial sector, the need to function as a unit in Geneva pushed the Six to make concessions to each other and achieve a final position. The Commission played a key role in setting the agricultural mandate. Thanks to its technical expertise and ability to engineer a compromise, the Commission played its part as package-broker to perfection. Moreover, it was able to structure the entire debate and, consequently, influence the final outcome in Brussels. Even if modified to meet the requests of the member states, the mandate reflected well the Commission's vision of the organization of world markets. Yet it was also the case that the Commission's preferences were exploited and manipulated by member states, primarily France, to enhance their own preferences.

The Second Round of Negotiations in Geneva: Not Much to Talk About

With the EEC's proposals put on the table at the end of July 1966, discussion concentrated on the self-sufficiency rate suggested by the Commission, together with a similar proposal by the United Kingdom. The United States and the other exporters rightly noted that the offer was to bind the ratio at a level substantially above the existing self-sufficiency rate, and only for three years. Second, contrary to the requests of exporters, there was no automatic link between exceeding the rate and corrective measures—a quantitative guarantee that the EEC refused to give. Third, exporters wanted precise commitments on the link between growth in consumption and growth in imports, so that they would increase in tandem. Finally, according to the EEC the rate was to be applied to exporters as well, but this rate would not make sense for exporters. The self-sufficiency rate had to assume a quantitative meaning to be applied only to importers, while exporters would bear obligations in case prices on the world market fell to the level of the minimum price. For them this represented an equitable commitment between exporters and importers. The exporting countries therefore considered the EEC's and Britain's offers meaningless in trade terms. Exporters analyzed the self-sufficiency rate from the point of view of creating reasonable access, which meant the assurance of an open market. Such a guarantee was absent from the European proposals. Given this unsatisfactory situation, the aim of the exporters became turning the self-sufficiency rate into an automatic mechanism to guarantee access.

---

[49]   CM2 1966/34 PV de la 188ème session du Conseil de la CEE, June 13–14, 1966; CM2 1966/148 PV de la 388ème session du CEREPER, June 15–17, 1966.

[50]   CM2 1966/48 PV de la 191ème session du Conseil de la CEE, July 22–23/26–27, 1966.

They suggested applying the rate only to importers, omitting the proviso that it would operate only when new surpluses rose, and fixing importers' ratio at the average achieved in a recent base period. However, these counterproposals led nowhere because of the already expected French veto.[51]

As for the other elements of the EEC's offers, the U.S. negotiators appreciated the fact that the EEC had suggested only a moderate boost in wheat prices, but opposed the setting of a reference price for feed grain. Washington looked at these commodities as an opportunity to enhance its exports to the EEC, and refused to set a minimum price. As for food aid, the EEC proposals linked food aid to the disposal of surplus. Washington rejected such a link and wanted a specific program, with each participant's contribution to it clearly defined. The United States suggested food aid of 10 million tons a year, to which it would contribute 40 percent.[52] Herter and Freeman had already made clear to Rey and Rabot that an outcome in which the United States gave massive food aid to LDCs while other countries retained commercial markets was impossible.[53]

The Commission's negotiator, Pierre Malvé, stated explicitly that the EEC could not give quantitative assurances. The self-sufficiency rate was not an engagement by importers to provide access to their markets, but rather a device to determine obligations if surpluses created imbalances in the world market. The Commission also insisted that the domestic policies of exporters be a topic of discussion. As for prices, exporting countries evaluated prices as they were established under the IWA. The EEC, on the contrary, considered the international reference price an instrument to bind the level of domestic support and, hence, freeze the level of current protection. On food aid, the EEC continued to claim that food aid had to be handled in connection with surpluses.[54]

The Commission was irritated that exporters continued to demand concessions without specifying what they were prepared to give in return. The EEC's negotiating partners differentiated between importers and exporters, rather than thinking in terms of a reorganization of world markets by linking domestic policies and international trade. Moreover, the EEC firmly supported the balancing of

[51]   AECB BAC 122/1991-5, Rapport 76 de la délégation de Commission pour les négociations du GATT, August 17, 1966; Memorandum from Roth to Herter, "Kennedy Round Matters for Your Discussion with Erhard," September 26, 1966, Herter Papers, box 8, JFKL.

[52]   PRO FO 371/189599, Anglo-French Economic Committee "Kennedy Round: Agricultural Products," Supplementary note by the Ministry of Agriculture, Fishery and Food, October 1966; ibid., Background paper for the visit of French Foreign Minister Couve de Murville, October 3–4, 1966 "Kennedy Round," September 30, 1966.

[53]   NARA 364 Recs of the USTR, box 5, Circular Telegram no. 2343 from State Department reporting conversation between Herter, Freeman, Rey and Rabot in Washington, May 27, 1966 and ibid., circular Telegram no. 2349 from State Department reporting conversation between Rey and Ball, June 27, 1966.

[54]   AECB BAC 122/1991-5 Rapport 76 de la Commission, August 17, 1966.

concessions within the Cereals Agreement negotiations, while exporters wanted to place these negotiations in the general framework of the round so that concessions on cereals would be compensated for by concessions in other sectors. The Commission categorically refused to accept that the Cereals Agreement depended on decisions on textiles or bicycles.[55]

The United Kingdom, the other big importer of grain, also offered to bind its self-sufficiency rate. However, as it suggested 86 percent, while its existing rate was 70 percent, it came under even stronger criticism than the EEC.[56] At the end of 1966, despite the new proposals of the EEC and the efforts at mediation by Wyndham White, positions remained far apart. A general willingness to negotiate some form of agreement existed, but it would probably be far from what Washington had hoped to achieve.[57]

The fundamental problem was that EEC had gathered in Geneva with proposals that had little chance of being accepted by their GATT partners and no chance of being modified in Brussels. Moreover, the adoption of the variable-levy system and the approval of a high common price for grain indicated that the EEC was moving toward greater protectionism. The French rejection of quantitative guarantees and the parallel German rejection of the reduction of UGPs showed that there was not much left to negotiate in the GATT. The EEC had set up an unchangeable CAP and had elaborated proposals that could not be modified because internal vetoes blocked alterations. Moreover, the role of the GATT in moderating CAP protectionism was weakened by the United States. The GATT could have posed a much more binding constraint for CAP policymakers, had the United States not decided not to challenge this common policy—considered as essential for European integration. As a result, the negotiations over grain in Geneva seemed doomed even before they started. When the negotiations started in Geneva, after a protectionist and non-negotiable CAP had been approved, there was not much to talk about.

Negotiations on Nongrain Agriculture: Between Failure and Stasis

From the outset of the Kennedy Round, negotiations in the Meat and Dairy groups moved at a slower pace than those in the Cereals Group. At the end of 1966 it

---

[55]   CM2 1966/16726 Comité 111, 248ème réunion "Sommaire des conclusions," October 3, 1966; AECB BAC 122/1991-6 Rapport 83 de la Commission, October 17, 1966.

[56]   NARA 364 Recs of the USTR, box 1, Background paper for the visit of Sir Richard Powell, undated but written in September 1966 and PRO FO 371/189599, Anglo-French Economic Committee "Kennedy Round: Agricultural Products," Supplementary note by the Ministry of Agriculture, Fishery and Food, October 1966.

[57]   ANF 724.713, box 7, Premier Ministre, Comité Interministrériel pour les questions de Coopération Economique Européenne, Note preparée par la DREE "Session du Conseil des CE des 21 et 22 Décembre," December 21, 1966.

became clear that agreements on these products were unlikely. While both sides of the Atlantic had an interest in reaching an arrangement on cereals, this was not the case for meat and dairy products. The United States was the biggest importer of beef, which it regulated through a quota system that needed the approval of Congress to be modified. The United States was disposed to accept quantitative engagements along the lines of the existing import quota legislation. However, it was not disposed to tariff cuts, to take engagements on domestic policy, to fix an international price of reference, or to negotiate on an MDS plan. Washington, supported by New Zealand and Australia, proposed setting exporting contingents by means of an annual negotiation that would take into consideration increases in consumption by the importing countries. In any case, the United States never pushed for an agreement on meat.[58]

The EEC was a major producer of, and trader in, beef. Although it was a net importer, its production was rising thanks to improvements in technology. France and the Netherlands produced a small surplus, while the other four members of the EEC remained importers. Italy and Germany imported meat from Argentina and Denmark in quantities that France and the Netherlands could have satisfied. However, Italy and Germany preferred the cheaper meat available from their traditional suppliers. The EEC and, above all, the Commission wanted to establish a commodity agreement so as to contribute to the stabilization of world markets through the binding of the MDS and the establishment of a reference price. An international agreement, the Commission believed, could conciliate the different trade interests among the Six. Yet at the end of 1966, positions remained too far apart, and the failure to reach a compromise was complete.[59]

Talks over dairy products also stalled. Participants in the Dairy Group had agreed to discuss butter, a heavily subsidized item for which a world surplus existed, but to exclude other products. Since 1958 the EEC had been self-sufficient in butter. All the member countries except Italy met their own needs, and the Dutch produced a large surplus. The Hague looked with much interest on a commodity arrangement that would organize trade and encourage access to world markets for its surplus. The Dutch target was to improve its share of the British market, now dominated by New Zealand, Denmark, and Australia, which received preferential treatment as members of either the Commonwealth or the EFTA. The position the EEC took in Geneva was complicated by the fact that the French and the

---

[58]   Memorandum for John Schnittker, Under Secretary of Department of Agriculture and Anthony Solomon, Assistant Secretary of Department of State from Roth, "US Recommendations for a World Grains Arrangement," September 28, 1966, Roth papers, box 2, LBJL; AECB BAC 122/1991-8, Communication de la Commission au Conseil NCG (66) 60 final, "Aspects Essentiels des Négociations au GATT (pays industrialisés)," December 20, 1966.

[59]   AECB Marjolin cabinet papers, BDT 144/92-780, "Résumé de la déclaration du représentant de la CEE devant le groupe des viandes," July 2, 1965 and AECB BAC 122/1991-6 Rapport 86 de la Commission GATT, November 7, 1966.

Dutch wanted to sell their large surpluses on the German and British markets. Bonn, however, wanted to continue to import from Denmark and considered the Dairy Arrangement an instrument to make quantitative concessions to the Danish, concessions that the Dutch and the French were not disposed to accommodate.[60]

The main obstacle to an arrangement was that the two big importers, the United Kingdom and the United States, had no great interest in reaching an understanding. The United Kingdom regulated imports through a quota, the bulk of which was granted to New Zealand. The British were happy with this system and had no intention to fix an international price of reference and to give up their quotas. By the same token, the United States was openly hostile to an arrangement and refused to engage in discussions on its domestic policy or to negotiate on MDS.[61]

On top of these complexities, France, Italy, and the Netherlands wanted to enhance their exports of cheese to the British, American, and Swiss markets, but the product was not considered in the Dairy Group. In Geneva the Commission tried to put pressure bilaterally on Britain, the United States, and Switzerland. However, it was difficult to ask for guarantees of access when the EEC refused to do the same for cereals.[62] The Dutch, with a major interest in gaining access to the British butter and cheese market, insisted that an arrangement had to be concluded and that the British had to make offers on cheese. The Dutch even claimed that an agreement was an essential condition for the positive conclusion of the Kennedy Round in both the industrial and the agricultural sectors. Supporting the Dutch, the Commission claimed that an arrangement on butter and the possibility of increasing the EEC's cheese exports were crucial elements that would influence the EEC's attitude on the entire Kennedy Round. Still the fact remained that the EEC had no power to move its partners. Under these circumstances, in March 1967 the failure of negotiations on dairy products was complete.[63]

---

[60]   AECB PV 345, January 19, 1966, Annex "Rapport de la Commission au Conseil sur les négociations commerciales au GATT"; AECB BAC 122/1991-25, Note de la délégation des Pays-Bas pour les négociations commerciales au GATT, "Groupe des produits laitiers," January 24, 1967.

[61]   PRO FO 371/189601, Telegram unnumbered from Board of Trade to Geneva, June 21, 1966 reporting conversation between Blumenthal, Hedges and Powell, Hughes and Kearns and PRO FO 371/189599 Anglo-French Economic Committee, "Kennedy Round: Agricultural Products," Supplementary note by the Ministry of Agriculture, Fishery and Food, October 1966.

[62]   CM2 1967/331, PV de la 226ème réunion du Comité 111, January 31, 1967; CM2 1967/331, Note, "Travaux effectué par le membres suppléants du Comité 111, 26/27 janvier 1967," February 7, 1967.

[63]   AECB BAC 122/1991-8, Communication de la Commission au Conseil NCG (66) 60 final, "Aspects Essentiels des Négociations au GATT (pays industrialisés)," December 20, 1966; AECB BAC 122/1991-9, Rapport no. 98 de la Commission (présenté par Rey et Marjolin), February 23, 1967; CM2 1967/329 PV de la 103ème session du Comité 111, March 31, 1967.

As for the rest of the agricultural products not covered by commodity groups, the negotiating situation was not much easier. The EEC aimed to organize world trade in agriculture with the MDS approach and insisted that domestic policies be part of the negotiations in Geneva. Despite the agreement reached between Mansholt and Herter in March 1965 to study the domestic policies of the Kennedy Round participants, this study went nowhere. Only the Commission gave indications. The other governments were reluctant to describe the domestic measures they used to support their agriculture and indicated that they would make offers only on barriers at international borders.[64]

For the EEC, setting up the list of offers for noncommodity group products was as difficult as the establishment of the list of exceptions for the industrial sector. Each of the Six, and in particular France and Italy, had its own products to protect. The Commission elaborated proposals for moderate reductions of protection and presented member states with a list of possibilities that required equitable and balanced sacrifices. It hoped that the all member states would accept the proposals as they stood and that a negotiating marathon would be avoided. Initially, the Commission had wanted to negotiate only on the MDS plan for all products. However, the strong opposition to this idea in Geneva and the difficulty in implementing it—as it was objectively difficult to set up reference prices for all products—led the Commission to suggest that member states also offer some tariff cuts. The Commission proposed minimum import prices for products entering the EEC so as to guarantee the stability of the internal market and gain the recognition of the CAP for these products in Geneva. It suggested minimum prices for eggs and chicken, fruit and vegetables, rice, cork wines and alcohols, tobacco, and fish, together with small tariff cuts that varied from 4 to 20 percent.[65]

The Six—primarily because of French opposition—were unable to accept the already limited Commission proposals as they stood. As a result, the Council of Ministers conducted a marathon discussion and, under French insistence, member states bargained product by product. France opposed any reduction of protections on fish, fruit and vegetables, wine, and tobacco. Italy was also unenthusiastic about conceding much to third countries, in particular with respect to rice, fruit and vegetables, for which it aimed to establish a protected Community market. However, Italian resistance also derived from dissatisfaction with the CAP. Until that moment this common policy covered mostly products of interest to other EEC members. Decisions were still pending on fruit—especially oranges—and vegetables, wines and other alcoholic products, tobacco, and cork, all sectors of

---

[64]   Letter from Roth to Thomas Curtis, July 1, 1965, Roth papers, box 1, LBJL; AECB Marjolin cabinet papers, BDT 144/92-780, Communication de la Commission au Conseil concernant la partie agricole des négociations commerciales au GATT, July 22, 1965.

[65]   AECB BAC 122/1991-5, "Introduction aux propositions d'offres de la Commission pour la négociation des produits du secteur agricole," undated, 1966; ibid., Note de la DG Agriculture, June 30, 1966; ibid., PV 366, July 6, 1966.

major interest to Italy.[66] The Commission's proposals also covered sectors for which the CAP had not been elaborated, putting at risk Italian interests. Thus before committing to anything, the Italians wanted to know what benefits they were to obtain from the CAP. It was only after Mansholt assured them that the Commission would soon present CAP regulations for products of interest to Rome that Italian minister of agriculture Tolloy seemed ready to accept the Commission's proposals, asking for only a few modifications. Benelux and Germany were not enthusiastic about the idea of setting a minimum import price, as this would represent a new trade barrier. However, they were ready to accept the Commission's proposals so that the EEC could show up in Geneva with offers in hand.[67]

To elaborate a final compromise, Rey and Mansholt presented new proposals reducing by one-fifth the EEC's concessions. Germany and Benelux promptly allied themselves with the Commission, concluding that, if it believed that the new proposals would create a valuable negotiating basis, they would accept them. After a last discussion item-by-item, France and Italy also accepted the new suggestions. In any case the EEC's offers remained incomplete, as they did not determine the minimum price for eggs and poultry, fruit and vegetables, and fish.[68] Only in new marathon talks at the end of December 1966 did the Six finally set these prices half way between the level demanded by the Netherlands and Germany and the higher level asked by France and Italy. Ultimately, as the Commission had suggested, the EEC offers consisted of the binding of a minimum price and small tariff cuts averaging about 5 percent. Thus the offers were grounded on the proposals of the Commission. As had been the case with grain, this institution played a crucial role thanks to its technical expertise and ability to suggest plausible solutions.[69]

At the beginning of August the agricultural offers on noncommodity groups were exchanged. When the EEC presented its offers, the Americans' pessimistic expectations proved to be accurate. The EEC made extensive use of minimum prices, which the U.S. negotiators rejected as an unacceptable basis for negotiations. Moreover, proffered tariff cuts were shallow and limited in scope.[70] Washington considered the EEC proposals on minimum price an attempt to obtain international acceptance of the reference price/variable levy system for major

---

[66]   Galli and Torcasio, *La partecipazione italiana alla politica agricola comunitaria*, 118–19.

[67]   CM2 1966/17511, Note S/527/66, Travaux du comité 111, July 14–15, 1966.

[68]   AECB BAC 122/1991-5, Note de la DG Agriculture, July 25, 1966. AECB PV 369, July 26, 1966; CM2 1966/48 PV de la 191 session du Conseil de la CEE, July 22–23/26–27, 1966; AECB BAC 122/1991-3, Note, "Project d'Expose de présentation des offre de la Communauté," September 13, 1966.

[69]   CM2 1966/90 PV de la 203ème session du Conseil de la CEE, December 21–22, 1966.

[70]   Administrative History of the Department of State, vol. I, Part VIII, "International Economic Relations," LBJL and Administrative History of STR, Narrative History, vol. 1, box 1, LBJL.

commodities; a number of token tariff offers had been included for this purpose alone. Washington had always maintained a pragmatic approach toward this system and had always claimed that, rather than quarrel over the CAP's compatibility with the GATT, it would negotiate with the EEC to set up mutually acceptable ways to protect U.S. trade interests. Unfortunately, the EEC offers did not lead in this direction. Washington concluded that the situation was serious and unpromising. A substantial improvement of offers by the EEC was needed.[71]

The circumstances for tropical products appeared to be not much better. For the EEC, making offers on these products was a complicated affair. It had an association agreement under the Yaoundé Convention that granted preferential treatment to the associated African countries and Madagascar. These countries opposed any reduction of their preferences and went so far as to claim in some cases that the EEC's customs duties had to be raised against other LDCs. Aware of this demand, the Commission proposed to the Six only small tariff cuts for tropical products. Among the Six, Germany and the Netherlands favored the greatest reduction possible so as to confirm the liberal attitude of the EEC; they wanted the Commission to propose drastic tariff reductions on coffee, cacao, bananas, and rum. For these two countries, the GATT talks had to reduce the difference between the treatment of the associated countries and that of the other LDCs. By contrast, the French rejected any proposals that could weaken the favorable conditions provided to the associated countries under the Youndé convention. Thus Couve de Murville took the view that, as long as a solution was found to the problem of access to markets and stabilization of trade flow, the French government would support the Commission's proposals on tropical products. Belgium, Luxembourg, and Italy held a middle ground. Eventually the Six agreed to consolidate duties to the level set by the Yaoundé convention and to make a 50 percent cut on some products, such as tea, on which duties had been suspended.[72]

The refusal of the EEC to meaningfully reduce the Yaoundé preference came under attack by the nonassociated LDCs, which held that there was little for them in the Geneva talks.[73] The British supported the LDCs' pressure on the EEC to improve offers, so as to compensate the Commonwealth countries for reductions

---

[71]   NARA 364 Recs of the USTR, box 6, Position paper, "Kennedy Round Confrontations on Agricultural offers," September 8, 1966; ibid., box 1, U.S. delegation to the Sixth Round of GATT Trade Negotiations "Part 1: Delegation Evaluation of Offers," November 1, 1966 and "Assessment of offers as of November 30, 1966 and comparison of the offers of the EEC and the USA."

[72]   AECB BAC 62/1980-59 PV de la 3ème session du Conseil d'Association CEE-EAMA, May 18, 1966; ibid., Note d'information, "Consultation des EAMA sur les négociations en cours dans le cadre du Kennedy Round," June 2, 1966; CM2 1966/34 PV de la 188ème réunion du Conseil de la CEE, June 13–14, 1966 ; PRO FO 371/189599, Note, "Tropical Products" by the Tariffs Division, October 1966.

[73]   Ibid.

in British tariffs.[74] As for the Americans, under the TEA they could reduce duties on tropical products, but only if the EEC did the same. Since the passing of the TEA, the Americans' aim was to reduce, and ultimately to eliminate, the tariff preferences extended by the EEC under the Yaoundé convention, allowing Latin American countries to increase their exports to the EEC and decrease pressure on the U.S. market. However, the refusal of the Six to make serious reductions to tariffs closed the way to any meaningful result in this sector.[75]

---

[74] PRO FO 371/189599, Note of Rot Denman (UK delegation in Geneva) to Carter (Board of Trade), October 7, 1966.

[75] NARA 364 Recs of the USTR, box 1, U.S. delegation to the Sixth Round of GATT Trade Negotiations, "Part 1: Delegation Evaluation of Offers," November 1, 1966; Administrative History of the Department of State, vol. I, Part VIII, "International Economic relations."

Chapter 7

The Final Bargain: Setting the Tone of European Regionalism in Global Trade

Troubles in Transatlantic Relations

The last phase of the Kennedy Round took place in a strained atmosphere across the Atlantic. De Gaulle's decision to quit the command structure of NATO in March 1966, his open criticism of Johnson's military effort in Southeast Asia, and French policy on the U.S. dollar added tension to the already difficult Franco–U.S. relations. The United States looked with apprehension at French policy. In July 1966, the Treasury Department concluded that France was "practicing economy warfare" against the United States "within a framework of a national policy that calls for the weakening of U.S. strength and influence in Western Europe as a necessary condition of establishing French hegemony over that area."[1]

Troubles existed also in American–German relations. The quarrel over the financing of U.S. troops in the Federal Republic and U.S. nonproliferation policy were major points of tension. Erhard's fall at the end of 1966 was followed by the formation of the Grand Coalition of Christian Democrats and Social Democrats, headed by the CDU leader, Kurt Kiesinger. The new chancellor, Foreign Affairs Minister Willy Brandt, and the minister of finance, Franz Joseph Strauss, had every intention of strengthening relations with France. While German–American relations worsened, the new German government seemed on the verge of performing a pro-Gaullist turn.[2]

With the U.S. balance-of-payments deficit increasing, the Johnson administration, the Treasury Department in particular, reproached the Six for failing to share the security burden and for not cooperating in supporting the U.S. dollar. Washington continued to link trade, security, and monetary issues despite the refusal by the Six to do the same. As a result, within the Johnson administration, discussions multiplied on whether the United States had to reduce its military presence in Europe. Moreover, Johnson had counted on an increase in exports through the Kennedy Round to improve the U.S. balance of payments ledger. However, the EEC had first slowed negotiations, stalled them with the crisis of the Empty Chair, and then refused to reduce protectionism in agriculture.

---

[1] Memorandum from Winthrop Knowlton to Fowler "France," 11 July 1966, Fowler Papers, box 68, LBJL.

[2] For the stance of the Johnson Administration towards the European allies see Schwartz, *Lyndon Johnson and Europe*.

In 1964, the U.S. trade surplus with the EEC started declining as a result of major increases in EEC exports. Exports continued to increase, but imports increased even faster.[3]

Against this background, doubts about whether it was in the U.S. interest to support European integration mounted. Since 1947, the United States had agreed to accept European economic discrimination as a way to unify Europe politically. However in mid-1966 the economic EEC regional system still lacked this political unity, while it increased trade discrimination with the implementation of the CAP. The United States had supported the EEC as a first step toward political union, supposing that it would remain an outward-looking influence. However, the EEC seemed to be heading in other directions. When in 1967 the German economics minister Schiller reminded the U.S. treasury secretary, Henry Fowler, that the EEC had been a "US 'baby,' with George Ball one of the fathers," Fowler was quick to note that that EEC had been designed as an "outward looking" baby.[4] With the failure of the EEC to achieve a higher level of political consolidation and U.S. economic troubles, it was becoming more difficult for the White House and the State Department to openly support European integration and subordinate trade policy to foreign policy considerations. Moreover, the protectionist mood in Congress was mounting. The Johnson administration was blamed for not protecting U.S. trade interests and was warned against selling out U.S. agricultural interests in Geneva.[5]

The U.S. reaction to the second British bid to join the EEC showed this changing mood. At the end of 1966, Prime Minister Harold Wilson informed the Americans about his intention to probe the Six on a new application.[6] The Johnson administration supported enlargement of the EEC for the same reasons that the Kennedy administration had. However, what was considered an insufficiently liberal EEC attitude in the Kennedy Round and the stance of the Six toward sharing the military burden reinforced American concerns. Secretary of the Treasury Fowler wondered whether the United States had to ask the Six to share monetary and military costs before supporting the enlargement.[7]

In this context of troubled transatlantic relations, a successful conclusion of the round remained crucial for the Johnson administration. It represented a major

---

[3]   OECD SITC Rev. 2—Historical Series 1961–90 (Paris: OECD 2000).

[4]   FRUS 1964–68, vol. VIII, General and Financial and Monetary Policy, document 129. Memorandum of Conversation between Fowler, Bator, Schiller and Schoellhorn, in Washington, June 19, 1967.

[5]   Zeiler, *American Trade and Power in the 1960s*, 230–31 and Alfred E. Eckes Jr, *Opening American Market. US Foreign Trade Policy since 1776* (Chapel Hill, NC, 1995), 190–94.

[6]   On the second British attempt to join the see Oliver Daddow (ed.) *Harold Wilson and European Integration. Britain's Second Application to Join the EEC* (London 2002).

[7]   Draft Telegram from the State Department to all diplomatic posts "US policy on EEC Association," January 1967.

element of U.S. trade and foreign policy, and a failure would have negative consequences for relations with the Europeans and domestically. The isolationist and protectionist mood within Congress would be strengthened and the liberal U.S. trade policy endangered. It was against this background that U.S. negotiators got ready to lead the final phase of the round.

Getting Ready for the Final Bargain

While transatlantic relations deteriorated, those between the Six improved. With the major decisions about the CAP having been made in July 1966, one of the main issues that had strained relations was removed from the EEC's agenda. Moreover, the fundamental decision to implement the customs union and the CAP starting July 1, 1968 had been made. At this point, no big confrontation lay ahead, at least for the moment.[8] With these key resolutions approved, tensions diminished, and the final phase of the Kennedy Round gave the opportunity to regain cohesiveness. The January–May 1967 period was characterized by a strong effort by the Six to stick together to defend their trade interests and by a clear awareness that concessions were necessary to maintain unity and elaborate a common position.

In the two Council of Ministers meetings of late December 1966 and mid-January 1967, the EEC worked out its strategy for the final phase of the round. In November 1966, the EEC had been the major recipient of warning lists from other participants in the round. It reacted in a flexible and pragmatic way to this muscle-flexing strategy. It did not want to risk a watering down of final concessions from other countries, an outcome that did correspond to its interest in reducing tariffs. Rey asserted that, as the Scandinavians and the Swiss had not offered exceptions in November 1964, a clear imbalance existed between them and the EEC. He also considered American and British warning lists unjustified. A qualitative comparison of the offers showed that they were equitable. Thus the lists were only a bargaining chip to which the EEC need not to respond with improved offers. The German secretary of state, Fritz Neef, however, reacted with alarm at the potential withdrawals by other countries. He feared a scaling down of offers and a reduction in trade liberalization. Neef was especially worried about Scandinavian and Swiss withdrawals, which would hit German interests harder than those of the rest of the EEC. Thus he pressured other members to improve offers to these countries. Neef also held that the EEC owed something to the British and the Americans. He could accept Rey's claim that concessions were already balanced, but for tactical reasons. Then the EEC had to be prepared to improve its offers.[9]

---

[8]   On the relations among the Six at the beginning of 1967 see Ludlow, *The European Community and the Crises of the 1960s*, 125–46.

[9]   CM2 1966/90 PV de la 203ème session du Conseil de la CEE, December 21–22, 1966 and CM2 1967/2 PV de la 205ème session du Conseil de la CEE, January 12, 1967.

The Germans, however, failed to get their EEC colleagues on board. Couve de Murville emphasized that the CET was lower than the tariff levels of the other countries and that the EEC offers were as generous as those of the Americans and the British. Since the beginning of the round, the French government had been worried that the Germans would bend to American pressure, and in the current climate it feared that Bonn could succumb to the American threat of withdrawing offers. The French minister recognized that an imbalance existed with the Nordic countries and Switzerland. However, negotiations with them depended on solutions to the ASP and disparities, two issues crucial in U.S.–EEC relations. The French minister held that the time was not ripe for concessions. Couve's strategy was to prevent the EEC from being pushed into a corner in Geneva and making concessions without trying to get reciprocal benefits, as the Germans tended to do. The French minister highlighted another key reason to oppose concessions at this stage. Three years of discussions had demonstrated the EEC's inability to keep its negotiating positions secret. If improved offers were elaborated now, they would inevitably be leaked and the negotiating strength of the EEC undermined. Couve de Murville thus raised a crucial problem that, as shown below, was linked to the negotiating authority of the Commission. Italy, meanwhile, as its minister of commerce Tolloy declared, was ready to improve the EEC's offers if other countries would reciprocate. The Benelux ministers concurred that it was desirable to make better offers to the Nordic countries and the Swiss, but because of the impossibility of keeping the EEC's negotiating position secret, they sided with Couve de Murville.[10]

The compromise over these positions was hinted at by Neef and immediately picked up by Rey as an opportunity to strengthen the Commission's negotiating position in Geneva and in the EEC's trade policymaking in general. The German secretary of state linked the problem of leaks to the bargaining authority of the Commission. To prevent leaks, Neef suggested giving more general and more flexible directives to the negotiating agent, rather than precise instructions. Building on this suggestion, Rey emphasized that, to effectively conduct the final phase, the Commission did not need a mandate but rather general guidance and more room to maneuver. Rey suggested allowing the Commission to negotiate ad referendum with the Nordics and the Swiss, the countries to which concessions had to be made. In this way the bargaining in Geneva could be speeded up and leaks would be, if not avoided, at least limited. Member states promptly approved Rey's suggestion, agreeing that, to reach satisfactory compromises with third countries, maneuvering room for the Commission was necessary.[11]

As a result, in mid-January 1967, the Council of Ministers recognized that an imbalance existed with the Swiss and Nordics. The Commission would negotiate ad referendum with them to explore how offers could be improved. Despite German doubts, the Council concluded that no inequity existed with the British

[10]   Ibid.

[11]   Ibid.

and the Americans. The EEC would not present a withdrawal list, in order not to risk the effectiveness of the round, but the Commission would take a severe line with Britain and the United States. Moreover, following a French suggestion, the Commission was instructed to focus negotiations with the British and the Americans on the critical questions of disparities and NTBs. For this task, the Council of Ministers allowed its negotiating agent the same flexibility it authorized with the small EFTA countries.[12]

Rey and Hijzen were satisfied with the flexibility they had obtained. For the first time, they could bargain from a nimble posture, a stance that could reinforce the role of their institution both within and outside the EEC. Because member states had decided that the Commission had to be given more freedom to act, the institution had finally achieved the prerogatives it had requested from the outset.[13] This decision represented a marked change from the beginning of the round. A trade-off took place between member states' control over the Commission, on the one hand, and the speed and efficiency of the decision-making process, on the other. In this final phase, when an agreement had to be reached in Geneva and with no linked issue pending in Brussels, member states allowed the Commission a greater flexibility. They increased its power because doing so was in their interest. Once again, the Commission was instrumental to national concerns, and the source of its power lay firmly in the hands of the member states.

Negotiating Round and Round

In preparation for the final phase, the Commission worked out the tactics it intended to follow. The Commission had to bargain on two fronts: in Brussels with the Six and in Geneva with the EEC's trading partners. Thus, it had to reassure member states that any deal it made in Geneva was satisfactory to them and, at the same time, convince other countries to accept its proposals. The Commission's primary tactic consisted in stretching out the bargaining until the very last moment. In this way it hoped to get last-minute concessions from trading partners who wanted to rescue the round from deadlock. Moreover, Hijzen believed that the French, as

---

[12]   Ibid.; NARA 364-130 Recs of the USTR, box 5, Telegram no. 3325 from Schaetzel to State Department, January 13, 1967 and ibid., Telegram no. 10499 from Bohlen to State Department reporting his conversation with the French officials Dromer and Corson, January 14, 1967; ibid., Telegram no. 3468 from Schaetzel to State Department, January 20, 1967.

[13]   For Rey's aim of getting more flexibility to negotiate in Geneva see AECB PV 386, January 6, 1967 and PV 387, January 10, 1967. For Rey and Hijzen's satisfaction about the results of the Council of Ministers see AECB PV 388, January 18, 1967; PRO BT 241/847, Telegram no. 1 from UK delegation to Brussels to Foreign Office, January 18, 1967; NARA 364-130 Recs of the USTR, box 5, Telegram no. 3468 from Schaetzel to State Department, January 20, 1967.

was typical of them, would compromise only at the last moment. Thus, delaying tactics seemed the appropriate route to follow.[14]

Once the bargaining restarted in Geneva, the Commission spent from January to March discussing the improvements the EEC could make and those that other countries could give in return. Only in the middle of April did it present the Council of Ministers with a list of fresh proposals. Faced with the general stalemate that gripped the talks, the U.S. negotiators, who bore the responsibility of moving the round ahead, adopted a confrontational attitude, creating an atmosphere of crisis and the possibility of failure, and seeking a showdown with the EEC in which it would be forced to give ground. Roth was convinced that the Europeans had both political and economic interests in bringing the negotiations to a successful conclusion.[15] However, four years of the Kennedy Round had demonstrated that tough pressure was necessary to make progress. Crisis, a hard line, and brinkmanship seemed the only path. Moreover, the Americans suggested the end of April as the deadline to conclude the negotiations, hoping that a time limit would lead the other governments to reach an agreement.[16] Yet by mid-April, little had been achieved. At this point, the Kennedy Round entered a crisis that lasted until mid-May, when a framework agreement was finally formulated.

Chemicals remained a major source of conflict. As a result of the Commission's increased flexibility, some progress was initially achieved. The Commission suggested that the Chemical Group negotiate with a new approach that eventually emerged as the final compromise. No exceptions were to be made to the 50 percent rule, and a ceiling would reduce rates that remained high even after a 50 percent reduction. The United States would convert the ASP rates into ad valorem rates, limit them to 40 percent, and then reduce the result by 50 percent. The EEC would cut duties on chemicals by 50 percent without claiming disparities and with virtually no exceptions. The U.S. delegation found this plan negotiable, but insisted that some concessions had to be made unconditionally, separate from the abolition of the ASP. Washington pushed for a separation, for a *decoupage* as the issue was labeled, into conditional cuts subject to the removal of the ASP and unconditional reductions. In this way, they would not be linked to Congress's decision on this NTB.[17] The Commission, however, opposed *decoupage* because it would reduce the U.S. incentive to ask Congress to abolish the ASP. In truth, the Commission

[14] PRO BT 241/849, Confidential note, "Kennedy Round: Chemicals" from Denman to Goldsmith, March 21, 1967 reporting conversation between Denman, Hijzen and Braun.

[15] Herter died on 30 December 1966. Roth, until that time Herter's deputy in Washington, became acting U.S. Trade Representative until March 1967, when he was officially sworn in by Johnson. On Roth's role in the Kennedy Round see Dryden, *Trade Warriors*, 97–113.

[16] Telegram no. 3299 from Roth to Bator, April 20, 1967, Roth papers, box 3, LBJL.

[17] Telegram no. 764 from Bator to Rostow for the President, April 24, 1967, NSF, National Security Council History, Kennedy Round crisis April–June 1967, Book 2, tabs 25–53, box 52, LBJL.

was not hostile to the plan, but it was not disposed to reach an early compromise, hoping to obtain the best possible counter-concessions in a last-minute acceptance of the two-package deal.[18]

While negotiations over the Cereals Agreement continued at a very slow pace, by the beginning of April it had become clear that no commodity agreement would be negotiated for meat and dairy products. This failure disappointed France and the Netherlands, which had hoped to use the agreements to increase their exports to the American and, above all, the British markets.[19]

In the meantime, talks between the Nordic countries and the EEC took a dangerous turn. After thorny discussions, in the middle of March, Hijzen presented the Nordic delegation with the improvements the Commission planned to suggest to the Council of Ministers. The Commission proposed a greater reduction in duties on basic paper from 16 to 12 percent, rather than the previously suggested 14 percent, and to increase the duty-free contingent on newsprint and the 5 percent contingent on aluminum. Hijzen also promised to do his best to convince the Council of Ministers to improve offers on live cattle, poultry, and eggs. In exchange, the Commission asked for the maintenance of the Nordic countries' original offers in the industrial sector and improvements in offers for fruit and vegetables.[20] These proposals disappointed the Nordic partners. Sweden remained dissatisfied with the lack of concessions on trucks, and Denmark felt thwarted by the imprecise engagements for agriculture. Convinced that the time had arrived to be tough and to demonstrate their weight as a negotiating bloc, on April 1 the Nordic countries withdrew 53 percent of their original offers, hitting, above all, German interests in the mechanical and transport equipment sectors.[21]

This move infuriated Rey and led to stormy meetings among the interested parties.[22] Relying on the authority to negotiate ad referendum, Rey hoped to reach a compromise that could be presented to the Council of Ministers. Here the Commission would need to convince member states of the reasonableness

[18]   PRO BT 241/849, Confidential note, "Kennedy Round: Chemicals" from Denman to Goldsmith, March 21, 1967 reporting conversation between Denman and Hijzen.

[19]   CM2 1967/331, Note, "Travaux effectués par le membres suppléants du Comité 111, 26/27 janvier 1967," February 7, 1967; AECB BAC 122/1991-9, Rapport no. 98 de la délégation de la Commission, February 23, 1967; CM2 1967/11 PV de la 210éme session du Conseil de la CEE, February 7, 1967; CM2 1967/329 PV de la 103ème session du Comité 111, March 31, 1967.

[20]   CM2 1967/328 PV de la 101 réunion du Comité 111, February 8, 1967. AECB BAC 122/1991-9, Rapport no. 99 de la délégation de la Commission, February 24, 1967 and AECB BAC 122/1991-9, "Négociations commerciales dans le cadre du GATT," Communication de la Commission au Conseil, April 4, 1967.

[21]   AECB BAC 122/1991-22, Délégation de la Commission pour les négociations commerciales au GATT, "Compte-rendu de la sixième réunion officieuse exploratoire entre la Commission et la délégation nordique, 17 mars 1967," March 18, 1967.

[22]   PRO BT 241/849 Telegram no. 312 from Melville to Foreign Office, April 8, 1967.

of its proposals and demonstrate the advantages of negotiating with flexibility. However, the Nordic move complicated the task: faced with withdrawals, member states were unlikely to respond with greater concessions. Equally important, the Nordic strategy could undermine the authority of the Commission to negotiate ad referendum. Member states could reproach their negotiating agent with failing to achieve reasonable results, its new freedom to act notwithstanding. Rey, however, did not modify the list of EEC improvements to be presented to the Council of Ministers, not wanting to risk a watering down of concessions.[23]

Despite the lack of progress in Geneva, at the Council of Ministers meeting of 1–12 April, the Six and the Commission expressed satisfaction with the EEC's performance. Rey noted that the cohesion that member states were showing would surely strengthen the EEC in the final bargaining. Neef and Tolloy announced their full confidence in the Commission and their satisfaction with the way it was conducting negotiations. Couve de Murville praised the solidarity and cohesiveness that characterized the talks within the EEC.[24]

For chemicals and grain, the Six expressed confidence in the ability of Rey and Mansholt to conclude the negotiations advantageously. Rey proposed improved offers to the Nordic countries and to the Americans, provided they reciprocated.[25] The commissioner wanted to avoid a new discussion by the Council on each single product in his proposals, as had occurred in 1964–66, when ministers spent hours discussing such issues as duties on canned asparagus. The Council of Ministers, warned the commissioner, had to make the difficult political decision to improve offers, accepting his proposals as they stood. Unfortunately, only Neef was disposed to do so, while representatives of the other governments had reservations. As for concessions to the Nordic countries, member states were stiff-necked. They showed genuine disappointment over the Nordic withdrawals. Particularly annoyed were the Dutch, who threatened to toughen their stance. They opposed concessions to the Danes on livestock and were annoyed by the failure of the Meat and Dairy groups, by the meager offers in the vegetable sector from the British and the small EFTA countries, and by the bilateral deal Denmark and Switzerland had reached on dairy products. Consequently, the Netherlands refused to grant additional concessions in either the agricultural or the industrial sector. As a result, this traditionally liberal

---

[23]   CM2 1967/17518, Note d'information, "Négociations commerciales multilatérales du GATT—Résultats des travaux effectués par le Comité spécial 111," April 5, 1967; AECB PV 397, April 3–6, 1967; AECB BAC122/1991-22, Délégation de la Commission pour les négociations commerciales au GATT, "Réunion entre la Commission et la délégation des pays nordiques, 6 avril 1967," April 11, 1967.

[24]   CM2 1967/17 PV de la 212ème session du Conseil de la CEE, April 10–12, 1967.

[25]   On the Commission proposals see AECB PV 397, 3 April 1967, "Négociations commerciales dans le cadre du GATT," Communication de la Commission au Conseil, April 4, 1967 and ANF 724.713, box 7, Premier ministre, Comité Interministériel pour les Questions de Coopération Economique Européenne, Note, "L'état actuel des négociations tarifaires de Genève," April 6, 1967.

country attended the last part of the negotiations with positions akin to those of France, the member state generally considered most troublesome and protectionist in the EEC.[26] Rey was worried about the stubbornness of the member states and feared they might even withdraw offers. His major preoccupation was to avoid an escalation of tactics that could reduce tariff liberalization. Therefore, he took care in underlining the tactical reasons behind the Nordic withdrawals. He proposed that the EEC offer improvements, especially for meat to the Danish and fish to the Norwegians, but on the condition that the Nordic countries reestablish all offers. The Commission would endeavor to persuade these trading partners to moderate their position and, together with the 111 Committee, would decide which improvements were to be made. Member states, aware of the need to unlock discussions with these countries, accepted Rey's proposals.[27]

The Commission recommended better offers on items of interest to the United States in the mechanical sector, among which excavating machines were important to Roth, and for tobacco, poultry, and fruit and vegetables. Rey hoped in this way to get the Americans to make concessions to the EEC on cheese and fruit and vegetables. Initially, Couve de Murville, Tolloy, and de Block did not want to give ground to the United States or request any further concessions. They opposed better offers in the agricultural sector, in parallel to the Americans' negative attitude on meat, dairy products, and fruit and vegetables. Despite this initial reservation, warned by Rey that some steps were necessary, the Council of Ministers determined that, if the Commission could demonstrate that a quid pro quo was possible, protections could be reduced on some items.[28] With these fresh instructions, the Commission entered into the final bargaining in Geneva.

Shuttling Back and Forth

The final weeks of negotiations in Geneva were characterized by informal bargaining between the Commission's officials—under of the direction of Rey—and the representatives of the GATT partners, above all the United States. Rey's leadership meant that the Commission was able to eliminate member states from direct representation in the discussions and to act as sole agent for both

---

[26] For the Dutch attitude towards the Nordic countries see CM2 1967/17519, Note informative, "Résultats des travaux effectués par le Comité spécial de l'article 111 lors de sa réunion en date 10 avril," April 10, 1967; NARA 364-130 Recs of the USTR, box 5 Telegram no. 5265 from Schaetzel to State Department, April 12, 1967; AAPD 1967 document 128 Drahterlass des Ministerialdirigenten Frank, April 13, 1967.

[27] CM2 1967/17 PV de la 212ème session du Conseil de la CEE, April 10–12, 1967. NARA 364-130 Recs of the USTR, box 5, Telegram no. 5265 from Schaetzel to State Department, April 12, 1967.

[28] CM2 1967/17 PV de la 212ème session du Conseil de la CEE, April 10–12, 1967 and AECB PV 398, April 13, 1967.

the industrial and the agricultural sectors. The need to conduct the negotiations efficiently led the Six to leave the bargaining to the Commission. At the same time, however, Rey was compelled to shuttle back and forth to Brussels to inform the Council of Ministers of events and to receive its guidance. As a matter of fact, even if the Commission had obtained greater freedom to act, any final decision remained firmly in the hands of the national governments. In Brussels member states showed readiness to follow the Commission's orientation, to approve its positions, and to delegate to it solutions of problems. They considered this attitude necessary to establish a common stance. However, they were also prompt to scrutinize the treatment of every single product and ensure that their interests would be protected.

On April 19, 1967, Rey, Hijzen, Roth, and Blumenthal restarted the bargaining.[29] In the industrial sector, Rey rejected *decoupage*. In the agricultural sector, the commissioner did not accept an independent food aid program, as Roth requested. As for the rest of the agricultural sector, Rey proposed a small increase in offers on the condition that Washington reciprocate. Roth and Blumenthal were surprised by Rey's requests, while Rey was stunned by the American refusal to reciprocate. Roth insisted that the EEC improve its token offers on nongrain agriculture—in particular fruit and vegetables, poultry, and tobacco—from the 5 percent average cut it had proposed to at least 13 percent.[30] He pressured Rey, stating that, unless agricultural concessions were made, the United States would "not conclude the Round." Rey did not seem very impressed and underlined that, if the U.S. government wished to take the responsibility for "scuttling the Kennedy Round that was an American business."[31] Assessing this situation, Roth wrote to Bator that Johnson would "shortly be faced with having to choose between a Kennedy Round with no offers of substance in non-group agriculture (and perhaps even no agreement) or no Kennedy Round agreement at all."[32]

In the meantime, Rey shuttled back to Brussels to get fresh instructions. His major task was to convince the Six to make additional concessions. Rey appreciated the clear way in which Roth had threatened withdrawals. He could make it plain to ministers that they had to increase offers or face the consequences.[33] The EEC

[29] For an excellent, even if a little gossipy, account of the final phase see Dryden, *Trade Warriors*, 97–113.

[30] Telegram no. 866 from Rusk to Roth, April 21, 1967, Roth papers, box 3, LBJL.

[31] Telegram no. 3299 from Roth to Bator, April 20, 1967, Roth papers, box 3, LBJL. PRO PREM 13/1869 Telegram no. 384 from UK delegation in Geneva to Foreign Office, April 21, 1967.

[32] Telegram from Roth to Bator, April 26, 1967, Bator papers, box 13, LBJL. See also Telegram no. 3390 from Geneva to Bator, April 26, 1967, NSF, National Security Council History, Kennedy Round crisis April–June 1967, Book 2, tabs 25–53, box 52, LBJL and PREM 13/1869 Telegram no. 402 from UK delegation to Geneva to Foreign Office, April 26, 1967.

[33] Telegram no. 3374 from Roth to Bator, April 25, 1967, Bator papers, box 13, LBJL.

negotiator was performing a tricky balancing act between the member states and his negotiating partners in Geneva.

The Council of Ministers meeting of May 2 resulted in fresh instructions to Rey. According to Rey, the fate of the round would be decided on discussions over chemicals and agriculture between the EEC and the United States. The small EFTA countries and the United Kingdom would acquiesce to the agreement the major economic powers reached. Hence, the Council of Ministers concentrated on these two problems. On chemicals, Rey asserted that the time had arrived to consider *decoupage*, as this plan seemed to be the only negotiating ground. Rey asked to be allowed to engage with some flexibility in discussions on the content of the two-package deal. Aware that suppleness was needed to unlock the bargaining, all six EEC countries quickly accepted Rey's request. They allowed the Commission to undertake exploratory discussions on which the Council of Ministers would then deliberate. However, the Six remained unmoved on cereals. Despite Mansholt's proposal for a 3-million-ton program of food aid in exchange for a U.S. agreement to fix prices of feed grain, the Belgian and German ministers for agriculture, Heger and Hoecherl, opposed the program. They asked to shrink the self-sufficiency rate (SSR), engaging the EEC in a much more limited food aid program. However, French opposition precluded a reduction of the SSR. The Council of Ministers decided to let Rey negotiate flexibly on the SSR and the size of the food aid program, bearing in mind the orientation of member states.[34]

Back in Geneva, Rey claimed to be ready to negotiate with more freedom, whereas Roth announced that he would to leave for good on the evening of May 9. If no agreement had been reached by that time, Washington would consider the Kennedy Round a failure. Roth hoped in this way to pressure the EEC to reach a final agreement.[35] From May 4 to 9, the negotiations were essentially bilateral bargaining on chemicals and agriculture between the Commission and the U.S. negotiators in Wyndham White's office.[36] Thus, in the last and crucial phase of the round, the Commission was able to escape the presence of the EEC's member states and to constitute their only negotiating agent.

By May 9 no agreement was in sight. In chemicals, since the Commission was now willing to discuss the *decoupage* formula, the question became how to fill the package. Facing an impasse, Wyndham White put forward a plan according to which the EEC would reduce its tariffs by 20 percent, unconditioned on the ASP removal and without claiming exceptions and disparities. The United States would

[34] CM2 1967/25 PV de la 215éme réunion du Conseil de la CEE, January 2, 1967.

[35] Memorandum for the President from Bator "Meeting tomorrow on the Kennedy Round," May 1, 1967, NSF, National Security Council History, Kennedy Round crisis April–June 1967, Book 2, tabs 25–53, box 52, LBJL; Memorandum for the President from Bator, May 4, 1967, NSF Subject File, Chronological Files, box 47, LBJL.

[36] ANF 724.713, box 7, Ministère de l'Economie et des Finances—DREE, Note, "Négociations commerciales multilatérales de Genève. Bilan succinct des travaux du 8 au 15 mai 1967," May 18, 1967.

reduce its duties by 50 percent without claiming disparities and exceptions. Then it would abolish the ASP, and in return the EEC would make a further 30 percent cut. The Commission took a favorable position regarding this proposal, while the Americans refused it, as they deemed the 20 percent reduction by the EEC inadequate in comparison to the U.S. 50 percent cut. In the rest of the industrial sector, Roth asked for stronger offers in the mechanical and electronic sectors and was prepared to reciprocate on the U.S. side. However, as Rey noted, these sectors were too sensitive for the EEC to budge, and no improvements could be expected.[37]

On nongrain products, to solve the impasse, Rey took the responsibility—without consulting the 111 Committee—for instructing the Commission's negotiator for agriculture, Rabot, to make concessions on tobacco and canned fruit, to which the U.S. delegation attached political importance. The original U.S.$39 million in offers was raised to U.S.$100 million. Roth demanded further jumps, to a total value of U.S.$200 million, making additional requests on 17 products and threatening, as an alternative, to fix the imbalance by reducing American offers.[38] Rabot warned Roth that, in the face of these threats, there was no possibility of further EEC concessions. The American move would leave him with no selling points to use with the EEC ministers in arguing for richer offers. Rabot announced that "no more could be said" and declined further discussion. However, in order not to complicate the negotiations, Rey and Rabot left the EEC's offers on the table. The move was surely a hazardous one, as the 111 Committee had not authorized it.[39]

For cereals, following four days of useless bargaining on the SSR, Roth decided to change the negotiating ground. He advanced the "revolutionary idea," as he put it, of giving up the U.S. request for access and confining the agreement to wheat prices and a 5- to 5.5-million-ton program of food aid. Roth grounded his proposal on the fact that effective and continual access to the EEC was not attainable. The EEC would consent only to a very high SSR. There was, therefore, no point in negotiating worthless concessions in exchange for which the United States had to undertake commitments on its domestic policy and prices for feed grain.[40] Such a breakthrough so late in the negotiations astonished Rey. Most importantly, he was disappointed because it eliminated the SSR and the MDS plan, two key elements the Commission itself had suggested. At this point, Rey's return to Brussels became inevitable, as the American proposals were too radical

---

[37]   CM2 1967/17519, Telegram from Schacht in Geneva (Consilium Genève) to Calmès and Megret (Consilium Bruxelles), May 9, 1967; Telegram no. 3565 from Roth to Bator, May 9, 1967, Roth papers, box 3, LBJL.

[38]   Telegram no. 3597 from Roth to Bator, May 10, 1967, Roth papers, box 3, LBJL.

[39]   CM2 1967/17519 Telegram from Schacht in Geneva (Consilium Genève) to Calmès and Megret (Consilium Bruxelles), May 9, 1967.

[40]   PRO BT 241/850 Telegram no. 446 from Melville to Foreign Office, May 9, 1967; Telegram no. 3597 from Roth to Bator, May 10, 1967, Roth papers, box 3, LBJL.

to be accepted—even ad referendum—by the Commission.[41] The case of grain, once more, showed that its representatives were able to take positions in response to developments in Geneva, going beyond the Council of Ministers' instructions. Yet any major decision required the intervention of member states.

On May 9, at four o'clock in the morning, the talks deadlocked, and the disagreement between the Commission and the American negotiators stalled the whole bargaining process.[42] After an attempt to force Rey to reach a broad ad referendum agreement before leaving for Brussels, thanks to the diplomatic mediation of the Swedish negotiator Montant, Roth consented to interrupt the negotiations—and not break them off—and give time to the commissioner to go back to Brussels. However, Roth obtained a fixed deadline by which to conclude the round, hoping in this way to push the EEC to make final decisions. Under U.S. and Commission instructions, Wyndham White released a public statement saying that all parties agreed that the final concluding date of the negotiations would be May 14, "win or lose."[43]

The Last Stage of the Kennedy Round in Brussels

In Brussels Rey submitted his fresh proposals to the Council of Ministers in order to get the final instructions to bring to an end the long Kennedy Round. In checking these proposals, the ministers of foreign affairs, commerce, and agriculture examined every single duty on every single item. However, there was no tension among them, but a full awareness that concessions were required. The issues of chemicals and cereals were rapidly solved. On chemicals, Rey asked the ministers to approve Wyndham White's suggestion. Couve de Murville's prompt endorsement paved the way for the Council of Ministers' rapid approval. In fact, it seemed difficult for the EEC not to follow suit. The GATT director general, Wyndham White, had put it forward, and the Commission had already approved his suggestion ad referendum.[44]

The Six speedily reached an agreement on cereals. Mansholt was disappointed that the United States had dropped the Commission's MDS plan and SSR suggestion. In the commissioner's view, in order not to make promises on domestic policy, Washington had to give up the opportunity to regulate world trade and freeze the level of protection. His plan had been written off by both the U.S. negotiators and

---

[41] CM2 1967/17519 Telegram from Schacht in Geneva (Consilium Genève) to Calmès and Megret (Consilium Bruxelles), May 9, 1967.

[42] PRO BT 241/850 Telegram no. 446 from Melville to Foreign Office, May 9, 1967; Telegram nos 3558 and 3359 from Geneva to Bator, May 9, 1967, NSF National Security Council History, Book 1-TABSI-6, LBJL.

[43] Telegram nos 3565 and 3577 from Roth to Bator, May 9, 1967, Bator papers, box 13, LBJL; Telegram no. 3573 from Roth to Bator, May 9, 1967, Roth papers, box 3, LBJL.

[44] CM2 1967/28 PV de la 216ème réunion du Conseil de la CEE, May 10–11, 1967.

the member states, who had failed to credibly defend it in Geneva, and had instead exploited the Commission's preferences to pursue their own agenda. Once again the Commission had no independent means to impose its opinion on the outcome of the negotiations. Mansholt bitterly recommended acceptance of the U.S. proposals as the only way to reach an agreement. He asked the Council of Ministers to give the Commission some flexibility, rather than precise directives, in order to bargain over the 5 million tons of food aid. The Dutch and the Germans, however, were reluctant to accept a program bigger than 3 million tons. The American move changed the attitude of Italy, France, and Luxembourg. With the prospect of setting up a food aid program not linked to the SSR, these three countries wanted an independent program so as to underline its character as a development policy. The program had to be considered an independent instrument of aid, rather than a commercial one, in order obtain all the political benefits in relations with LDCs. To this end, Tolloy, Faure, and Gregoire wanted commitments on food aid separate from the rest of the round, and not to incorporate the agreement in the GATT framework. The 3 million tons had to be minimum contributions. Faure, again demonstrating that the French were willing to give the Commission freedom to act when doing so corresponded with their trade interests, were prepared to allow the Commission to negotiate without issuing any mandate. In the face of these stances, Dutch and, above all, German opposition was rapidly removed. There was nothing the Germans could do to avoid the food aid program unless they wanted to stir up serious trouble in Geneva. As a result, the Council of Ministers agreed to give the Commission flexibility to establish a program of 3–4 million tons of food aid. At this point the two thorniest questions—the treatment of chemicals and cereals—had been answered.[45]

By contrast, an agreement on other issues was not so quick, even though all the EEC's member states made efforts to compromise and maintain cohesion. In nongrain agriculture, as the Americans had requested improvements on a list of 17 products, Rey presented a report to the Council containing new offers on 14 products. To pressure ministers to approve the plan without changes, Rey warned that such concessions were vital to a successful round. In the final bargaining with the Americans, the Commission would have to bear in mind the major worries of the national governments. The commissioner aimed to avoid a new time-consuming confrontation among member states, in which his institution might present global proposals and member states ask to pull out. None of the member states criticized Rey for having presented offers for which he lacked authorization. They considered his initiative necessary to move the discussions ahead. However, not all of them intended to approve the report as it stood. Germany opened the way by firmly opposing a reduction in duties on poultry and unmanufactured tobacco. Couve de Murville did not share Rey's belief that the EEC's attitude on nongrain agriculture would determine the success or failure of the round. It was a simple question of salesmanship, "une simple opération de 'bazardage,'" declared the French minister.

---

[45]   Ibid.

Thus he objected to reducing levies on sugar, fish, poultry, canned asparagus and peaches, and cigarettes. The Italian minister, Tolloy, objected to the reduction in the unmanufactured tobacco tariff from 28 to 24 percent and the cut in the duties on cigarettes, and aligned himself with all French requests. The Belgian Heger and the Dutch de Block could accept the Commission report as it stood if this might push Washington to make counter-concessions on cheese and potatoes. After further negotiations within the 111 Committee and a last round of discussions in the Council of Ministers, where the national governments checked and double-checked every single product, member states eventually decided to approve almost all of the Commission's proposals. Couve de Murville gave up French reserves. The German minister, Schiller, successfully pressured Tolloy to accept a reduction of duties on cigarettes from 180 to 100–105 percent, and not 117 percent, as Italy had requested, leaving the Commission free to negotiate the final rate. However, Germany and France refused to make further concessions on poultry.[46]

Rey presented proposals to reduce tariffs in the mechanical sector. The commissioner had declined the majority of the U.S. requests for additional offers, but could not reject all of them. Again, Rey did not want the Council of Ministers to discuss the list item by item, as this would require a rigid negotiating position in the GATT. Instead, members would express their orientation, and the Commission would bear these preferences in mind. Benelux approved the proposals as they stood, while Germany was prepared to increase concessions and France and Italy wanted to reduce them, in particular duties on machines for public work. In any case, Tolloy and Couve de Murville expressed their full confidence in the Commission and its conduct of the negotiations. They accepted Rey's request to be given flexibility.[47]

The discussions hit a wall on questions related to the small EFTA countries. Member states displayed a rigid attitude, believing that these countries had not reciprocated the EEC's offers. The Commission presented a list of improvements touching, among other things, on aluminum and paper. While Germany and Luxembourg were ready to accept it as it stood, the other members had objections. With respect to paper, Italy, France, Belgium, and the Netherlands objected to concessions, whereas the additional offers on aluminum met the predictable opposition of France. To benefit Norway, the Commission proposed to reduce from 18 to 15 percent the duty on frozen filleted fish. This concession was considered so important in Oslo that the Norwegian delegation subordinated to it the reduction of the duty on cars. However, France raised an objection on the ground that a common fishery policy had not yet been set. Moreover, France opposed new concessions to the Swiss on watches and the Netherlands on cotton textiles. Rey was worried about this restrictive position. He believed that these concessions were indispensable and warned that it was time for difficult political decisions. The commissioner exerted what pressure he could and warned that member states

---

46 Ibid.
47 Ibid.

were putting at risk the entire round. Rey's efforts to convince the four recalcitrant governments received the support of the Germans and were, in the end, partially successful. Italy and Belgium showed flexibility and decided to give up all their opposition. Couve de Murville and de Block, however, remained resistant. At this point, Rey once again warned that the reserves would complicate negotiations with EFTA countries, which might withdraw offers on such crucial sectors as cars, shoes, glass, and machinery. He assured the representatives that he would not offer a decrease in the duty on aluminum and would keep in mind member states' stance on paper. Eventually, the Council of Ministers agreed to leave to the Commission the responsibility for negotiating the best solution possible, while bearing in mind the orientation of the six governments. Eventually, Rey attained better offers and some flexibility in bargaining.[48]

Rey was highly satisfied with the result of the Council of Ministers meetings. Member states had given flexible directions, accepted a large proportion of his requests, and displayed confidence in the Commission's judgment and capacity to defend members' trade interests. All the Six showed a willingness to conclude the round, and above all saw the need to maintain cohesiveness.[49] Aware that concessions and flexibility were indispensable to the round, and confident in Rey's opinions and negotiating skills, member states accepted the Commission's proposals. In this sense, the fact that the national governments aimed at reaching an agreement at all costs facilitated the final compromise and the role of the Commission. At this point, the last stage of the Kennedy Round in Brussels was over. Now it was up to Rey to conduct the last talks in Geneva. At the conclusion of the session a standing ovation was given to Rey. However, as Rabot put it, after the agreement in Brussels, Rey had "to get out of the trenches" and meet Roth.

Agreement, at Last

As the last set of talks started in Geneva, a breakdown in the bargaining was unlikely. As a matter of fact, despite the many matters still unresolved, both the EEC and the United States had the political will to conclude the round. The United States, which had been leading the negotiations from the outset, was especially determined to bring the talks to a useful conclusion. Bator and the State Department held that, for economic and political reasons, the round had to be terminated, and President Johnson shared their considerations.[50] As Bator put it, Washington would lose a considerable economic benefit in the industrial sector if the round were abandoned. Moreover, failure could lead to the kind of commercial

---

[48]   Ibid.

[49]   Interview with Paul Luyten, Brussels, 7 July, 2003.

[50]   Memorandum for the records "Positions taken at the Meeting with the President on the Kennedy Round," May 11, 1967, and Memorandum of conversation between Roth and Bator, May 11, 1967, Bator papers, box 12, LBJL.

warfare in which the United States, as a trade surplus country, had a great deal to lose. In effect, the central point was not the level of tariffs, but maintaining "a reasonable set of trade rules without which international trade would become a jungle warfare," remarked Bator. The failure of the Kennedy Round would lead to a spiraling of protectionism, with parliaments holding the whip hand. Moreover, noted the White House assistant, transatlantic relations would deteriorate, and the EEC could turn into an isolationist and anti-U.S. bloc. The LDCs would be further alienated from the world trade regime.[51]

By the same token, Secretary of State Rusk believed that a breakdown of the negotiations would be synonymous with the failure of U.S. leadership of the Western world and would encourage highly destructive economic rivalries. "The Atlantic partnership concept would be weakened; Gaullist nationalism strengthened; developed and developing countries further divided," claimed Rusk. Divisions over trade in Western Europe would be aggravated and the chance to benefit from a generalized reduction in intra-European tariffs would be lost. Failure would also call into question the GATT rules for regulating the trading regime. It might compromise chances for agreement on international monetary reform and presage an eventual return to the economic nationalism and autarky of the years preceding World War II. An unsuccessful Kennedy Round would reverse a 30-year trend of progress in trade liberalization and would unleash the forces of protectionism, "driving the USA back to the Smoot–Hawley act."[52]

The fact that both the EEC and the United States were eager to reach an agreement did not imply that a rapid conclusion was just around the corner. A final compromise remained tricky, and the bargaining between the EEC and the United States was fierce. The final stages of the negotiations in Geneva consisted of nonstop bartering from May 12 to 16, 1967, during which Wyndham White successfully put on the table his package deal to hammer out an accord.

The only area to be rapidly settled was that of interest to the LDCs. As for cotton textiles, the LDCs accepted an extension of the LTA for three years. In return, both the United States and the EEC agreed to slightly enlarge the quota but to make only a 20 percent reduction in tariffs, not a full 50 percent, in order to compensate themselves for the quota enlargement. The 20 percent reduction— remarkably lower than the 35 percent average cuts of the Kennedy Round—and the small increase in the quota confirmed the unwillingness of industrialized countries to make concessions to LDCs, despite the statement of 1963 that the Kennedy Round would be a major breakthrough for trade and development. As for tropical products, the EEC did not make any meaningful reduction in the Yaoundé preferences. The LDCs left out of this preferential system criticized it fiercely,

---

[51]   Memorandum for the President from Bator "Your Meeting Tomorrow on the Kennedy Round," May 10, 1967, NSF National Security Council History, Book 1-TABSI-6, box 52 LBJL.

[52]   Memorandum of the State Department written by Hinton, May 10, 1967, Bator papers, box 12, LBJL.

with the support of the United Kingdom and the United States. However, the refusal of the EEC to make serious reductions closed the door to any meaningful results in this area.[53]

In the industrial sector, Roth threatened massive withdrawals unless the EEC improved its offers on paper, aluminum, and the mechanical sector and gave up half of its disparities claims. The Commission improved offers by one-third of what the U.S. delegation demanded for the mechanical sector and reduced the disparities list. On aluminum, Rey offered to bind an annual tariff quota of 130,000 tons at 5 percent. In response Roth decided to reduce the U.S. duty by 20 and not 50 percent. Norway was highly disappointed by the maintenance of the CET at 9 percent. Also dissatisfied by the small reduction of the CET on frozen filleted fish from 16 to 15 percent, and not to 11 percent, Norway cut its duty on cars from 10 to 8 percent rather than to 5 percent. With respect to paper, the Nordic countries reluctantly accepted the Commission's offers.[54] The British also maintained their offers on passenger cars despite the EEC exceptions on commercial vehicles and their parts. In effect, if the United Kingdom excepted cars, the EEC would follow suit, and this would mean no tariff reductions on motor vehicles. However, as the EEC market for cars was important to the British—the trade surplus in motor cars and components was in their favor—the EEC reduction in the duty on cars could not be forsaken.[55]

Chemicals and agriculture remained to be patched up. On chemicals, Roth aimed at a *decoupage* formula that would give the U.S. government some presentational advantages before Congress. By contrast, the Commission wanted to keep to a minimum any unconditional concessions and to make exceptions on plastics. The Commission's stance provoked a hostile reaction from the British, who threatened to increase their duty on plastics if the EEC made exceptions.[56] For grain, the dropping of the SSR, the MDS, and the price of feed grain removed the major obstacles to an agreement. Only the price of wheat and the size of food aid remained open.[57] On nongrain agriculture, an agreement snagged on the EEC's concessions to the United States. Roth stuck firmly to his requests on the 17 products and threatened to reduce U.S. offers. Rey suggested improvements, but Roth judged them insufficient.[58]

---

[53]   Department of State—Administrative History, vol. I, Part VIII, LBJL and Administrative History of the Department of Commerce—vol. I, Part III "Report of Trade Policy Activities," undated, box 2, LBJL.

[54]   AECB BAC 122/1991-12 "Négociations commerciales dans le cadre du GATT," communication de la Commission au Conseil, NCG (67)35, May 31, 1967.

[55]   PRO PREM 13/1869, Note for the Prime Minister, "The Kennedy Round" C(67)35, undated but written in March 1967.

[56]   Telegram no. 3652 from Roth to Bator, May 13, 1967, NSF, Subject file—Trade Negotiations, box 47, LBJL.

[57]   Telegram no. 3668 from Roth to Bator, May 15, 1967, Roth papers, box 3, LBJL.

[58]   Telegram no. 3655 from Roth to Bator, May 14, 1967, NSF National Security Council History, Book 1-TABSI-6, box 52 LBJL.

Facing this deadlock across the board, on May 14 Wyndham White decided that the time had arrived for a package deal containing joint concessions unpalatable to all parties. He first worked to fix the minimum price of wheat (Hard Winter No. 2) at U.S.$1.73 a bushel, against the U.S.$1.85 asked by exporters and the U.S.$1.65 asked by Japan and United Kingdom, and the maximum price at U.S.$2.13. The agreement on wheat opened the way for a package deal for chemicals and food aid, and EEC offers on agriculture.[59]

In chemicals, Roth and Blumenthal persuaded Wyndham White to put on the table a *decoupage* package, elaborated by them, as his own suggestion. The EEC and United Kingdom would reduce tariffs by 20 percent generally, and by 30 percent on rates higher than 25 percent, unconditionally and as part of the Kennedy Round. The United States would make a 50 percent cut generally and 20 percent on rates of 8 percent or below. Japan and Switzerland would make a full 50 percent reduction. For the conditional ASP package, the EEC, the United Kingdom, and Switzerland would make additional commitment on NTBs and a further 30 percent reduction (so as to achieve a full 50 percent reduction); the United States would convert the ASP and lower rates where indicated to a general 20 percent level. As for the NTBs, Italy, France, and Belgium agreed to remove their road tax, while the British offered a 25 percent reduction in the tobacco preference. This last concession could significantly enhance the chances of congressional action on ASP, as the American tobacco industry would be willing to support removal. As a result, an appropriate compromise was made and the log-jam was broken.[60]

As part of the Wyndham White package deal, the arrangement on cereals would include a food aid program of 4.5 million tons, higher than Rey had been authorized to accept in Brussels. The United States would contribute 42 percent of the program, the EEC 23 percent, Canada 9 percent, Australia, the United Kingdom, and Japan 5 percent, and other countries 11 percent. As the EEC requested, the arrangement would be set up outside the Kennedy Round. Indeed, the text of the International Grains Agreement was developed in Rome at the International Wheat Conference of July and August 1967. It was composed of two parts. The Wheat Trade Convention set minimum and maximum prices for wheat and established procedures to be followed when prices reached minimum or maximum levels so as to maintain and stabilize prices within the specified range. The Food Aid Convention put exporters and importers into a partnership on the food aid program of 4.5 million tons annually, as agreed in Geneva.[61]

[59]   Ibid.
[60]   Telegram nos 3660, 3663, 3668 from Roth to Bator, May 14/15, 1967, Roth papers, box 3, LBJL; Memorandum, "The Kennedy Round Crisis April–June 1967," NSF National Security Council History, Book 1—TABSI-6, LBJL.
[61]   Ibid.; Administrative History of the Department of Agriculture, vol. I, chapter III, International Trade, "The Sixth Round of Trade Negotiations," undated. See this document for a full and technical analysis of the IGA agreement.

An eleventh-hour agreement was reached on nongrain agriculture thanks to the fact that Rey, on his own responsibility—as he had not asked the 111 Committee's authorization—decided go further than the Council of Ministers had agreed. Rey improved the EEC offers on tobacco, cigarettes, canned salmon, grapefruit, canned fruit, poultry, offal, and whisky. In response, Roth improved offers on tomatoes and cheese, but made no changes on olive oil.[62]

The various proposals of Wyndham White's package were discussed at the 111 Committee meeting of May 15. Germany, Belgium, and Luxembourg were ready to accept them, Italy and the Netherlands were reluctant to make further concessions on nongrain agriculture, and France asked for time to reflect. After a telephone conversation with Couve de Murville in Paris and Neef in Bonn, and after further improvements on tobacco, cigarettes, and offal undertaken to accommodate the Americans, Rey accepted the package deal.[63] In the end, in the early morning of May 16, a framework agreement was reached. At this point the director general could announce to the press that the bargaining was over.[64]

Despite the announcement, only an oral and framework accord had been formulated. The agreement had to be put on paper, and numerous details had to be specified before June 30, 1967, the date agreed for the signatures on the final act. As noted, in order to reach an accord with the United States, Rey had presented unauthorized offers and accepted a bigger food aid program than that envisaged by the Council of Ministers.[65] When at the end of May the EEC's list of offers was put on paper, member states realized that details they had not agreed to had been conceded. Italy, France, and the Netherlands objected. Rey's actions presented the Council of Ministers with a *fait accompli*, for he had given concessions that they opposed. Consequently, they asked for removal of certain items from the list. The Dutch complained about the eleventh-hour concessions to the Scandinavians with respect to fish. Italy and France objected to the offers to the British in food, even if, in return, the EEC had obtained better tariffs on fruit and vegetables. The Commission tried to avoid any discussion of such specifics, warning that changes to agreements on any products would cause other countries to retaliate by reducing

---

[62]   ANF 724.713, box 7, Ministère de l'Economie et des Finances—DREE, Note, "Négociations commerciales multilatérales de Genève. Bilan succinct des travaux du 8 au 15 mai 1967," May 18, 1967; AECB BAC 122/1991-12 "Négociations commerciales dans le cadre du GATT," communication de la Commission au Conseil, May 31, 1967 and CM2 1967/16726 PV de la 284ème réunion du Comité 111, May 30–31, 1967.

[63]   ANF 724.713, box 7, Ministère de l'Economie et des Finances—DREE, Note, "Négociations commerciales multilatérales de Genève. Bilan succinct des travaux du 8 au 15 mai 1967," May 18, 1967.

[64]   PRO PREM 13/1869, Note, "The Kennedy Round," May 16, 1967.

[65]   CM2 1967/17936, Telex no. 23.05/01 from Consilium in Geneva to Consiluim in Brussels, May 23, 1967, "Communication de M. Rey aux représentants permanents le 18 mai 1967, en ce qui concerne la conclusion des négociations commerciales multilatérales dans le cadre du GATT."

their concessions to the EEC.[66] The final agreement on the concessions was reached at the Council of Ministers meetings of June 26–27 1967. Here member states confirmed the greatest part of the concessions, and only minor changes were made. Once the agreement had been reached, under the suggestion of Rey, the Council of Ministers instructed Hijzen to sign the Final Act of the Kennedy Round.[67]

The agreements were signed on June 30, only hours before the expiration of the five-year tariff-cutting authority conferred on the U.S. president by the TEA of 1962. At this point, the Kennedy Round was truly over.[68]

The EEC in the Multilateral Trading System: A Liberal Actor and a Stumbling Block

The results of the negotiations were notable, if mixed. In the industrial sector, they produced the remarkable average reduction of duties of 35 percent, applied to U.S.$40 billion worth of goods, with about two-thirds of the cut reaching 50 percent. Even if the goal of a 50 percent linear cut had not been achieved, the reductions were greater than those negotiated in previous rounds. In 1972, at the end of the implementation period, Japan would have an average tariff level of 11.5 percent, the United Kingdom 10.4 percent, the United States 9.4 percent, and the EEC 8.2 percent. Tables 7.1–7.3 show the reductions in tariffs on major products by the EEC, the United States, and the United Kingdom. Achievements varied across different sectors. With an average reduction of 45 percent, machinery was the sector where the greatest cuts were made—a major concession by the EEC, for American and British products were competitive, and the existing CET was already low, between 6 and 12 percent. The EEC, however, because of French and Italian opposition, excepted business machines and electronics, two new industries that it did not want to subject to U.S. competition. In the automobile sector, the EEC reduced the CET from 22 to 11 percent on cars, but refused to make cuts on heavy commercial vehicles and tractors, to the displeasure of the British.[69] Only limited results were achieved for textiles, steel, paper, and aluminum.[70]

---

[66]   CM2 1967/16726 PV de la 284ème réunion du Comité 111, May 30–31, 1967.

[67]   AECB BAC 122/1991-12, "Négociations commerciales dans le cadre du GATT," communication de la Commission au Conseil, May 31, 1967; AECB PV 409, May 26–28, 1967; CM2 1967/48 PV de la 224ème session du Conseil de la CEE, June 26–27, 1967; CM2 1967/54 PV de la 225ème session du Conseil de la CEE, July 10/11, 1967.

[68]   Memorandum, "The Kennedy Round Crisis April–June 1967," NSF National Security Council History, Book 1—TABSI-6, LBJL.

[69]   ANF 724.713, box 7, Premier ministre, Comité Interministériel pour les Questions de Coopération Economique Européenne, Note, "Négociations commerciales dans le cadre du GATT," May 16, 1967.

[70]   For a detailed description of the Kennedy Round results sector by sector, see Preeg, *Traders and Diplomats*, 204–36; Curtice and Vastine, *The Kennedy Round and the Future of American Trade*.

With the significant reduction in tariff barriers, NTBs became the major obstacle to trade exchanges. In this sense, the antidumping code the United States, the EEC, the United Kingdom, Japan, Canada, and most of the EFTA countries signed and the effort to eliminate other NTBs paved the way to a more extensive inclusion of NTBs in the following GATT negotiations, the Tokyo Round (1974–79).

However, tariffs were not rendered redundant by the Kennedy Round. As Tables 7.1–7.3 show, in some sectors they remained high. In effect, some areas remained immune to liberalizing efforts, as all governments protected certain trade products. The rule of exceptions allowed governments to pull out of the linear cut the most sensitive industrial sectors, while opening others to increased competition. In this sense, the rule permitted the pursuit of neomercantilist policies that characterized states' commercial policies and gave the latter a peculiar mixture of liberalism and protectionism.

In the industrial sector the interest of all the major participants in lowering others' tariffs led to a reciprocal substantial reduction, both across the Atlantic and within Western Europe. The Kennedy Round enhanced economic integration in the industrial sector, and for its part the EEC fully contributed to the liberalization of trade. While maintaining its regionalism, it was not a stumbling block to freer trade.

Table 7.1   EEC average ad valorem percentage incidence of import duties before and after the Kennedy Round

	Pre-Kennedy Round	Post-Kennedy Round
All chemicals	14.3	7.6
Leather manufactured goods	9.2	5.7
Rubber manufactured goods	15	7.8
Wood and cork manufactured goods, except furniture	10.9	8.8
Paper and board manufactured goods	10.7	7.5
Textiles	16	15.6
Mineral manufactured goods	9.4	5.5
Iron and steel	9.4	6.7
Manufactured metal goods	12.8	7.2
Machinery other than electrical	11.1	6.4
Electrical machinery	14.2	9.1
Transport equipment	15.4	9.9
Footwear	17.8	12.4
Instruments	13.3	8.4

Source: Data taken from Preeg, *Traders and Diplomats*, 209 and GATT, *Legal Instruments Embodying the Results of the 1964–1967 Trade Conference* (Geneva, 30 June 1967).

Table 7.2   U.S. average ad valorem percentage incidence of import duties
before and after the Kennedy Round

	Pre-Kennedy Round	Post-Kennedy Round
All chemicals	17.8	9.3
Leather manufactured goods	16.2	10.4
Rubber manufactured goods	11.3	6
Wood and cork manufactured goods, except furniture	7.1	6.8
Paper and board manufactured goods	10.9	5.5
Textiles	21.4	20.1
Mineral manufactured goods	9.9	7.5
Iron and steel	6.5	5.7
Manufactured metal goods	14.7	7.7
Machinery other than electrical	11.9	6
Electrical machinery	13.6	7.1
Transport equipment	7.1	3.5
Footwear	21.1	12.1

Source: Preeg, *Traders and Diplomats*, 208 and GATT, *Legal Instruments Embodying the Results of the 1964–1967 Trade Conference* (Geneva, 30 June 1967).

Table 7.3   UK average ad valorem percentage incidence of import duties
before and after the Kennedy Round

Products	Pre-Kennedy Round	Post-Kennedy Round
All chemicals	18.8	9.4
Leather manufactured goods	17.7	13.1
Rubber manufactured goods	13.6	7.8
Wood and cork manufactured goods, except furniture	15.2	7.3
Paper and board manufactured goods	16.6	13.2
Textiles, except clothing	20.6	16.9
Mineral manufactured goods	9.3	4.8
Iron and steel	11.3	9.2
Manufactured metal goods	12.8	9
Machinery other than electrical	14.2	8.6
Electrical machinery	20.1	12.4
Transport equipment	20.1	11
Building parts and fittings	15.8	9.2
Footwear	22.8	14.7
Instruments	26.4	13.5

Source: Preeg, *Traders and Diplomats*, 210 and GATT, *Legal Instruments Embodying the Results of the 1964–1967 Trade Conference* (Geneva, 30 June 1967).

In marked contrast were the results in the agricultural sector. For the first time in an international commercial conference, agricultural trade had been a key issue. A commodity agreement on wheat and a food aid program of 4.5 million tons per year had been agreed to, and token tariff cuts were made on poultry, fruit and vegetables, and offal, and more substantial cuts on tobacco. However, the protectionist trend was not reversed.

As the U.S. undersecretary of agriculture John Schnittker noted, the "[CAP] system, which insulates home producers from the effects of outside competition regardless of the difference in efficiency, is perhaps the greatest unsolved problem in international trade today." The EEC was able to achieve its aim of reducing tariffs in the industrial sector while maintaining its protectionism in agriculture. It ended the round with the CAP intact, which now became a major obstacle in world agricultural trade. The GATT had not been able to overcome the EEC's protectionism, with major consequences for international markets. In the following 10 years, the EEC shifted from being the largest importing bloc to being the largest exporting one.

Within the EEC, the Commission was the actor most disappointed with the results of the agricultural talks and the abandonment of the MDS plan. Mansholt had considered the round an opportunity to organize agriculture at the world level, binding the existing level of protectionism and reducing the protectionist effects of the CAP. This chance was missed. According to Mansholt, the negotiations failed because exporters had not abandoned the classical concept of access and quantitative assurance. They preferred short-term guarantees to arranging real cooperation, keeping a controlled level of protectionism in the sector.[71] Yet Mansholt's explanation is partial. First of all, none of the EEC member states really believed in the MDS plan. They had supported it only to give a bargaining chip to the EEC, not because they were convinced of the feasibility of the plan. In effect, they never complained about the U.S. decision to drop it. Equally important, the adoption of the variable-levy system and the approval of a high common price for grain had already indicated that the EEC as a whole was moving toward increased protectionism. Then the French veto of quantitative guarantees and the Germans' parallel opposition to the reduction of grain prices showed that there was not much left to negotiate in Geneva. Italy, the Federal Republic, and the Netherlands concerned themselves with maintaining imports from outside the EEC, but this purpose was not strong enough to push them to modify in Geneva the agreement that had been previously reached on the CAP in Brussels. All of the Six gave priority to the EEC regional market and the protection of their farmers.

A last aspect of the round is worth considering. Despite the meager results in the agricultural sector, the industrialized countries were satisfied with the outcome. The GATT had proven to be a suitable framework in which to reduce trade barriers

---

[71]   AECB BAC 209/1980-297 PV 409, May 31, 1967 "Dixième rapport general." For the Commission's dissatisfaction on agriculture see also ANF 724.713, box 7, Ministère de l'Economie et des Finances—DREE, Note, "Négociations commerciales multilatérales de Genève. Bilan succinct des travaux du 8 au 15 mai 1967," May 18, 1967.

among the industrialized countries. Completely different was the position of the LDCs. Despite the initial promise of a breakthrough in trade that would favor the interests of the LDCs, they were once again largely set aside. As the round entered its final phase, the problems these countries faced were moved to a lower level of priority, and developed countries consistently ignored their requests. The LDCs accused the developed countries of disregarding their interests. In response to this chorus, Wyndham White issued a statement noting that the actions taken had fallen far short of the expectations of the LDCs, making their disappointment with the GATT clearer than ever.[72]

The results of the round set the tone for the international trade regime. They led to freer trade in the industrial sector and protectionism in agriculture. They marked the position the EEC would hold in the world trading regime, and confirmed that the GATT was a "rich-man's club."

The EEC in International Trade Relations

At the first Council of Ministers meeting after the negotiations in Geneva, Rey thanked member states for the confidence they had shown in him. He affirmed that, without this support and the cohesion that had characterized the internal work of the Community in the last months, it would not have been possible to reach positive results.[73] Rey's remarks referred to the two most noteworthy aspects of the EEC in the last phase of the round: the confidence of the member states in the Commission, and their cohesiveness.

The Kennedy Round strengthened the solidarity of the Six and marked their emergence as a single unit in world trade. One year after the end of the crisis of the Empty Chair, the Six had been able to maintain cohesion during the last phase of the round. They had all made concessions in Brussels so as to achieve a common position from which to negotiate in Geneva. As the French and the Germans noted, facing other countries across the negotiating table helped the EEC member states to become more aware of their common interests and maintain their unity in the final phase of the round.[74] The Six found themselves in conflict

---

[72]   ANF 724.713, box 7, Ministère de l'Economie et des Finances—DREE, Note, "Négociations commerciales multilatérales de Genève. Bilan succinct des travaux du 8 au 15 mai 1967," 18 May 1967; Telegram from State Department to various posts, 22 May 1967, Bator papers, box 13, LBJL; CM2 1967/48 PV de la 224ème session du Conseil de la CEE, 26–27 June 1967.

[73]   CM2 1967/39 PV de la 221ème session du Conseil de la CEE, June 5–6, 1967.

[74]   ANF 724.713, box 7, Premier ministre, Comité Interministériel pour les Questions de Coopération Economique Européenne, Note, "Négociations commerciales dans le cadre du GATT," May 16, 1967. See also ibid., Ministère de l'Economie et des Finances—DREE, Note, "Négociations commerciales multilatérales de Genève. Bilan succinct des travaux du 8 au 15 mai 1967," May 18, 1967; AAPD 1967, document 170.

over many issues that corresponded to different national economic interests and different commercial policies. Nevertheless, these disagreements did not preclude a common stance or common commercial policy. They were aware that speaking with a unified voiced reinforced their bargaining strength and that concessions to achieve the necessary compromise to negotiate as a sole entity were indispensable. They shared trade interests in staying together in a Community and, consequently in bargaining as a unit and making necessary concessions.

For the Six, attending the round as a unit meant elaborating a common commercial policy that depended on reciprocal concessions motivated by different trade interests. The GATT negotiations favored the elaboration of the common commercial policy. The early definition of the EEC commercial policy was the result of a compromise among the different and diverging trading interests of the Six, and this position was prompted by the GATT talks. In effect, by responding to the U.S. initiative for a new GATT round, the Six were forced to define a common position concerning the multilateral trading system. Moreover, the Kennedy Round marked the EEC's new role as a single powerful actor on the world stage. Despite frequent and intense internal quarrels, the EEC was able to participate in important international negotiations with a single voice and finished the talks as one of the leading commercial actors in the multilateral system. It was through the implementation of a common commercial policy that the EEC became an international actor.

The Kennedy Round was a major confrontation between the EEC and the United States. In the discussions, the commercial negotiating power of the United States was matched by that of the EEC, which emerged as an equivalent commercial heavyweight. However, the EEC was not yet able to lead a major negotiation, and this task still remained the responsibility of Washington, for ongoing internal conflicts prevented the EEC from being able to move the GATT talks ahead. Moreover, in assessing reasons to successfully conclude the round, the EEC members seemed concerned only with the economic advantages they could obtain. By contrast, Washington also considered the impact that failure or success could have on the world trading regime and the GATT. The Six did not seem to have this orientation.

As for the confidence of the member states in the Commission, this issue is related to the role of this institution and the Council of Ministers in the EEC's trade policymaking. One of the aims of the Commission in attending the Kennedy Round was to establish itself as the sole negotiator on behalf of the EEC. The round strengthened the role of the Commission in international trade relations. In Brussels, during the last phase of the negotiations, member states were inclined to defer to Rey's opinions. In Geneva, step by step, the Commission was first able to reduce the role of the representatives of the member states that attended the discussions and then, finally, to remove them altogether from the discussions. In practice, the last phase of the negotiations was conducted by Rey and the other Commission negotiators, while representatives of the member states waited outside the bargaining room to be informed of the results. In the last phase the Commission was able to achieve its goal, confirming once more that the crisis of the Empty Chair had had no effect on its role in so fundamental a field as trade relations with countries outside the EEC. In 1963, Germany and the Netherlands had often challenged the Commission by asking to attend the bargaining in Geneva. As for the French, during the crisis of the Empty Chair they had strongly complained about the actions of the Commission. However, they had never questioned the latter's negotiating role or its right to bargain in the absence of the member states. This had been the hands-off attitude of the French government before June 1965, and it remained so after January 1966. In 1967, the Six were very well aware that, to enhance their trade interests, the EEC had to be represented by the Commission, which alone could talk in Geneva with a single voice. Thus member states allowed it to strengthen its role because doing so was in line with their trade interests.

The Commission passed the test posed by the Kennedy Round. In Brussels, it showed the necessary technical expertise and innovative thinking to generate ideas needed to reach a compromise; it was able to structure and set the terms of the bargaining and to steer the negotiations forward. The Commission used persuasion and the management of information to influence the perceptions of the member states and to assure them of its aims. Member states relied on its proposals and mediating role. In Geneva, the Commission affirmed its status as the sole EEC negotiating agent even in sectors for which it lacked legal authority, and member states proved increasingly inclined to defer to its judgment. In this way the Commission was able to perform, and even go beyond, the role the Treaty of Rome had assigned to it in 1957. It is worth noting that the sector in which the influence of the Commission was stronger was indeed agriculture, despite the fact that the Treaty of Rome did not authorize it to negotiate with other countries. The Commission bargained in Geneva on the basis of a plan it had itself negotiated, and member states never questioned its authority. On the contrary, they respected the opinions of Mansholt and Rabot on the agricultural sector.

Yet this account of the Commission's achievements needs to be qualified. They should be considered in light of the fact that member states had a priority interest in reaching an agreement. As a matter of fact, they aimed to attend the GATT talks as a trading unit and to successfully conclude the negotiations in Geneva. Both goals provided them with a strong incentive to compromise in both Brussels and Geneva and, consequently, eased the role of the Commission. Moreover, the Commission had its own preferences and attempted to enhance them through the presentation of proposals in Brussels and the manner in which it negotiated in Geneva. Yet there were clear limits to its capacity to determine the final outcome. In Brussels, the long meetings by the Council of Ministers, COREPER, and the 111 Committee, during which national governments questioned every single item from canned peaches to canned asparagus, demonstrated that trade policymaking remained in the hands of member states. The Commission was able to enhance its preferences only when they appealed to the Council of Ministers. The latter decided what outcome was acceptable, and the Commission had no autonomy in setting the content of the mandate. Its actions were constrained by the preferences of the member states.

In Geneva, it was the Council of Ministers that outlined the scope and limits of the Commission's room to maneuver, and the autonomy of the latter varied considerably over time as a function of the phase of the negotiations in Brussels and in Geneva. Whereas from 1963 to early 1967 member states strictly controlled the Commission, in the final phase they increased the discretion of their negotiating agent in order to improve the efficiency of the EEC's decision-making process. The representatives of the member states that attended the discussions in Geneva first silenced themselves, and then they left the negotiating room. Once member states decided that the round had to be concluded and there were no critical issues pending in Brussels, they granted the Commission the flexibility required to negotiate the last phase, although Rey was compelled to shuttle back and forth to Brussels to receive instructions. Yet the withdrawal and granting of concessions not authorized by member states and the fact that the Commission had a degree of autonomy to decide tactics show clearly that the latter was not simply acting as a messenger for the Council of Ministers. Member states pragmatically set limits to the EC's actions, guided by the principle of trade self-interest. Eventually, they allowed the Commission a stronger role because doing so coincided with their best interests.

Conclusions

This book has analyzed the participation of the EEC in the Kennedy Round. Its central argument is that these negotiations marked the emergence of the EEC as a world trading power, enshrined its international trade policy, and shaped its stance in world trade. To sum up the analysis, this concluding chapter will restate the main empirical findings in order to underline the key insight for each of the three domains of investigation with which I have been concerned.

The first domain is the bargaining among the EEC's members in Brussels to establish a common position from which to negotiate in Geneva. I have argued that member states had a major interest in attending the round as a regional trading unit, an orientation emanating from the factors that had led to the creation of the Community with a customs union as its foundation. This shared interest held the Six together, allowing them to overcome differences and reach the compromises necessary to formulate a common position. Crucially, the upcoming GATT talks spurred member states to reconcile their conflicting trade interests so as to converge on a common commercial policy that could be deployed in Geneva.

To be sure, the elaboration of a common position was not an easy goal to achieve. The Six agreed that too drastic a reduction in trade barriers would endanger the regionalism of the EEC and its unified identity. However, they had also divergent interests in the treatment of specific sectors. As Chapter 5 illustrated, member states bargained fiercely on the exceptions lists to be presented in Geneva, but at the same time they were all eager to pursue their collective aims, and thus were motivated to compromise. By the same token, Chapter 6 shows how the Six were able to come to an understanding over agriculture, despite the diverging interests of France and the other five countries. They were able to reach a final resolution because they were driven to negotiate with a single voice. This major interest led them to compromise.

Equally important, the Six were able to develop a common stance despite the many quarrels that strained their relations in areas other than the particulars of trade. As was shown in Chapter 3, the member states reached a common position under which to attend the two GATT ministerial meetings that launched the trade talks, notwithstanding the tensions caused by the French veto of the British request for membership and the negotiations over the CAP. As emerged in Chapter 4, even during the crisis of the Empty Chair, the Six were able to maintain their unity in Geneva despite the French boycott of the meetings in Brussels. Then, in the strained aftermath of the crisis, they were able to adopt a common position for the final part of the round. During the last phase of the talks, the Six stuck together impressively in the confrontation with the United States to defend their trade interests. This shows the fundamental importance of trade integration in the politics and economics of the member states, an aspect historians have often underestimated. Strong commercial interests held the Six together, despite the tensions that existed in other fields.

This ability to maintain unity permitted the EEC to speak with one voice and so become an international actor and a world trading power. Pooling sovereignty over trade relations and acting as a collective helped the Six to defend their trade interests and acquire a predominant position in world trade. As shown in Chapter 7, the EEC by the end of the Kennedy Round had emerged as a major actor capable of confronting the United States on equal terms. In this sense, the round confirmed the role of the EEC on the world stage and represented its first act of foreign policy.

Yet, while emerging as a commercial heavyweight and a powerful international actor, the EEC was not yet able to lead a major round of negotiations. Internal conflicts prevented the EEC from being able to move the talks ahead, a task that remained the responsibility of Washington. The limits of the EEC's leadership were also made evident by the attitude of its members, who seemed concerned only with the economic advantages they could obtain, toward the trade talks. By contrast, Washington also considered the impact that failure or success could have on the world trading regime, the GATT, and the transatlantic alliance. The United States bore the major responsibility for an outcome that it conceived in broad economic, diplomatic, and strategic terms.

The second domain of analysis in this book has been the EEC's trade policymaking. I have explored the role of the EEC's institutions in setting policy. Moreover, I have illustrated the Commission's effort to affirm its role as the sole negotiating agent on behalf of the EEC and strengthen its position both internally and externally, and have explained what led member states to grant to the Commission this role in most cases. The Commission had its own preferences distinct from those of member states and tried to advance them through its right of presenting proposals in Brussels, its technical and mediating skills, and its role as negotiating agent. In Brussels the Commission played a significant role in formulating the 1963 mandate, as shown in Chapter 3. Then, as Chapter 5 demonstrates, it played an important part in elaborating the list of exceptions for the industrial sector by presenting proposals and framing compromises that all six members could accept. As emerged in Chapters 3 and 6, thanks to its technical skill and vision of how trade in agriculture should be managed, the Commission was able to elaborate a plan that the Six accepted as the EEC's negotiating position in Geneva. Member states relied on the Commission for its proposals and brokering role, and the institution played a significant role in setting the policy outcome in Brussels.

Yet these achievements need to be more finely delimited. First, the fact remains that member states made all final decisions, and the Commission had to function within a mandate issued by the Council of Ministers after prolonged negotiations. The long and exhausting meetings of the Council of Ministers, COREPER, and the 111 Committee, during which national governments controlled and questioned the treatment of every single item in the mandate, plainly show that the elaboration of commercial policy remained in their hands. Moreover, the Commission's mediating role was surely eased by the fact that member states were interested in reaching a common position and therefore were willing to compromise. Equally important, as Chapter 5 showed, the Commission did not always favor mediation between national interests, and in some cases stuck to its original proposals, which contained measures to advance its preferences. In these instances, however, member states sidelined the supranational institution and reached a common stance without making use of its technical skills and proposals. Moreover, in the case of textiles and papers, for which the Commission based its proposals on an elaboration of the common industrial policy, member states ignored suggestions that did not suit them. Thus, there were clear limits to the capacity of the Commission to influence the final outcome of internal decision-making. It could promote its preferences only when they appealed to the Council of Ministers, and it could act only within the constraints imposed by the member states. Mediation and technical skills were not enough to write the Commission's own ideas into policy outcomes.

As for its role as negotiating agent, member states pragmatically set the scope and limits of the Commission's room to maneuver, guided by the principal objective of enhancing their own trade interests. Whereas in the Dillon Round the Six had curtailed the Commission's role by attending sessions with speaking rights, in the Kennedy Round they ultimately allowed it to become the sole negotiating agent even in sectors for which it lacked legal authority under the Treaty of Rome, because this tactic aligned with their interests. Speaking with a single voice, the EEC's negotiating agent reinforced the strength of individual national positions, for an EEC stance carried far more political weight than any one member country's opinions. Moreover, because it was the Commission as agent that faced other countries across the bargaining table, member states were isolated from pressures and could hide their divergent positions. Thus, the Brussels institution solidified its role by exploiting the interests of the Six in negotiating as a unit, and because member states allowed it to assume an active role.

The Commission's degree of freedom to maneuver varied over the course of the trade talks. From 1963 to early 1967, member states strictly controlled the Commission, which acted more or less as their porte-parole. There were two reasons for asserting this control. First of all, with the CAP issue still pending, France had no intention of giving flexibility to the Commission just to reach a compromise in Geneva. Second, the process of negotiating as a unit created a great deal of rigidity and caused significant delays in the talks in Geneva. The Six coordinated their position in Brussels through long meetings, as a result of which the Commission often showed up at the GATT negotiations with no room to shift its stance. Some member states—especially France—found this stultifying system useful, exploiting the rigidity in the EEC's policymaking to stretch out the bargaining until trading partners were more willing to offer concessions. Thus, the EEC could afford to keep its negotiators in Geneva on a tight leash, leaving little room for autonomy and discretion. As shown in Chapter 3, in 1964 the Commission tried to influence the outcome of the agricultural talks by exploiting its role as negotiating agent. The French reaction to this audacity demonstrates that member states had the necessary instruments to reign in their representative whenever it attempted to impose its own preferences or escape their control.

In the last phase of the talks, when concessions had to be exchanged in order to conclude the round, and with the CAP issue now settled, member states increased the discretion of their negotiating agent in order to improve the efficiency of the EEC decision-making process. As emerged in Chapter 7, they allowed the Commission to negotiate ad referendum and left the bargaining room. In many cases, the Commission presented to its negotiating partners concessions that the Council of Ministers had not authorized, going beyond the directives received. This was possible also because able commissioners and officials—such as Rey, Marjolin, Mansholt, Colonna di Paliano, Rabot, and Malvé—were able to win the confidence of the member states.

Member states had a pragmatic approach toward the Commission, considering how their trade interests might best be represented. Thus governments that openly criticized supranationalism, such as Paris, supported the Commission throughout the round because it had an almost identical vision on trade issues. By contrast, The Hague and Bonn, in theory supporters of supranationalism, often questioned the role of the Commission, as it did not represent the EEC in accordance with their wishes. In determining their position toward the supranational institution, member states did not consider airy ideological issues, but concrete trade interests. The pragmatism of member states was demonstrated by their attitude toward the Commission in the Empty Chair crisis. France never questioned the negotiating role of the Commission during and after the crisis, and it was during the last phase of the round that EEC's representative gained autonomy. Thus, despite what is often claimed, the crisis did not weaken its negotiating role. On the contrary, the economics and politics of a particular sector were the factors that determined what powers the Commission held. Thus, it negotiated over agriculture, NTBs, and Poland's application for GATT membership—all issues for which it lacked authority according to the Treaty of Rome—because member states desired to speak with one voice in these sectors. By the same token, these same states negotiated nationally over quantitative restrictions in textiles and in talks with Japan, with which they regulated trade by means of quantitative restrictions, despite the Commission's attempt to gain authority over these issues.

The struggle between member states and the Commission over the allocation of power in the conduct of foreign commercial policy in the Kennedy Round was only the first act of a longer play. Throughout the GATT/WTO rounds attended by the EEC/EU, the two actors continued to quarrel over the boundaries of their respective authority. As the international trade agenda shifted from tariffs and other border measures to NTBs, which had become the major obstacle to the free circulation of goods, and as new fields of international trade such as services, investments, and intellectual property were added to the GATT/WTO rounds, member states and the Commission repeatedly had to find a new settlement to their differences.

In the third domain of analysis, I examined the history of the GATT and international trade and the role the EEC played. I explained under which conditions the EEC reduced its trade barriers and, therefore, its contribution to the liberalization of international trade. I showed why the EEC became a liberal actor in the industrial sector, but a stumbling block in the agricultural sector.

The Kennedy Round was significant for the EEC because it set the tone of its international trade relations, established the patterns of its regional and multilateral integration, and defined its place in world trade. For the Six, attending the new GATT talks meant agreeing on the direction of their external trade relations by defining how open to world trade the EEC would be. Moreover, setting a common position from which to negotiate in Geneva required that the Six define in Brussels a common policy for manufactured goods and agricultural products. Thus, the EEC did not define its trade policy and its stance in the world trade regime in isolation in Brussels. The U.S. initiative for a far-reaching liberalization of trade and the GATT talks coincided with this definition and, at the same time, advanced it. At the same time that the EEC established a customs union, it also decided how liberal its customs union would be.

The EEC adopted a liberal stance on trade in manufactured goods, but complete protectionism on agriculture. As I showed in Chapters 2 and 5, in the industrial section of the round, the Six were prepared to reduce tariffs. An interest in enhancing their exports to other developed countries led them to adopt a liberal approach so as to obtain, on a reciprocal basis, a reduction in other countries' trade barriers. Thus they accepted lower tariffs and delineated the CCP along freer trade lines, contributing to the liberalization of international trade, even though differences existed among the Six. As illustrated in Chapter 7, the EEC substantially reduced its tariffs, and ended the round with lower average tariff protection than the United States, the United Kingdom, and Japan. In the case of the industrial sector, the creation of the EEC regional agreement had positive effects on the multilateral trade regime, as it favored liberalization.

The trade talks shed revealing light on the trade policy of each of the six member states. In general, France and Italy were more protectionist than Germany and the Benelux countries and preferred smaller tariff reductions than did the latter. However, France and Italy were not countries with "protectionism in their blood," as the Americans and the British put it. From behind the wall of the CET, they accepted a reduction in their tariffs, complementing the reductions they were already implementing to set the CET level of protection. This instance confirms the liberalizing role regional trade can have. Moreover, the Benelux countries and Germany also had products to protect for which they were unwilling to reduce barriers. None of the Six favored either free trade across the board or full protectionism; rather, each had sectors where the goal was reduced barriers, and other sectors it was determined to defend.

The round did not achieve any degree of liberalization in agriculture, nor even any regulation, apart from the International Wheat Agreement and token tariff reductions on some products. The priority of all EEC members in this area was to set up a CAP that would support the welfare of farmers and establish a regional market. None of them had any intention of compromising on this basic aim, and German agricultural policy could be as protectionist as French policy. Equally important, the CAP came to represent the sum of all of the protectionist policies of the Six, with the net result that the CAP was more protectionist than the individual national policies of the member states. The Netherlands, Germany, and, to a lesser extent, Italy had hoped to use the Kennedy Round to reach an understanding with other countries that would allow the EEC states to maintain their cheap imports of food from outside the EEC. The refusals of the Germans to set a lower price for grains and of the French to grant quantitative assurances to third countries precluded this wished-for result and, in general, a less protectionist common policy. As Chapters 6 and 7 demonstrated, when the negotiations started in Geneva, after a protectionist and non-negotiable CAP had been approved, there was not much to talk about. The EEC concluded the round with its CAP intact and remained free to increase its protectionism in the following years. The EEC became a stumbling bloc in agricultural trade and soon transitioned from a major world importer to a major world exporter. The trade talks were a lost opportunity to come to an agreement on the regulation of agriculture and to keep the protectionism of the CAP from becoming even more rigid.

The EEC's lack of interest in enhancing its exports and the higher priority it gave to a welfare policy in agriculture through the establishment of the CAP explain the total lack of bargaining power on the part of the GATT and the United States when it came to pushing the EEC to reduce trade barriers. Washington had nothing to offer the Six to entice them to decrease protectionism in this sector. In any case, its own GATT waiver, obtained in 1955, made it difficult for Washington to present itself as the sponsor of trade liberalization. Moreover, for security reasons—that is to say, to support European integration—the United States had chosen not to question the principle of the CAP, further weakening its bargaining stance.

The round did, however, pinpoint the direction that had to be followed in order to reduce discrimination in agriculture. It made clear that domestic policies had to be included in the negotiations if protectionism was to be reduced. The problems of world agriculture had clearly surfaced, while the political willingness to resolve them had not yet matured. Discussions on the agricultural sector identified the barriers, and the nature and the size of the system of protection. The Tokyo Round (1973–74) again made it abundantly clear that the traditional way of tackling the agricultural sector in multilateral GATT negotiations—that is, at the level of import border measures—could never free up trade in major agricultural products. In the early 1980s, the OECD started producing basic studies on overall support levels of the developed countries. These studies helped the GATT in the Uruguay Round (1986–94) to begin dealing with agriculture by encompassing all relevant measures: customs tariffs, domestic measures of support, export subsidization, and sanitary and phytosanitary regulations. In effect, in the Uruguay Round some initial, albeit limited, results were achieved. In the meantime the EU began to accept changes in the CAP mechanism with the McSharry reform of 1992. Agriculture, however, still remains a major barrier to the liberalization of international trade. The Doha Round, initiated in 2001, is still attempting to reduce discrimination in this sector.

The Kennedy Round achieved a 35 percent average tariff reduction, substantially higher than what had been achieved in previous GATT talks. However, not all areas of trade were affected in the same way, as the developed countries had sectors they wanted to shelter. The GATT's flexibility made it a suitable instrument to promote the internationalization of trade among developed countries. As protectionism and freer markets coexisted in the political economy of the developed countries, the GATT's flexible rules permitted the neomercantilism that characterized their commercial policies. Moreover, it well revealed the interaction between international institutions and national policies operating in trade policy areas.

The GATT proved its usefulness as an international, multilateral framework to enhance cooperation among governments at the crucial moment when the EEC regional agreement came into existence. It was to the multilateral framework of the GATT that the Eisenhower and then Kennedy administrations looked to reduce EEC discrimination. And it was again to the GATT that the Nixon administration turned in 1973 to smooth the effect of the EEC's growth in membership. In this sense, regionalism and multilateralism have always proceeded hand in hand throughout the history of the GATT.

While the GATT provided a suitable framework for industrialized countries to address their trade relations, LDCs remained unsatisfied. The problems of LDCs were considered in the Kennedy Round, even though no results were achieved, beyond further alienating LDCs from the international regime. The developing countries maintained that the industrialized nations had not devoted as much attention to their trade problems as had been promised. In truth, the latter had no intention of making concessions in the two types of goods crucial for the LDCs, textiles and tropical products. At the same time, it should be recognized that the nonreciprocity rule, ostensibly a feature that protected the LDCs, did not help them reach their aims. The GATT worked like a bazaar, and to obtain concessions, it was necessary to give them in return. Nonreciprocity rules marginalized the LDCs at the negotiating game. It would only be during the Uruguay Round in the 1980s that LDCs decided to more actively participate in the GATT and the liberalization of international trade.

While focusing primarily on the three domains just described, I have also considered the U.S. stance toward European integration. Two aspects are worth underlining. First, the United States began the round believing it would find allies in the Commission, Italy, Benelux, and above all Germany, which would lend strength to the American vision of the round against that of the French. In particular, the United States considered the Germans the "good ally" that would push to advance the talks in Brussels, and the French the "bad ally" that would throw up roadblocks. When the round started, however, Washington discovered that the interests of its presumed collaborators made them more friendly to the French than to the Americans. Even if these countries rejected de Gaulle's policies toward the United States, when it came to trade, they too wanted to defend the regionalism of the EEC, and sided with Paris, not Washington. By the same token, the Germans, with their foot-dragging on the UGP, revealed themselves to be something less than the welcome partner the United States had expected. The French, however, were not the troublemakers Washington had assumed they would be. As shown in Chapter 4, they allowed trade talks to go ahead despite the lack of agreement on the UGP, and during the crisis of the Empty Chair, France did not prevent the EEC from negotiating.

Second, promotion of an open, nondiscriminatory international economic system at the end of World War II went hand in hand with American support for a unified Europe. The U.S. position in the Kennedy Round was dictated by this dual strategy: to advance its trade interests and, at the same time, European unity. American support mitigated extant hostility toward the EEC and in certain instances even eased relations among the Six. This was clearly demonstrated in 1958, when the Treaty of Rome was presented to the GATT and, thanks to U.S. support, its inconsistency with the GATT's rules was not formalized. The Johnson administration conducted the round in such a way as to help the EEC's members to maintain their unity, and the Commission to retain its role in the Community's trade policymaking. The U.S. decision not to challenge the CAP or oppose unified grain prices in 1964 overrode German arguments against the UGP and generally eased the way for establishment of this policy. During the Empty Chair crisis, the Johnson administration waited for a resolution before continuing and concluding the round. This decision was surely dictated by the fact that proceeding without the EEC did not make sense, but also by U.S. interest in maintaining a framework within which the EEC could regain unity and the Commission could negotiate. The round enhanced European integration, and EEC regionalism emerged stronger from the Kennedy Round. In this sense, the U.S. desire to support a single European voice in trade was realized.

The problem for Washington, however, was that while it favored European integration and encouraged the EEC to speak with one voice, when that single voice spoke up, it was not always pleasant to hear. The EEC's politics were not necessarily in tune with American expectations. The Treasury, Agriculture, and Commerce departments, which, in contrast to the State Department, were more attentive to U.S. domestic interests than security interests, were especially concerned. By the end of the Kennedy Round, American worries about the direction European integration was taking were already evident. The deficit in the balance of payments and, for the first time since 1893, the transformation of the U.S. trade merchandise surplus into a deficit in 1971, compounded by strains over monetary and security relations, the protectionist mood of the U.S. Congress, the failure to reduce CAP protectionism, and the toughness with which the EEC had defended its regionalism, raised mistrust over European integration. All of these factors complicated the U.S. government's effort to justify to a domestic audience its toleration of trade discrimination on the part of—as Congress put it—powerful, healthy, and selfish allies. It was no longer possible to declare that the United

States had to subordinate its economic interest to the strengthening of European integration.

This shift became evident during the EEC's negotiations over adding new members from 1969 to 1972, when under the Nixon administration the American position turned openly hostile. Hence, U.S. support evolved alongside the progressive development of the EEC. Eisenhower's main concern in 1958 was to put the EEC on track, and, therefore, he uncritically accepted it. During the 1960s, the EEC began to exercise its ability to stand up to the United States as a partner of equal strength. By the time Nixon entered the White House, the EEC had clearly demonstrated that it did not need U.S. support to exist. The Nixon administration was freer to consider the problems the EEC raised and, therefore, to openly criticize its institutions and its growth. In this sense, the Kennedy Round marked the end of a period of two decades during which the United States actively promoted the unity of Western Europe.

Bibliography

Archival Sources

EU Archives

EC Council of Ministers, Brussels:
111 Committee minutes 1962–69
COREPER minutes 1962–69
Councils of Ministers minutes 1962–69
Dossiers on the Kennedy Round:
– CM2 1963/32-541-558-946-947-948-949
– CM2 1964/390-888-
– CM IA 1.824.52

EC Commission, Brussels
Commission minutes 1961–69, parts 1 and 2
Commission reports on 111 Committee meetings, 1961–69
Commission reports on COREPER meetings, 1961–69
Commission reports to the Council of Ministers on the Kennedy Round (1963–68)
Dossiers on Kennedy Round: BAC 118/83; BAC 62/1980; BAC 122/1991; BAC 38/194; BAC 62/1980; BAC 26/1969
Mansholt *cabinet* papers
Marjolin *cabinet* papers

Historical Archives of the European Union, Florence
Dossiers on the Kennedy Round: CEAB 5/1169; BAC 026/1969; BAC 9/1967
Edoardo Martino papers
Emile Noël papers
Jean Monnet papers
Max Konstahm papers
Ministère des Affaires Etrangères Français (MAEF) Secrétariat Général, Entretiens et Messages, vols 17–22
Olivier Wormser papers

France

724.70/10, 1964–67 Kennedy Round, boxes 1–4
Archives Nationales Contemporaines, Fontainebleau
Couve de Murville cabinet papers

DREE files 1963–69
Ministère des Affaires Etrangères (Quai d'Orsay), Paris, Série Europe 1961–66
Série DE-CE 1961–66: GATT 929-930-931-932-949
SGCI files 1963–69

United Kingdom

Public Record Office, London
Board of Trade's files (BT 241, 303, 258)
Cabinet (CAB 147, 164)
Foreign Office files (FO 371)
Prime Minister's files (PREM 13)
Treasury (T 312)

United States

Kennedy Library
Ball papers
Herter papers
Pre-presidential papers

Johnson Library
Ball papers
Bator papers
Roth papers
Solomon papers
Administrative History of the Office of the Special Representative for Trade
    Negotiations, State Departments, Agricultural Departments, Treasury
    Departments, Agricultural Departments, Commerce Departments
Annual report of the President of the United States of trade programme, 1961–68
NSF – Europe and USSR, France, box 170
NSF Subject Files
WHCF

National Archives and Records Administration (NARA)
NA 364 Records of US Trade Representatives on Kennedy Round
NA 59 State Department, CDF 1960–63
NA 59 State Department 1964–66 Ecin 3
Na 59 State Department Central file subject numeric
NA 59, GRDS, CFPF
NA Congressional Records 1962–69
NA State Department, Central Files, FT 4 US/TEA
NA State Department, Presidential Memoranda of Conversation: Lot 66 D 149

Personal Archives

Jean Rey's personal papers, Université Libre de Bruxelles (JRPP)

Published official documents

Akten zur Auswärtigen Politik des Bundesrepublik Deutschland (AAPD) 1963–69
Documents Diplomatiques Français (DDF), 1963–65
Foreign Relations of the United States:
– Kennedy Administration (Europe and Canada)
– Johnson Administration 1964–68 (vol. VIII, International Monetary and Trade Policy; vol. XII, Western Europe; vol. XIII, Western Europe Region)
– Nixon Administration 1969–76 (vol. I, Foundations of Foreign Policy; vol. III, Foreign Economic Policy, 1969–72; International Monetary Policy, 1969–72; vol. IV, Foreign Assistance, International Development, Trade Policies, 1969–72)
GATT Basic Instruments and Selected Documents, 1958–72

Statistical collections

Direction of Trade Statistics Historical, 1948–1980 (Washington, DC: International Monetary Fund, 2002)
Foreign Agricultural Trade of the United States, U.S. Department of Agriculture, Economic Research Service.
Foreign Trade Related to Various Measures of Production: 1869–1970.
OECD SITC Rev. 2 – Historical Series 1961–1990 (Paris: OECD, 2000) *Political and Economic Planning. Atlantic Tariffs and Trade* (London: George Allen and Unwin, 1962; Research Service, March 1970)
Statistical Office of the European Communities 1954–78
Survey of Current Business (United States Department of Commerce, Bureau of Economic Analysis), October 1972, June 1975, June 1976.
United States Bureau of Census, *The Statistical History of the United States. From Colonial Times to the Present* (New York: Basic Books, 1976)

Interviews

Paul Luyten, Brussels, July 7, 2003
Jean-Michel Jacquet, Brussels, July 12, 2003
Valéry Giscard d'Estaing , Florence, October 27, 2004
Richard Gardner, Florence, May 3, 2005

Secondary sources

Aggarwal, Vinod K., and Fogarty, Edward A., *EU Trade Strategies. Between Regionalism and Globalism* (Basingstoke: Palgrave Macmillan 2004).

Alkema, Ynze, *Regionalism in a Multilateral Framework. The EEC, the United States and the GATT. Confronting Trade Policies, 1957–62* (EUI Ph.D. dissertation, 1996).

Alkema, Ynze, "European–American Trade Policies, 1961–1963," in Douglas Brinkley and Richard T. Griffiths (eds), *John F. Kennedy and Europe* (Baton Rouge, LA: Louisiana State University Press, 1999), 212–34.

Alting von Geusau, Frans A.M., *Economic Relations after the Kennedy Round* (Leyden: Sijthoff, 1969).

Ambrosius, Gerold, "The Federal Republic of Germany and the Common Market in Industrial Goods in the 1960s," in Regine Perron (ed.) *The Stability of Europe. The Common Market: Towards European Integration of Industrial and Financial markets? (1958–1968)* (Paris: Presses de l'université de Paris-Sorbonne, 2004), 47–61.

Anderson, Kym, *The External Implications of European Integration* (New York: Harvester Wheatsheaf, 1993).

Anderson, Kym, and Blackhurst, Richard (eds), *Regional Integration and the Global Trading System* (London: Harvester, Wheatsheaf, 1993).

Asbeek Brusse, Wendy, "The Americans, the GATT, and European Integration, 1947–1957: A Decade of Dilemma," in Francis H. Heller and John R. Gillingham (eds), *The United States and the Integration of Europe. Legacies of the Postwar Era* (New York: St Martin's Press, 1992), 221–49.

Asbeek Brusse, Wendy, *Tariff, Trade and European Integration 1947–1957. From Study Group to Common Market* (New York: St Martin Press, 1997).

Avery, William P. (ed.), *World Agriculture and the GATT* (Boulder, CO: Lynne Rienner, 1993).

Bairoch, Paul, *Economics and World History: Myths and Paradoxes* (New York: Harvester Wheatsheaf, 1993).

Balassa, Bela, "Tariff Protection in Industrial Countries: An Evaluation," *The Journal of Political Economy* 73, 6 (1965), 573–94.

Balassa, Bela, *Trade Liberalisation Among Industrial countries. Objectives and Alternatives* (London: McGraw Hill, 1967).

Balassa, Bela (ed.) *European Economic Integration* (Amsterdam: North-Holland, 1975).

Balassa, Bela, and Kreinin, Mordechai E., "Trade Liberalization Under the Kennedy Round: The Static Effects," *Review of Economics and Statistics* 49, 2 (1967), 125–37.

Baldwin, Richard, *A Domino Theory of Regionalism* (Cambridge: NBER, 1993).

Baldwin, Richard, and Wyplosz, Charles, *The Economics of European Integration* (London: McGraw Hill, 2009).

Baldwin, Robert E., *Trade Policy in a Changing World Economy* (New York: Harvester Wheatsheaf 1988).

Baldwin, Robert E., and Krueger Ann O., *The Structure and Evolution of Recent US Trade Policy* (Chicago, IL: University of Chicago Press, 1984).

Ball, George W., *The Past has Another Pattern* (New York: Norton, 1984).

Ballini, Pier Luigi, and Varsori, Antonio (eds), *L'Italia e l'Europa (1947–1979)* (Soveria Mannelli: Rubbettino, 2004).

Bange, Oliver, *Picking Up the Pieces* (Ph.D. dissertation, London University, 1997).

Barton, John H., Goldstein, Judith L., Josling, Timothy E., and Steinberg, Richard H., *The Evolution of the Trade Regime. Politics, Law, and Economics of the GATT and WTO* (Princeton, NJ: Princeton University Ptress, 2006).

Basevi, Giorgio, "The US Tariff Structure: Estimates of Effective Rates of Protection of US Industries and Industrial Labour," *Review of Economics and Statistics* 48 (1966), 147–60.

Benoit, Emile, *Europe at Sixes and Sevens. The Common Market, the Free Trade Area Association and the United States* (New York: Columbia University Press, 1961).

Block, Fred L., *The Origins of International Economic Disorder. A Study of United States International Monetary Policy from World War II to the Present* (Berkeley, CA: University of California Press, 1978).

Borden, William S., "Defending Hegemony: American Foreign Economic Policy," in Paterson, Thomas G. (ed.), *Kennedy's Quest for Victory: American Foreign Policy, 1961–1963* (New York: Oxford University Press, 1989).

Bordo, Michael D., and Eichengreen, Barry J. (eds), *A Retrospective on the Bretton Woods System: Lesson for International Monetary Reform* (Chicago, IL: University of Chicago Press, 1993).

Bozo, Frédéric, *Two Strategies for Europe: De Gaulle, the United States and the Atlantic Alliance* (Lanham, MD: Rowman and Littlefield, 2001).

Brinkley, Douglas, and Griffiths, Richard T. (eds), *John F. Kennedy and Europe* (Baton Rouge, LA: Louisiana State University Press, 1999).

Brown, William, A., *The United States and the Restoration of World Trade: An Analysis and Appraisal of the ITO Charter and the General Agreement on Tariffs and Trade* (Washington, DC: Brookings Institution, 1950).

Calandri, Elena, "L'Italia e l'assistenza allo sviluppo dal neoatlantismo alla Conferenza di Cancun del 1981," in Federico Romero and Antonio Varsori (eds), *Nazione, interdipendenza, integrazione. Le relazioni internazionali dell'Italia (1917–1989)* (Bari: Carocci: 2006), 253–70.

Calleo, David, and Rowland, Benjamin M., *America and the World Political Economy: Atlantic Dreams and National Realities* (Bloomington, IN: Indiana University Press, 1973).

Camps, Miriam, *European Unification in the Sixties. From Veto to the Crisis* (Oxford: Oxford University Press, 1967).

Caporaso, James A., *The European Union. Dilemmas of Regional Integration* (Boulder, CO: Westview Press, 2000).

Casadio, Gian Paolo, *Transatlantic Trade: USA–EEC Confrontation in the GATT Negotiations* (Farnborough: Saxon House, 1973).

Cohen, Benjamin J., *Organizing the World's Money: The Political Economy of International Monetary Relations* (London: Macmillan, 1978).

Coleman, William D. and Tangermann, Stefan, "The 1992 CAP Reform, the Uruguay Round and the Commission: Conceptualizing Linked Policy Games," *Journal of Common Market Studies* 37, 3 (1999), 385–405.

Coombes, David, *Politics and Bureaucracy in the European Community: A Portrait of the European Commission* (London: PEP, 1970).

Coppolaro, Lucia, "East–West Trade, the General Agreement on Tariffs and Trade (GATT) and the Cold War: Poland's Accession to GATT (1957–1967)," in Jari Eloranta and Jari Ojala (eds), *East–West Trade and the Cold War* (Jyväskylä: University of Jyväskylä Press, 2005), 124–48.

Coppolaro, Lucia, "The Empty Chair Crisis and the Kennedy Round of GATT Negotiations (1962–1967)," in Jean Marie Palayret, Helen Wallace and Pascaline Winand (eds), *Visions, Votes and Vetoes: The Empty Chair Crisis and the Luxembourg Compromise Forty Years On* (Brussels: Peter Lang, 2006), 219–42.

Coppolaro, Lucia. "The European Economic Community and the United States of America in the GATT Negotiations of the Kennedy Round (1964–1967): Global and Regional Trade," in Antonio Varsori (ed.) *Inside the European Community. Actors and Policies in the European Integration 1957–1972* (Baden-Baden: Nomos, 2006), 347–68.

Coppolaro, Lucia, "The United States and the EEC Enlargement (1969–1973): Reaffirming the Atlantic Framework," in Jan van der Harst (ed.), *Beyond the Customs Union: The European Community's Quest for Deepening, Completion and Enlargement, 1969–1975* (Brussels: Nomos, 2007), 135–62.

Coppolaro, Lucia, "U.S. Payments Problems and the Kennedy Round of GATT Negotiations, 1961–1967," in David M. Andrews (ed.), *Orderly Change: International Monetary Relations Since Bretton Woods* (Ithaca, NY: Cornell University Press, 2008), 120–38.

Coppolaro, Lucia, "The Six, Agriculture, and GATT. An International History of the CAP Negotiations (1958–1967)," in Kiran Patel (ed.), *Fertile Ground for Europe? The History of European Integration and the Common Agricultural Policy since 1945* (Baden-Baden: Nomos, 2009), 201–219.

Coppolaro, Lucia, "U.S. Policy on European Integration during the GATTKennedy Round Negotiations (1963–67): The last Hurrah of America's Europeanists" *The International History Review* 33, 3 (2011), 409–29.

Costigliola, Frank, "The Failed Design. Kennedy, de Gaulle, and the struggle for Europe," *Diplomatic History* 8 (1984), 227–51.

Costigliola, Frank, *France and the United States: The Cold Alliance since the World War II* (New York: Columbia University Press, 1992).

Costigliola, Frank, "Kennedy, de Gaulle, and the Challenge of Consultation," in Robert O. Paxton and Nicholas Wahl (eds), *De Gaulle and the United States: A Centennial Reappraisal* (Oxford: Oxford University Press, 1994), 169.

Craft, Nicholas, and Toniolo, Gianni., *Economic Growth in Europe since 1945* (Cambridge: Cambridge University Press, 1996).

Couve de Murville, Maurice, *Une Politique Etrangère 1958–1969* (Paris, Plon 1971).

Curtice, Thomas B., and Vastine, John R. Jr, *The Kennedy Round and the Future of American Trade* (New York: Praeger, 1971).

Curzon, Gerard, *Multilateral Commercial Diplomacy: The General Agreement on Trade and Tariffs and its Impact on National Commercial Policies and Techniques* (New York: Praeger, 1965).

Daddow, Oliver J. (ed.), *Harold Wilson and European Integration. Britain's Second Application to Join the EEC* (London: Frank Cass, 2002).

Dallek, Robert, *Flawed Giant. Lyndon Johnson and his Times* (Oxford: Oxford University Press, 1998).

Dam, Kenneth W., *The GATT: Law and International Economic Organization* (Chicago, IL: University of Chicago Press, 1970).

De Bièvre, Dirk, and Dür, Andreas "Constituency Interests and Delegation in European and American Trade Policy," *Comparative Political Studies* 38, 10 (2005), 1271–96.

Deighton, Ann, and Milward, Alan S. (eds), *Widening, Deepening and Acceleration: The European Economic Community 1957–1963* (Baden-Baden: Nomos, 1999).

De Melo, Jaime, and Panagariya, Arvind (eds), *New Dimensions in Regional Integration* (Cambridge: Cambridge University Press, 1993).

Destler, I.M., *American Trade Politics* (Washington, DC: Institute for International Economics/New York: Twentieth Century Fund, 1992).

Diebold, William Jr, *The End of ITO* (Ann Arbor, MI: University of Michigan, 1981).

Diebold, William Jr, "A Watershed with Some Dry Sides," in Douglas Brinkley, and Griffiths, Richard T. (eds), *John F. Kennedy and Europe* (Baton Rouge, LA: Louisiana State University Press, 1999), 250–63.

DiLeo, L., "George Ball and the Europeanists in the State Department, 1961–1963," in D. Brinkley and R.T. Griffiths (eds) *John F. Kennedy and Europe* (Baton Rouge, LA: Louisiana State University Press, 1999), 263–80.

Dinan, Desmon, *Origins and Evolution of the European Union* (Oxford: Oxford Univeristy Press, 2006).

Dryden, Steven, *Trade Warriors: USTR and the American Crusade for Free Trade* (Oxford: Oxford University Press, 1995).

Dür, Andreas, and Zimmermann, Hubert, "Introduction: The EU in International Trade Negotiations," *Journal of Common Market Studies* 45, 4 (2007), 771–87.

Eckes, Alfred E. Jr, *Opening American Market. US Foreign Trade Policy since 1776* (Chapel Hill, NC: The University of North Carolina Press, 1995).

Eckes, Alfred E. Jr, *Revisiting U.S. Trade Policy. Decisions in Perspective* (Athens, OH: Ohio University Press, 2000).

Eichengreen, Barry J., "Institutions and Economic Growth. Europe after World War II," in N. Crafts and G. Toniolo (eds), *Economic Growth in Europe since 1945* (Cambridge: Cambridge University Press, 1996).

Eichengreen, Barry J., *The European Economy since 1945: Coordinated Capitalism and Beyond* (Princeton, NJ: Princeton University Press 2007).

Eichengreen, Barry J., *Exorbitant Privilege: The Rise and Fall of the Dollar and the Future of the International Monetary System* (Oxford: Oxford University Press, 2011).

Elsig, Manfred, *The EU's Commercial Policy* (Aldershot: Ashgate, 2002).

Erhard, Ludwig, *Germany's Comeback in the World Market* (London: Allen & Unwin, 1954).

Evans, John W., *The Kennedy Round in American Trade Policy: Twilight of the GATT?* (Cambridge, MA: Harvard University Press, 1971).

Fauri, F., "Italy and the Free Trade Area Negotiations 1956–1958," *Journal of European Integration* 4, 2 (1988), 47–66.

Fauri, Francesca, *L'Italia e l'integrazione economica europea 1947–2000* (Bologna: Il Mulino, 2001).

Federico, Giovanni, *Feeding the World. An Economic History of Agriculture (1800–2000)* (Princeton, NJ: Princeton University Press, 2006).

Findlay, Ronald and O'Rourke, Kevin, *Power and Plenty: Trade, War and the World Economy in the Second Millennium* (Princeton, NJ: Princeton University Press 2007).

Finger, Michael J., "Effects of the Kennedy Round Tariff Concessions on the Exports of Developing Countries," *Economic Journal* 86, 341 (1976), 87–95.

Frank, Isaiah, *The European Common Market. An Analysis of Commercial Policy* (New York: Praeger, 1961).

Galli, Rosemary, and Torcasio, Saverio, *La partecipazione italiana alla politica agricola comunitaria* (Rome: IAI, Il Mulino, 1976).

Gardner, Richard N., *Sterling–Dollar Diplomacy in Current Perspective: The Origins and the Prospects of our International Economic Order* (New York: Columbia University Press, 1980).

Gavin, Francis J., *Gold, Dollars, and Power. The Politics of International Monetary relations, 1958–1971* (Chapel Hill, NC: University of North Carolina Press, 2004).

Geary, Michael J., *The European Commission and the First Enlargement of the European Union: Challenging for Power?* (London: Palgrave and Macmillan, forthcoming).

Gilpin, Robert, *The Political Economy of International Relations* (Princeton, NJ: Princeton University Press, 1987).

Golt, Sidney, *Developing Countries and the GATT System* (London: Trade Policy Research Centre, 1978).

Granieri, Ronald J., *The Ambivalent Alliance. Konrad Adenauer, the CDU/CSU, and the West 1948–1966* (New York: Berghahn Books, 2002).

Griffiths, Richard T., "The Common Market," in *The Netherlands and the Integration of Europe 1945–1957* (Amsterdam: NEHA, 1990), 183–208.

Griffiths, Richard T., *The Netherlands and the Integration of Europe 1945–1957* (Amsterdam: NEHA, 1990).

Griffiths, Richard, T. (ed.), *Exploration in OEEC History* (Paris: Organisation for Economic Co-operation and Development, 1997).

Griffiths, Richard, T., and Girvin, Brian (eds) *The Green Pool and the Origins of the Common Agricultural Policy* (London: LP, 1995).Grosser, Alfred, *The Western Alliance: European–American Relations Since 1945* (New York: Vintage Books, 1982).

Hachez-Leroy, Florence, *L'aluminium français: l'invention d'un marché, 1911–1983* (Paris: CNRS, 1999).

Harryvan, Anjo G. "A successful Defence of the Communitarian Model? The Netherlands and the Empty Chair Crisis," in Jean Marie Palayret, Helen Wallace, and Pascaline Winand (eds), *Visions, Votes and Vetoes: The Empty Chair Crisis and the Luxembourg Compromise Forty Years On* (Brussels: Peter Lang, 2006), 129–152.

Harryvan, Anjo G., *In Pursuit of Influence: The Netherland's European Policy during the Formative Years of the European Union, 1952–1973* (Brussels: Peter Lang 2009).

Harryvan, Anjo G., and van der Harst, Jan, "For Once a United Front. The Netherlands and the 'Empty Chair' Crisis of the Mid-1960s," in Wilfried Loth, *Crises and Compromises: The European Project 1963–1969* (Baden-Baden: Nomos, 2001), 167–91.

Hayward, David J., *International Trade ad Regional Economies. The Impacts of European Integration on the United States* (Boulder, CO: Westview Press, 1995).

Hedges, Irwin, R., "Kennedy Round Agricultural Negotiations and the World Grains Agreement," *Journal of Farm Economics* 49 (1967), 1332–44.

Hendriks, Gisela, "The Creation of the Common Agricultural Policy," in Ann Deighton and Alan S. Milward (eds), *Widening, Deepening and Acceleration* (Baden-Baden: Nomos, 1999), 143–56.

Henig, Stanley *External Relations of the European Community: Associations and Trade Agreements* (London: Political and Economic Planning, 1971).

Hieronymi, Otto, *Economic Discrimination against the United States in Western Europe* (Geneva: Droz, 1973).

Hilf, Meinhard, Jacobs, Francis G., and Petersmann, Ernst-Ulrich, *The European Community and GATT* (Deventer: Kluwer, 1986).

Hine, Robert C., *The Political Economy of European Trade. An Introduction to the Trade Policies of the EEC* (Brighton: Wheatsheaf Books/New York: St Martin's Press, 1985).

Hoda, Anwarul, *Tariff Negotiations and Renegotiations under the GATT and the WTO. Procedures and Practices* (Cambridge: Cambridge University Press, 2001).

Hoekman, Bernard, and Kostecki, Michael M., *The Political Economy of the World Trading System. The WTO and Beyond* (Oxford: Oxford University Press, 2009).

Holloway, Steven T., *The Aluminium Multinationals and the Bauxite Cartel* (Basingstoke: Macmillan, 1987).

Hudec, Robert E., *The GATT Legal System and World Trade Diplomacy* (New York: Praeger, 1975).

Irwin, Douglas A., "The GATT in Historical Perspective," *American Economic Review* 85, 2 (1995), 323–8.

Irwin, Douglas A., Mavroidis, Petros C., and Sykes, Alan O., *The Genesis of the GATT* (Cambridge: Cambridge University Press, 2008).

Jackson, John H., *World Trade and the Law of GATT* (Indianapolis, IN: Bobbs-Merrill, 1969).

Jackson, John H., *The World Trading System. Law and Policy of international Economic Relations* (Cambridge, MA, MIT Press, 1992).

James, Harold, *International Monetary Cooperation Since 1945* (Washington, DC: International Monetary Fund, 1996).

Johnson, Lyndon B., *The Vantage Point: Perspective of the Presidency, 1963–1969* (New York: Holt, Rinehart and Winston, 1971).

Johnson, Michael, *European Community Trade Policy and the Article 113 Committee* (London: Royal Institute of International Affairs, International Economics Programme, 1998).

Josling, Timothy E., Tangermann, Stefan, and Warley, T.K., *Agriculture in the GATT* (London: Macmillan/St Martin's Press, 1996).

Kerremans, Bart, and Switky, Bob, *The Political Importance of Regional Trading Blocs* (Aldershot: Ashgate, 2000).

Knudsen, Ann-Christina L., *Farmers on Welfare: The Making of Europe's Common Agricultural Policy* (Ithaca, NY: Cornell University Press, 2009).

Kock, Karin, *International Trade Policy and the GATT 1947–1967* (Stockholm: Amlquist and Widsell, 1969).

Kohlhase, Norbert, and Schwamm, Henri (eds), *La négociation CEE Suisse dans le Kennedy round* (Lausanne: Centre de recherches europeennes, 1974).

Kostecki, Michael M., *East–West Trade and the GATT System* (London: Macmillan, 1979).

Kraft, Joseph, *The Grand Design: From Common Market to Atlantic Partnership* (New York: Harper, 1962).

Krause, Lawrence B., *Europe Economic Integration and the United States* (Washington, DC: Brookings Institute, 1968).

Krueger, Ann O. "Trade Policy and Economic Development: How We Learn," *American Economic Review* 87 (1997), 1–22.

Lambert, John, "The Constitutional Crisis of 1965–1966," *Journal of Common Market Studies*, 4 (1966), 221–3.

Lappenkueper, Ulrich, "'Ein Europa der Freien und der Gleichen': La politique européenne de Ludwig Erhard (1963–1966)," in Wilfred Loth (ed.), *Crisis and Compromises: The European Project, 1963–1969* (Baden-Baden: Nomos, 2001), 65–91.

Laschi, Giuliana, *L'agricoltura italiana e l'integrazione europea* (Bern: Peter Lang, 1999).

Lee, Donna, *Middle Powers and Commercial Policy. British Influence at the Kennedy Round* (New York: St Martin's Press, 1999).

Loth, Wilfried, *Crises and Compromises: The European Project 1963–1969* (Baden-Baden: Nomos, 2001).

Ludlow, N. Piers, *Dealing with Britain. The Six and the First UK Application to the EEC* (Cambridge: Cambridge University Press, 1997).

Ludlow, N. Piers, "Challenging French Leadership in Europe: Germany, Italy, the Netherlands and the Outbreak of the Empty Chair Crisis of 1965–1966," *Contemporary European History* 8, 2 (1999). 231–48.

Ludlow, N. Piers, *The European Community and the Crises of the 1960s: Negotiating the Gaullist Challenge* (London: Routledge, 2006).

Ludlow, N. Piers, "The Emergence of a Commercial Heavy-weight: The Kennedy Round and the European Community of the 1960s," *Diplomacy and Statecraft* 18, 2 (2007), 351–68.

Lundestad, Geir, *"Empire" by Integration: The United States and European Integration, 1945–1997* (Oxford: Oxford University Press, 1998).

Lynch, Francis M.B., *France and the International Economy: From Vichy to the Treaty of Rome* (London: Routledge, 1996).

Lynch, Francis M.B., "De Gaulle's First Veto: France, the Rueff Plan and the Free Trade Area," *Contemporary European History* 9, 1 (2000), 111–35.

Ly Van Luong, Matthieu, "L'aluminium européen dans les négociations commerciales du Kennedy Round," *Cahiers d'Histoire de l'Aluminium* 28 (2001), 43–60.

Mathias, Jorg, *Regional Trade Agreements in the GATT/WTO. Article XXIV and the Internal Trade Requirements* (The Hague: TMC Asser Press, 2002).

Mayer, Frank A., *Adenauer and Kennedy: A Study in German–American relations, 1961–1963* (London: Macmillan, 1996).

McCalla, Alex F., "Protectionist in International Agricultural Trade, 1850–1968," *Agricultural History* 43 (1969), 329–43.

McKenzie, Francine, "GATT–EEC Collision: The Challenge of Regional Trade Blocs to the General Agreement of Tariffs and Trade, 1950–1967," *International History Review* 33, 3 (2010), 229–52.

Metzger, Stanley D., *Trade Agreements and the Kennedy Round* (Fairfax, VA: Coiner, 1964).

Meunier, Sophie, *Trading Voices. The European Union in International Commercial Negotiations* (Princeton, NJ: Princeton University Press, 2006).

Milward, Alan S., "Tariffs as Constitutions," in S. Strange and R. Tooze (eds), *The International Politics of Surplus Capacity: Competition for Market Shares in the World Recession* (London: Allen & Unwin, 1981).

Milward, Alan S., *The Reconstruction of Western Europe, 1945–51* (London: Methuen, 1984).

Milward, Alan S., "Was the Marshall Plan Necessary?," *Diplomatic History* 13 (1989) 231–53.

Milward, Alan S., "The Origin of the Fixed-rate Dollar System," in Jaime Reis (ed.), *International Monetary System in Historical Perspective* (Basingstoke/New York: Macmillan/St Martin's Press, 1995).

Milward, Alan S., *The European Rescue of the Nation-state* (London: Routledge, 2000).

Milward, Alan S., and Brennan, George, *Britain's Place in the World Import Controls 1945–60* (London: Routledge 1996).

Milward, Alan S., *The United Kingdom and the European Community. The Rise and Fall of a National Strategy* (London: Frank Cass, 2002).

Milward, Alan S., Lynch, Francis M.B., Ranieri, Ruggero, Romero, Federico, and Sorensen, Vibeke, *The Frontier of National Sovereignty. History and Theory* (London: Routledge, 1993).

Moravcsik, Andrew, *The Choice for Europe: Social Purpose and State Power from Messina to Maastricht* (Ithaca, NY: Cornell University Press, 1998).

Moravcsik, Andrew, "De Gaulle Between Grain and Grandeur: The Political Economy of French EC Policy, 1958–1970," *Journal of Cold War Studies* 2–3 (2000), 4–68.

Nême, Jacques, and Nême, Colette, *Economie Européenne* (Paris: Presses universitaires de France, 1970).

Norwood, Bernard, "The Kennedy Round: A Try at Linear Trade negotiations," *Journal of Law and Economics* 12 (1969), 297–319.

Paemen, Hugo, and Bensch Alexandra, *From the GATT to the WTO. The EEC in the Uruguay Round* (Leuven: Leuven University Press, 1995).

Palayret, Jean-Marie, Wallace, Helen, and Winand, Pascaline (eds), *Visions, Votes and Vetoes: The Empty Chair Crisis and the Luxembourg Compromise Forty Years On* (Brussels: Peter Lang, 2006).

Patel, Kiran (ed.), *Fertile Ground for Europe? The History of European Integration and the Common Agricultural Policy since 1945* (Baden-Baden: Nomos, 2009).

Paterson, Thomas G., *Kennedy's Quest for Victory: American Foreign Policy, 1961–1963* (New York: Oxford University Press, 1989).

Patterson, Gardner, *Discrimination in International Trade: The Policy Issues 1945–1965* (Princeton, NJ: Princeton University Press, 1966).

Petrini, Francesco, *Il liberismo a una dimensione: la Confindustria e l'integrazione europea, 1947–1957* (Milan: Franco Angeli, 2005).

Peyrefitte, Alain, *C'était de Gaulle* (Paris: Fayard, 1994).

Phillips, Peter W.B., *Wheat Europe and the GATT* (New York: St Martin's Press, 1990).

Pizzorni, Geoffrey J., *L'industria chimica italiana nel Novecento* (Milan: FrancoAngeli, 2006).

Political and Economic Planning, *Atlantic Tariffs and Trade* (London: George Allen and Unwin, 1962).

Pollack, Mark, *The Engines of European Integration: Delegation, Agency, and Agenda Setting in the EU* (Oxford: Oxford University Press, 2003).

Pomfret, Richard W.T., *The Economics of Regional Trading Arrangements* (Oxford: Oxford University Press, 2001).

Prate, Alain, *Les batailles économiques du Général de Gaulle* (Paris: Plon, 1978).

Preeg, Ernest H., *Traders and Diplomats: An Analysis of the Kennedy Round of Negotiations under the GATT* (Washington, DC: Brookings Institute, 1970).

Ramírez Pérez, S.M., "The Role of Multinational Corporations in the Foreign Trade Policy of the European Economic Community: The Automobile Sector Between 1959 and 1967," *Actes du Gerpisa*, no. 38 – "Variety of Capitalism and Diversity of Productive Models."

Ranieri, Ruggero, "Italian Industry and the EEC," in Ann Deighton and Alan S. Milward (eds), *Widening, Deepening and Acceleration: The European Economic Community 1957–1963* (Baden-Baden: Nomos, 1999), 185–96.

Ranieri, Ruggero, "The Origins and Achievements of the EEC Customs Union (1958–1968)," in Antonio Varsori (ed.), *Inside the European Community. Actors and Policies in the European Integration 1957–1972* (Baden-Baden: Nomos, 2006), 257–81.

Reis, Jaime (ed.), *International Monetary System in Historical Perspective* (Basingstoke/New York: Macmillan/St Martin's Press, 1995).

Romero, Federico, "Interdependence and Integration in American Eyes: From the Marshall Plan to Currency Convertibility," in Milward, Alan S. (ed.), *The Frontier of National Sovereignty. History and Theory 1945–1992* (London: Routledge, 1994), 155–82.

Romero, Federico, and Varsori, Antonio, *Nazione, Interdipendenza, Integrazione. Le relazione internazionali dell'Italia (1917–1989)* (Rome: Carocci, 2006).

Rosamond, Ben, *Theories of European Integration* (Basingstoke/New York: Macmillan/St Martin's Press, 2000).

Sanderson, Fred H. (ed.) *Agricultural Protectionism in the Industrialized World* (Washington, DC: National Center for Food and Agricultural Policy, 1990).

Schaetzel, Robert, *The Unhinged Alliance* (New York: Harper & Row, 1975).

Schlesinger, Arthur M., *A Thousand Days: John F. Kennedy in the White House* (Boston, MA: Houghton Mifflin, 1965).

Schulte, Markus, "Industrial Interest in West Germany's Decision against the Enlargement of the EEC. The Quantitative Evidence up to 1964," *Journal of European Integration History*, 3, 1 (1997), 35–61.

Schulte, Markus, "Challenging the Common Market Project: Germany Industry, Britain and the Europe, 1957–1963," in Ann Deighton and Alan S. Milward (eds), *Widening, Deepening and Acceleration: The European Economic Community 1957–1963* (Baden-Baden: Nomos, 1999), 167–83.

Schwartz Thomas A., *Lyndon Johnson and Europe: In the Shadow of Vietnam* (Cambridge, MA: Harvard University Press, 2003).

Serra, Enrico (ed.), *Il rilancio dell'Europa e i trattati di Roma* (Brussels: Bruylant, 1989).

Shonfield, Andrew, *International Economic Relations of the Western World, 1959–1971 Vol. 1, Politics and Trade* (London: Oxford University Press for the Royal Institute of International Affairs, 1976).

Shonfield, Andrew (ed.), *International Economic Relations of the Western World, 1959–1971 Vol. 2* (London: Oxford University Press for the Royal Institute of International Affairs, 1976).

Snape, Richard H., "History and Economics in GATT's Article XXIV," in Kym Anderson and Richard Blackhurst (eds), *Regional Integration and the Global Trading System* (London: Harvester Wheatsheaf, 1993), 273–91.

Sorensen, Ted, *Kennedy* (New York: Harper and Row, 1965).

Soutou, Georges H., *L'alliance incertaine: les rapports politico stratégiques franco-allemands, 1954–1996* (Paris: Fayard, 1996).

Stern, Robert M. (ed.) *The Multilateral Trading System: Analysis and Option for Change* (New York: Harvester Wheatsheaf, 1993).

Strange, Susan, *International Monetary Relations of the Western World, 1959–1971* (London: Oxford University Press, 1976).

Taber, George M., *John F. Kennedy and a Uniting Europe: The Politics of Partnership* (Bruges: College of Europe, 1969).

Talbot, Ross B., *The Chicken War. An International Trade Conflicts between the United States and the European Economic Community, 1961–1964* (Ames, IA: Iowa State University Press, 1978).

Tracy, Michael, *Government and Agriculture in Western Europe, 1880–1988* (New York: Harvester Wheatsheaf, 1989).

Triffin, Robert, Europe *and the Money Muddle: From Bilateralism to Near-convertibility, 1947–1956* (Westport, CT: Greenwood Press, 1976).

Türk, Henning, "'To Face de Gaulle as a Community' – The Role of the Federal Republic of Germany in the Empty Chair Crisis," in Jean Marie Palayret, Helen Wallace, and Pascaline Winand (eds), *Visions, Votes and Vetoes: The Empty Chair Crisis and the Luxembourg Compromise Forty Years On* (Brussels: Peter Lang, 2006), 113–28.

Vaisse, Maurice, *La Grandeur: Politique Etrangère Du General De Gaulle, 1958–1969* (Paris: Fayard 1998).

Van der Harst, Jan (ed.), *Beyond the Customs Union: The European Community's Quest for Deepening, Completion and Enlargement, 1969–1975* (Brussels: Nomos, 2007).

Varsori, Antonio, *L'Italia nelle relazioni internazionali dal 1943 al 1992* (Rome: Laterza 1998).

Varsori, Antonio, *Il Comitato Economico e Sociale nella costruzione europea* (Venice: Marsilio, 2000).

Varsori, Antonio (ed.), *Inside the European Community. Actors and Policies in the European Integration 1957–1972* (Baden-Baden, Nomos, 2006).

Viner, Jacob, *The Customs Union Issue* (New York: Carnegie Endowment for International Peace. 1950).

Wahl, Nicholas, and Paxton, Robert, *De Gaulle and the United States: A Centennial Reappraisal* (Oxford: Berg, 1994).

Warley, Thorald K., "Western Trade in Agricultural Products," in Andrew Shonfield (ed.), *International Economic Relations of the Western World* (London: Oxford University Press for the Royal Institute of International Affairs, 1976), 287–402.

Weiss, Frank D., *Trade Policy in West Germany* (Tübingen: J.C.B. Mohr, 1988).

Wilcox, Clair A., *Charter for World Trade* (New York: Macmillan, 1949).

Wilkes, George, *Britain's Failure to Enter the European Community, 1961–1963: The Enlargement Negotiations and Crisis in European, Atlantic, and Commonwealth Relations* (London: Frank Cass, 1977).

Willis, Roy F., *France, Germany, and the New Europe 1945–1967* (Stanford, CA/ Oxford: Stanford University Press/Oxford University Press, 1968).

Winand, Pascaline, *Eisenhower, Kennedy and the United States of Europe* (New York: St Martin's Press, 1993).

Woll, Cornelia, "The Road to External Representation: The European Commission's Activism in International Air Transport," *Journal of European Public Policy* 13, 1 (2006), 52–69.

Zeiler, Thomas W., "Free-trade Politics and Diplomacy: John Fitzgerald Kennedy and Textile," *Diplomatic History* 11 (1987), 127–42.

Zeiler, Thomas W., *American Trade and Power in the 1960s* (New York: Columbia University Press, 1995).

Zeiler, Thomas W., "Managing Protectionism. American Trade Policy in the Early Cold War," *Diplomatic History* 22 (1998), 337–60.

Zeiler, Thomas W., *Free Trade Free World* (Chapel Hill, NC: University of North Carolina, Press, 1999).

Zimmermann, Hubert, *Money and Security. Troops and Monetary Policy in Germany's Relations to the United States and the United Kingdom, 1950–71* (Cambridge: Cambridge University Press, 2002).

Zimmermann, Hubert, *Wege zur Verhandlungen um die Aufnahme Chinas in die WTO, 1985–2001* (Baden-Baden: Nomos, 2007).

Zoumaras, Thomas, "Plugging the Dike: The Kennedy Administration Confronts the Balance-of-Payments Crisis with Europe," in Douglas Brinkley and Richard T. Griffiths (eds), *John F. Kennedy and Europe* (Baton Rouge, LA: Louisiana State University Press, 1999), 170–86.

Index